STING

The Secret Life of Gordon Sumn

Wensley Clarkson

Thunder's Mouth Press
New York

Published in the United States by
Thunder's Mouth Press
841 Broadway, Fourth Floor
New York, NY 10003

Originally published by Blake Publishing Ltd., London

Library of Congress Cataloging-in-Publication Data

Clarkson, Wensley.
Sting: the secret life of Gordon Sumner/by Wensley Clarkson.—
1st US ed.
p.   cm.
Originally published: London: Blake, 1996.
Includes discography/filmography (p.   ) and index.
ISBN 1-56025-226-X
1. Sting (Musician)   2. Rock musicians—England—Biography.
I. Title.
ML420.S847C53   1999
782.42166′092—dc21

[B]   98-46736
                                                        CIP
                                                        MN

Manufactured in the United States of America

NOTES OF GRATITUDE

In a Nutshell

I OWE MY DEEPEST THANKS to the many individuals who have helped to make this book possible. All told, I interviewed more than a hundred people, among them friends, acquaintances, writers, directors, producers, editors, artists, lawyers, publishers, record store clerks, musicians, agents, strippers, private eyes, accountants, reporters and middle-aged hippies.

Some of these sources have chosen to remain anonymous. To them I offer a note of appreciation for the help they have provided.

However, there are many others who don't mind being thanked out loud. First and foremost, my heartfelt thanks must go to Sting's good friends in Brazil: Deborah Cohen, Gilda Matoso and Carlos Paiva, whose help and guidance were unswerving. Also, the inimitable Harold Emert whose optimism and kind words were a constant source of encouragement. In Newcastle, Ronnie Pearson was a source of many great stories about Sting, especially from his time with the Last Exit band and during his frustrating years as a young teacher. Pearson has remained close to Sting and clearly remembers the problems they both faced as struggling musicians.

Andy Hudson was Sting's first ever manager and he kindly revealed some fascinating details about the years when Sting was at the bottom of the pile. Hudson patiently endured my many questions and, unlike many people in showbusiness, always returned my calls graciously and swiftly.

Rik Walton provided marvellous descriptions of Sting's early performances in the seedier clubs of the North East. His off-the-wall accounts gave me a unique insight into the life that Sting was leading at that time.

Terry Ellis was wonderfully helpful because he gave me an honest, unbiased version of those early days, which is so essential to an incisive biography like this. Some of Terry's colleagues on the Newcastle jazz scene also provided an interesting appraisal that was of enormous benefit.

A number of Sting's friends from his early days on the London New Wave scene came up with details of his struggle for recognition and his involvement with the seedy side of life.

The section on the extraordinary success of The Police owes much to the behind-the-scenes efforts of observers like Gordon Blair who provided much of the information that lies at the heart of that part of the book.

In Brazil, I had the good fortune to bump into Jean-Pierre Dutilleux who provided much of the backbone of the real story behind Sting's adventures in the rainforest. I also enjoyed a cuppa and a chat with the world's most famous ex-pat, Ronnie Biggs.

The wonderfully accommodating Quentin Crisp also deserves a special note of thanks for agreeing to meet a complete stranger and talk for many hours about his impressions and experiences with Sting.

On the editorial front there are a number of people to thank, particularly my publisher, John Blake, whose enthusiasm from day one has been magnificent and inspiring. Many thanks also go to Sadie Mayne for keeping up the pressure when all around her were faltering.

Others who deserve many, many thanks include: Peter Miller, Gavin Taylor, Dave Wood, John Harker, Gerry Richardson, John Glatt, Mark Sandelson, Martin Dunn, Jon Ryan, Graeme Gourlay, Rupert Maconick, Pete Pickton, Judy Maguire, Denis Wright, Rosie Ries, Piers Thompson, Michael Seymour, Jessica Brass, Phil Sutcliffe, Nick Cooper, Herman Rojas, Gerardo Moro, Ruth De Aquino and Toby, Polly, Rosie and Fergus Clarkson for keeping an eye out for anything interesting in the mountain of magazines they plough through every week.

The Academy of Motion Picture and Science Library (Los Angeles), St Catherine's House, London, the BBC, the Lincoln Center (New York), the LA *Times*, Associated Newspapers, News

International, the New York *Times*, the Boston *Globe*, *Vanity Fair*, *GQ*, *Sky*, *Entertainment Weekly*, *Los Angeles Magazine*, *Variety*, *Hollywood Reporter*, *Premiere*, *Melody Maker*, *Sounds*, *Empire*, *Playboy* and the Mirror Group provided much of the background material, as did books on The Police including *Police Confidential*, published by Macdonald, *Sting* by Steve Gett, published by Cherry Lane Books, *Sting* by Marsha Bronson, published by Exley, and Phil Sutcliffe's excellent book *The Police, Outlandos d'Amour*, published by Bobcat Books.

Finally, I owe a huge debt to Sting's indefatigable solicitor, Christopher Burley, for reading my final manuscript and helping me to correct numerous, inevitable factual errors.

To my mother Pamela

Contents

CONTENTS

INTRODUCTION

EVERY BREATH HE TAKES

READER BEWARE! This is a book about a rock'n'roll icon who has never shied away from speaking his mind. It does not reveal all of Sting's most secret or outrageous opinions but it is the most fascinating account of his life you are ever likely to read.

Who is the man behind the public face of one of the world's premier solo recording artists? Whence comes his love of life's darkness, his apocalyptic drive? How was it possible for someone with such a difficult background to make it to the very top?

I first encountered Sting when he came spitting on to the stage at a rough-and-tumble pub called The Nashville Rooms in West London in 1977. It was one of The Police's first gigs and they were trying to give the distinct impression that they were a rowdy punk outfit. They looked far too talented to be convincing, however, and I knew it would only be a matter of time before the band became a force to be reckoned with.

Sting is one of the few rock stars in the world who has proved that he has staying power. There is no simple way to explain this global mania. Perhaps, as Sting himself might say, the question is best explored from different points of view.

The surest way for an artist to achieve adulation and visibility beyond the limits of their chosen discipline is to have extraordinary sexual charisma. A seemingly neverending youthfulness, combined with a mystical air of danger, has undoubtedly helped Sting along the way.

Sting is the sort of guy who would never go unnoticed in a crowd.

His sharp features have appeared on the cover of just about every magazine around the world as a result. His audiences still lap up everything he sings about and many of them have remained loyal to him for almost twenty years.

Sting's astonishing success may be at least partly due to his unusual name. Sting is short and sharp and very memorable. Sting might sound to some like a brand name but his music is far from predictable. Intriguingly, his willingness to experiment has never lost him support, despite the constant fears of his record company and management.

However, he does have his critics. In recent years they have accused him of being too middle-of-the-road, too safe. Despite what his detractors say, though, there is a great deal more to Sting than meets the eye. His use of his own emotions in his compositions has become one of the most misunderstood aspects of Sting's work. His approach to music means that he frequently needs to suffer pain in order to deliver the goods.

His skill lies in coaxing his audiences into joining in with his own emotions. He admits he is a control freak which means that he adores the way his songs provoke such adulation.

Sting's work as both a rock star and actor is all cut from the same cloth. He tries to use his highs and lows to drive him onwards and upwards towards greater heights. He is also on a neverending quest to prove he is the best.

Although, in person, Sting may seem a rather overintense man, it is the openness of his finest compositions, their callous laughter at our darker moments, that has made him a truly global celebrity. Yet, as his icon status grows, he has actually become more approachable and now exudes the easy charm of one completely aware of his position. It's as if he's saying, 'If I can do it, so can you ...'

ONE

L'Enfant Terrible

> *'I liked swimming because it was
> the only way I got clean.'*
> - STING

THE ODDS AGAINST STING EVER MAKING IT to even the bottom rung of the ladder of musical stardom were enormous. If he surmounted that hurdle, any of the bookmakers where he was later to spend much of his leisure time would still have given astounding odds against him becoming one of the world's top solo performers.

How many children from a background of backstreet slums and near poverty have made it to the top in any decade this century? Certainly few enough to talk in terms of a million-to-one shot. No wonder he was considered rather smug and self-serving after he won his battle to be considered a real star.

'Privilege' was not a word the Sumner family was familiar with when Gordon Matthew Sumner came into this world on 2 October 1951. Life in the cold, hard, industrial borough of Wallsend, an ancient settlement so called because it was at the eastern end of Roman Emperor Hadrian's Wall across the north of

1

England, was not going to be easy by any means.

Wallsend, a grey, sprawling, rundown shipbuilding district near Newcastle, had already gone into decline following the boom years of World War II when ships were in overwhelming demand. The region suffered the worst of the nation's withdrawal symptoms as the great heavy industries went into a steep nosedive. In the 1950s, Tyneside tended to lead the nation in pollution, drunkenness, bad housing and unemployment. The weather always matched the bleak outlook — grey blustery days and brief summers that never seemed to feature more than a handful of sunny days.

The town of Wallsend was dominated by shipbuilders Swan Hunter, a social club where darts and cribbage played a vital role and numerous bingo halls. There were five cinemas in the town at that time. Trams came hurtling through the main streets on a loop line from Newcastle. In the centre of the town lay a massive air raid shelter, a relic of the countless bombing raids inflicted on the area by Hitler less than ten years earlier.

There was even a chap called Geordie Morgan who roamed the streets with his horse and cart picking up old bits of scrap. Wallsend remained busy mostly because it was the main ferry point for trips across the Tyne.

The Sumners lived at number 80 Station Road, a traditional double row of back-to-back houses near the great river. They rented their house from Swan Hunter and there was a permanent reminder of the huge company's influence just fifty yards from the house, thanks to the towering hulls of vast ships which cast a deep, dark shadow over the entire area as they were meticulously constructed.

Gordon's father, Ernest Matthew Sumner, had been a fitter in a local engineering works when he married attractive young hairdresser Audrey Cowell. Shortly afterwards, he changed career to become a milkman.

Later, after Gordon turned six, the family moved a short distance to a flat above the small dairy his father ran on Gerald Street, still in Wallsend. His mother Audrey also changed jobs and became an auxiliary nurse. She was just eighteen years of age when Gordon was born and she then stopped work for some years while achieving three further pregnancies in relatively fast succession.

The only memorable thing that had ever happened to any member of the Sumner family up until this point was when Uncle Joe was decorated for playing his accordion and keeping up the morale of his fellow soldiers on Crete during the World War II invasion of the island. Everyone rather liked the idea that he had a medal for *not* killing people.

When Gordon Sumner was born on that grey October day, the Festival of Great Britain was in full swing and a general election was looming. For Ernie and Audrey, however, the only things that mattered were the birth of their first child and getting through the bitter winter weather on Ernie's weekly wage of just eight pounds.

The Sumners were never destitute but they could barely afford any more than mere essentials. By the time brother Philip and sisters Angela and Anita were born, the house had become an overcrowded mass of hysteria, with shouting and screaming a regular occurrence.

To young Gordon, the family always seemed to be on the point of breaking up. There were constant fights, many of them caused by the financial strain that fell upon the shoulders of Ernest Sumner who was trying to bring up a large family on a tiny wage.

As the oldest child, Gordon felt more to blame for the anguish and unhappiness that seemed to underline life at home. He constantly worried about what would happen if his parents split up. He also wondered why on earth his mother and father had ever got married since they seemed to hate each other so much.

'Who the fuck would I go with if my mother ran off?' explained Sting years later. 'Stay with me dad? Nah. And who would take the television? I was very concerned about that.'

Sting used the television as a form of escape from his unhappy childhood. It became the epicentre of his early life. He would spend hours glued to the black-and-white box that took pride of place in the tiny front room of their home. He followed the adventure programmes with particular interest. Sometimes he would even talk back to the set, urging his favourite characters to win a gun battle or whatever.

Sting also spent much of those early childhood years on the lean, mean streets of Wallsend. There was no place else to go. Football would be played in the scruffy lane behind their home. Sometimes they would chase girls and chuck stones at them when they taunted them. There were also fights between the kids — still well under the age of ten — hanging around outside pubs and the chip shop on the corner, not to mention the Ritz cinema in the High Street. Sting and his pals would often stop complete strangers in the street and ask them if they would take them in to see 'A' certificate films. On Saturday mornings, there were the sixpenny matinees that featured cartoons and showed films like *The Lone Ranger* and Abbott and Costello adventures.

Special treats tended to revolve around watching football matches at Newcastle United and ship launches at the nearby yards.

Brother Phil remembers the early days well. He shared a bedroom with Sting and both boys dreaded the days when their dad would make them go and help him out at the dairy. 'The phone would go at some ungodly hour in the morning after Dad had gone to work. It always meant that someone hadn't turned up and, as Gordon was the eldest, he had to go and help out,' recalls Phil.

Sting was in big demand for delivering pints of milk with his father because he had large hands and could carry ten bottles at a time, much to the wonderment of his kid brother and sisters. However, he was often eaten up with jealousy about the other kids who worked for his father. Some of them seemed to be Ernie's favourites. Gordon was just the awkward, lanky son.

All this meant that Sting had to fight doubly hard for acceptance by his father and this eventually inspired him to try to do well in the classroom and at sport. Sting was particularly keen on swimming and would spend his threepence at the local baths every night. His mother was keen on it too, because it was the only way he got clean. Sting was fiercely competitive and would hold unofficial races in the pool with any boys who looked vaguely about his size.

At the age of seven, Sting became an altar boy at St Columba's Roman Catholic Church and had to learn the full Latin service as well as looking like an innocent cherub for the duration of Mass. At the beginning he never once questioned the wisdom of the church and used to enjoy singing the loudest and pretending to be fluent in Latin.

At school, Sting excelled at English but little else. He surprised teachers with his ability to write beautifully constructed sentences from the age of eight. For the rest of the day, however, he tended to daydream in class.

Sting's interest in literature had been nurtured a couple of years earlier when he became particularly close to his grandmother, Agnes Sumner, the one and only 'culture vulture' in the family. She introduced Sting to *Treasure Island* at the age of five and then encouraged her grandson to read dozens of the other books and magazines, like the satirical *Punch*, that were always lying around her house.

Sting read anything he could get his hands on. He loved the written word and would re-read favourite passages from books over and over again just for the sheer pleasure of it.

This love affair with reading set Sting a bit apart as far as his playmates at the time were concerned. They preferred to kick a ball around rather than bury themselves in a book. Sting soon became uninterested in team activities. He preferred solo pursuits and was becoming increasingly intrigued by music. His earliest 'Lawrentian memory', as he now calls it, is of sitting under the piano at home listening to his mother play a tango. 'She was very good, but she gave it up soon after that. Weird. I dunno why ...'

Sting tried to play the piano himself as soon as he could reach the keys. He was convinced that if he just hammered away at it the music would come out eventually. It was an attitude that was to stay with him for the rest of his life.

The young Sting constantly hummed songs to himself. In junior school he would run around the playground with self-created tunes playing in his head. He just couldn't get some melodies out of his mind, yet there was no one at home pushing him even to consider music as a hobby.

When Sting was eight, his Uncle John emigrated to Canada and left his guitar at the family house. Sting's eyes lit up when he saw it and he asked his parents if he could borrow it. He soon learned how to play some basic tunes and began performing for relatives. 'He used to drive us mad with that guitar,' recalled Audrey years later.

Ernie Sumner eventually agreed to let Sting have guitar lessons just so that the rest of the family could get some peace and quiet. 'I sent him to a well-known music teacher called Mr Bianti. I think it cost ten bob an hour — a lot at the time. You can imagine how angry I was when Mr Bianti phoned to say: "Your son is wasting my time and your money. He will not be taught!"' remembered Ernie years later.

The problem was that Sting would not conform sufficiently to play the sort of tunes his guitar teacher thought suitable. He never went back to Mr Bianti and Ernie Sumner certainly wasn't going to throw away good money on any more lessons.

However, it wasn't just Sting's prowess on a guitar that was concerning the Sumners. By the age of nine he was extraordinarily tall and was treated like a freak of nature at school. He suffered many strange comments at home as well.

Still dressed in short trousers, despite his height, Sting looked ridiculous; a lanky, tall, awkward beanpole. Not surprisingly, he eventually picked up the nickname Lurch after the ponderous butler in the *Addams Family* comic horror TV show.

In the school football team Sting was stuck in goal on the basis that no one would be able to shoot the ball past him. Sadly, they were wrong. He was a dreamer who often completely failed to wake up in time to prevent the softest of goals.

Sting's nerdy appearance and his schoolmates' constant jibes drove the youngster into a self-imposed solitary confinement. He began to conceal elements of his character and started suppressing his opinions on many subjects for fear that his views might land him in trouble. The long-term result of all this was that Sting had few real friends when he was a child. No one seemed to understand him. He actually felt closest to his favourite characters on TV and that confused those around him even further.

One time he was watching TV with a friend called Kevin when a Western called *Bronco Lane* was on. In this particular episode, a cowboy called Tenderfoot (the hero of another Western series at the time) was making a guest appearance. However, Tenderfoot was also on his own show on the other channel at the same time and Kevin asked Sting, 'How can he be on both sides at once?'

Sting looked at his friend incredulously and thought, 'You're not very clever are you? You're stupid.' He then explained to Kevin that neither of these programmes was televised live.

Sting's addiction to TV also sparked a natural curiosity about certain subjects. Once he was watching a programme about skiing and flying and he turned to his parents to ask them about it. 'That's what posh people do,' came his father's terse reply. The class divisions which existed in places like Newcastle forty years ago were crystal clear.

Increasingly, Sting found he had to lower himself to the same level as his contemporaries so that his friends and family would not treat him as some kind of weirdo because of his deep knowledge and understanding of subjects they knew nothing about.

At school, unfortunately, this attitude created more problems than it solved. He came over as a very conceited child and even convinced himself that he did not have to work hard to succeed. In the comparatively mundane end-of-term exams, Sting frequently came out in the last five of the class. Yet, when it came to the eleven-plus exam — a very abstract intelligence test — he sailed through.

Passing the eleven-plus marked an important turning point in Sting's life because if he had failed it and gone on to secondary modern school, he would probably have ended up as a juvenile delinquent, or a milkman, miner or shipyard worker if he was lucky.

His parents were so delighted when he passed that they bought him a brand-new red bicycle. Despite Ernie's financial struggles, he always managed to make sure the family was well provided for.

On the other hand, Sting's teachers were infuriated by his success because he seemed to have achieved it on his own terms. When one of them found out he had passed his eleven-plus, he dragged Sting out in front of the class and said, 'This boy is going to St Cuthbert's! To a direct-grant grammar school! And I think it's a damned disgrace! Sit down boy!'

In those days direct-grant schools were establishments which took both the fee-paying children of wealthier parents and others, like Sting, who were considered 'talented' and were covered by a local authority grant to the school. Ernie Sumner was just on the income borderline and had to pay the princely sum of fifteen pounds towards the first year of schooling at St Cuthbert's, but nothing after that.

The worst, and best, thing about St Cuthbert's was that it was in the West End district, on the opposite side of Newcastle to where the Sumners lived. That involved a journey of almost one hour each way. It was the first major upheaval in Sting's young life and provoked a volatile combination of arrogance and pained vulnerability. His social opinions about things like poverty and politics had already started to form and he was determined not to conform completely in any environment, especially not one as middle class as his new school.

The very first example of this attitude came on the second day of attending his new, 'posh' school. Sting had failed to wear the regulation cap and was spotted by one of the priests who ran the school.

'Where's your cap, boy?'

'I lost it, sir.'

'Buy a new one, boy.'

'My mother says she can't afford it.'

That reply completely stumped the priest and Sting never wore a cap again. However, he did wear the rest of the uniform which consisted of a scarlet jacket, grey trousers and a tie.

Attending St Cuthbert's set Sting apart from the other kids back in the narrow streets of Wallsend, as did learning Latin, chemistry and

French. His few friends at home soon disappeared and he was treated like a leper. If he walked home and saw them playing football in the back lane, they would ignore his greetings. The fashion code of the neighbourhood kids at that time consisted of skintight drainpipes, brothel creepers and slicked-back hair, while Sting was still lurching along awkwardly in his stiff, hot, flannel uniform.

However, the loneliness Sting felt gave him the incentive to be a free spirit and he constantly lost himself in his own thoughts and fantasies. When the family moved to a smart new house on the brand-new Marden Farm Estate, near the coast at Tynemouth, his life as a loner seemed complete. By this time Sting's father owned the dairy which was doing well although he had kept the business at a relatively low level. Mr Sumner even took out a mortgage to buy the family's brand-new house and he also managed to buy himself a car for the first time.

For Sting there were other, more vivid, memories than his father's car or a new house. He never forgot how his attractive mother — who was still a relatively young woman even when Sting hit his teens — would provoke wolf whistles when they went out shopping in the nearby town centre. It greatly embarrassed Sting at the time, but he also felt immense pride in the fact that his mother was so beautiful that she drew such admiration.

Elements of Sting's close relationship with his mother were to cloud his later choice of girlfriends and wives. Audrey was not only a very pretty woman, she also had a strong hold over her elder son and insisted on approving any girl he dated. She even went as far as to encourage Sting to pick up pretty girls when they were out together. Often, she would engage the girls in conversation and then introduce them to her handsome son.

Frequently, Audrey would badger Sting to go on dates with the daughters of certain people who lived locally and she was always most interested in how those dates had gone when Sting got home. Some of Sting's few friends at the time found Audrey's attitude a little unnerving but then few of them fully appreciated just how close mother and son were. Certainly, Audrey took a lot of pride in her son's appearance and she considered her Gordon to be a handsome fellow who would be a fine catch for any local girl.

Years later, when Sting reached his late teens and early twenties, Audrey would cheekily encourage her son to tell her every detail of what had happened on various dates. Sting never flinched from telling her everything.

Back at their newly built house, Sting, now in his teens, and Phil found themselves sharing a room once again. Sting had posters of Bob Dylan, the Beatles and Tamla Motown stars on the wall. Phil preferred pictures of his favourite local soccer heroes. It perfectly illustrated the difference between the two boys.

However, the Sumner brothers did attend Cubs together — and both hated it. The crunch came one evening when they were learning how to tie knots during a particularly laborious meeting. Phil explains, 'Every time I tied a special knot one of Gordon's mates would distract me while another would untie the knot. After about half an hour I got sick of it. It ended up in a massive fight — with Gordon taking my side — and the terrible indignation of being banned from the Cubs.'

Sting never really liked that brand-new house on the Marden Farm Estate. He sneeringly referred to it as 'the little box' and kept telling anyone who would listen that he preferred the house at Wallsend, although he did begrudgingly admit he liked living nearer to the sea.

However, that house was especially significant because it marked the moment when Sting began to appreciate fully the importance of social class and how it was likely to alter his life. He noticed that kids behaved differently in the clean, tree-lined streets near the new house. He could tell that keeping ahead of the class system provided certain opportunities. He also saw that his parents behaved completely differently after the move to the new house. His mother — whom he clearly idolised — even spoke with a posher accent whenever she talked to any of the neighbours. It was hardly Millionaire's Row, but the family's move was the equivalent of going from the terraced properties of TV's *Coronation Street* to the immaculately modern, sanitised atmosphere of *Brookside*.

Sting also began working on his accent. He believed he would get further at grammar school if he dropped his strong Geordie vowels. He systematically began to train himself to talk posh. Every day, on the way to school, he would teach himself to speak differently by regularly repeating certain words to himself. Eventually, he developed the much stronger, more purposeful voice, with only a hint of the North East, that he has kept to this day.

Even then, Sting was determined not to remain rooted in Newcastle. He didn't have much of that legendary north-eastern pride. The success or failure of the local football team, Newcastle United, meant very little to his personal happiness. In his own mind, Newcastle was a dump. He saw it as a slum left over from the hard days of the industrial revolution. It was a place to escape from, not adore.

Sting's ambitions were already centred around finding a way out of that ordinary existence, but he still had a long way to go.

TWO

School Daze

'I wanted to be an adult for a long time.
The older I got, the better I felt.'
— Sting

By HIS EARLY TEENS, Sting was in a state of adolescent confusion. He wanted to further himself in every way, but he also found it difficult to obey authority and he particularly detested the snobbish kids who surrounded him at grammar school. The result was that he had a number of serious clashes with his teachers at St Cuthbert's. Some of them looked on him as an upstart milkman's son made good; a rough diamond from the wrong side of the tracks. Sting could not escape that fact and the more he tried to fight it, the more it got him into trouble.

He used his own natural instinct and intelligence to defend himself from teachers and pupils alike but even though he was in the top stream at school, he continued to be pinpointed as a troublemaker.

Not surprisingly, his problems were turning him into an even more introverted personality and he started to spend increasing amounts of time alone in his room at home, avoiding the family. However, his loneliness certainly fuelled a genuine interest in a range of music that was wide for someone so young.

In the fourth form he borrowed some jazz records from an older friend. 'I didn't like any of the records, but I thought it would do me good. I'd listen to album after album of Thelonious Monk piano solos and I thought, "This must be doing a world of good because it's just awful." Gradually, it just grew on me. It was the same with the blues. I'd listen to loads of the blues and I just didn't like them. But I persevered because I thought they were doing me good. It was like having to take some kind of medicine. I desperately wanted to be hip.'

Back at St Cuthbert's, things were going from bad to worse. Sting's entire class was suspended for ten days for stealing equipment from the chemistry laboratory. More incidents followed and, by the end of that particular term, all teachers were refusing to give lessons to Sting and his classmates.

Sting, then still plain Gordon Sumner, even earned himself a new nickname, 'Noddy', thanks to a craze at the school for reversing names. Thus, he became Nodrog Renmus, or Noddy for short.

Because he was so tall, Sting started fronting expeditions to local bookmakers to gamble on horses. Most of the kids were accustomed to spending much of their Saturdays hanging about outside bookies while their fathers had a flutter. It seemed only natural, therefore, that Sting should walk into a bookies and lay a few bets on behalf of his pals.

Even at that early age Sting liked the thrill of gambling. Naturally, he liked to win but he was also philosophical enough to realise that he was unlikely to come out a winner every time. By the time he had reached his mid-teens he would make a trip to the local bookies at least once a week and it was to become a habit — some might call it a passion — that would stay with him for life.

Sting achieved a pathetic thirteen per cent average over all his exams that term and came into direct conflict with his class master, Father Walsh, a man who Sting believed had been put on this earth to strike fear into naughty schoolboys. He was renowned for terrifying his pupils and his favourite weapon was the cane.

The first time Sting was punished was for the relatively harmless offence of talking in class. Walsh had already pinpointed Sting as a troublemaker and was determined to make an example of him. It seemed to Sting, and also to some of his classmates, that Walsh definitely derived some sadistic pleasure from punishing his pupils. His eyes would glaze over with sheer enjoyment as he lashed a young boy's bare bottom.

That term, Sting set the record for canings at forty-two strokes. It became such a common occurrence in the youngster's life that he would be undoing his trousers and dropping them virtually before Father Walsh had even yelled out his punishment. Being caned on the backside was pretty undignified, to say the least. Sting never forgot the sly smile that would flicker across Father Walsh's face as he looked down at the terrified youngster before taking a vicious swipe.

Sting tried to be a rough, tough, macho boy by not crying out as each stroke sliced into his buttocks but by the third swipe he would be screaming in agony and that was when Father Walsh would hit even harder. Sometimes, the strokes were so hard that streaks of blood would form on Sting's buttocks and he had to go to the lavatories to dampen the pain with toilet paper dipped in water. Often he was in such pain that he found it hard to walk, but his pride kept him going more than anything else. No one, not even the nightmarish Father Walsh, could take away his pride. His head was always held up high as he left the priest's office and he usually still gave a wink or two to his classmates who held him in awe for soaking up so many dreadful punishments.

However, Sting paid the price in many other ways. He was the only pupil in the sixth form who was not made a prefect. This meant that while everyone else wore regulation black gowns of office, he continued in the ordinary school uniform. Sting, however, saw it all in a completely different light. He was rather proud not to be a prefect because it made him different from the rest.

Sports-wise, team activities had long since lacked importance for Sting, but when it came to solo sports like running, he was still determined and gifted. He became Northumberland champion at 100 and 200 yards. He even learned a different, faster style of running by watching another boy sprinting on his toes. Not only did he copy that boy, he became better than him. Sting was nothing if not a fast learner.

Sting was still far more interested in excelling in intellectual terms. He adored out-thinking and out-reading his mostly middle-class schoolmates by quoting the avant-garde literature and music which had percolated down to British schools by the mid-sixties, such as the beatnik novels of Jack Kerouac, the new English poetry of Philip Larkin and Ted Hughes and the jazz albums by Charlie Mingus and Thelonius Monk which he had first borrowed at a remarkably young age.

There was also Bob Dylan. Sting was particularly turned on by Dylan's poetry, such as 'Masters Of War'. He began practising Dylan songs at home on his guitar and could do all eight verses of 'When The Ship Comes In' from the 1964 album *The Times They Are A-Changin'*.

At nearly six feet tall, Sting was regularly mistaken for at least sixteen while he was still as young as twelve. One of the most disturbing aspects of this was that he took drugs for the first time before he had even reached his thirteenth birthday.

Some friends in the neighbourhood got hold of a small quantity of cannabis and three of them went down to the beach at Whitley Bay one wintery day and haphazardly rolled up and smoked two joints among them. Sting's first and incredibly early experience of drugs was imprinted on his mind forever. He enjoyed smoking the cannabis and promised himself he would do it again. He liked the fact that drugs helped to loose him from the everyday tedium that seemed to dominate everyone's lives in Geordieland. His only regret was that the cannabis was not stronger, enabling him to eclipse reality completely for a short period and find out what was happening on the 'other side' of the world. His interest in exploring new pastures was definitely fuelled by those first experiences with drugs.

By the time Sting had reached his early to mid-teens, amphetamines (speed) were also available and cheap and drugs began to play a fairly regular role in his life. At the local pub he was commissioned by friends to buy the beers because he could pass for an adult. His friends also organised the purchase of the blue tablets of speed which were bought for three or four shillings each.

Meanwhile, Sting's interest in jazz was gradually turning into genuine love. One of Sting's pals, Pete Brigham, gave him an electric bass guitar which consisted of only two working strings (the remaining ones just buzzed). The instrument was constructed from a plank of wood but Sting didn't care just as long as it worked. He loved playing the blues in his bedroom.

Sting's musical influences did not stop at jazz. He loved the soul music on the Tamla and Stax labels, and he was particularly fond of The Beatles. Their influence was far-reaching and Sting adored playing their songs on his acoustic guitar. He saw his first live band — the Graham Bond Organisation — in 1965 at the infamous Club A Go Go in Newcastle when he was still thirteen years old. The band included the legendary Jack Bruce, probably the greatest bass player in the world at that time. His influence worked its way into groups as diverse as John Mayall's Bluesbreakers, Manfred Mann and Cream. Sting studied Jack Bruce closely and felt a strange affinity with him. Just as when he copied the boy he saw running on his toes as an athlete, he homed in on the skills of Jack Bruce and tried to emulate him too.

Over the following couple of years, Sting regularly visited the Club A Go Go to see a whole range of bands including The Animals, Pink Floyd and the incredible Jimi Hendrix and he never forgot how the master guitarist rammed his instrument through the roof of the club after a particularly outstanding rendition of 'Purple Haze'. Sting also watched another, slightly lesser known, group at the same venue, called Zoot Money And The Big Roll Band, with baby-faced guitarist Andy Summers.

At home, Sting's musical development was inconsistent to say the least. He had abandoned piano lessons in his early teens because his parents sold their piano and he found it impossible to learn without practice. However, the sessions on his acoustic guitar at least created some sort of bond between himself and his father.

Ernie Sumner liked to strum along with his son on the rare days when he wasn't completely wiped out with exhaustion from the incredibly long hours he worked at the dairy. Sting was delighted at first, but elements of rivalry soon started to creep in between father and son. Sting constantly tried to prove he could play better than his father. Ernie was not impressed. He couldn't understand why such things mattered to his son but Sting took it all very seriously.

During his school holidays Sting would help his father on his milk round, which should have brought them closer together. However, despite being the oldest child, Sting never seemed to get the love and appreciation that was heaped on his younger brother and two sisters. Ernie Sumner was hard on his older son. He had little time for his sensitive nature and suspected that Gordon needed to be toughened up so that he would survive in the outside world.

Meanwhile, it continued to seem as if Sting and his mother Audrey were joined at the hip. She would heap non-stop attention and praise on her eldest child. In her eyes he could do little wrong but that same overprotectiveness had the knock-on effect of making Ernie Sumner grow increasingly resentful towards the boy. He wanted Sting to fend for himself instead of being a stereotypical mummy's boy.

The situation reached a head in a way no one else in the family could have predicted. Sting had grown accustomed to burying himself in his room and strumming away on his guitar. He would spend hours each evening, up there on his own, ignoring pleas to come down for supper. Ernie Sumner complained bitterly to his wife about this and, amid much shouting, Audrey was dispatched to make the boy come down and join the family.

When Audrey knocked at the door of her elder son's room, to try to persuade him to stop playing and come downstairs to eat like any normal child, the sulky teenager threw a tantrum. Downstairs, Ernie Sumner threatened to come up and spank the boy. Audrey was caught in the middle, infuriated by Sting's stubbornness. With her husband's harsh words ringing in her ears, she flipped, charged into Sting's bedroom, snatched the guitar and smashed it into little pieces by flinging it against the door over and over again. Sting watched in silence. He felt like grabbing the guitar from his mother and smashing her over the head with it but he was so shocked by what she was doing that he could not move. He remained glued to the spot, close to tears, staring coldly at his mother until she dropped the remains of the guitar on the floor and walked out of the room, haunted by the look she saw in her son's eyes. Audrey felt guilty about what she had done because she knew how much that guitar meant to her son. She also knew that it marked a low point in his relationship with his parents. She had always felt close to Sting but, suddenly, in the space of a few hysterical seconds, all that warmth had crumbled.

Sting's reaction that day is worth noting. He did not chase after his mother. He did not shout obscenities at her. He just walked calmly down the stairs, past his brother and sisters and out of the front door. He did not come home for two days.

He wandered the streets, thinking deeply about what his mother had done, actually able to see both sides of what had happened. However, he also felt that circumstances had brought the situation to a head so he decided, there and then, that one day he would move away from the North East and never return.

At the time he felt immensely frustrated by his family, his school, his life. No one actually took the time to try to understand his motivation. No one seemed interested. The incident with his guitar simply confirmed his suspicion that he would have to get out into the big wide world and make it on his own. No one was going to help him. Most people would actually just get in his way and try to convince him not to be so naïve. From that day onwards, Sting devoted his every thinking moment to achieving success and escaping the drudgery of his homelife. It was a mission that would never end.

Sting has always been highly inconsistent about his attitude towards St Cuthbert's, claiming that he rebelled against it and detested the élitist attitudes of a grammar school. Yet his sister Angela remembers, 'He often talked of the school with fondness.'

In the early 1980s, Sting became involved in an act of kindness that perfectly emphasises his sister's point.

The school wanted an old boy to present the Duke of Edinburgh awards to the sixth form. Someone suggested asking Sting and he accepted. At the prize giving he added a lovely touch by wearing a school tie. 'I don't think he would have kept that if his school memories had been sour ones,' says old school friend David Stapleton.

Throughout his youth, certain images inspired Sting, such as the sight of Jack Bruce on stage holding his own with that magical bass guitar; the thought of clean streets and successful people; the freedom that creativity could bring. Sting realised that he had to concentrate on playing the bass guitar. He was convinced it would be his key to escape.

At home, he began playing his forty-fives at 78 rpm to bring out the bottom line so that he could clearly hear the bass rhythms on all the biggest records of that era. Upstairs in his tiny room, isolated from the rest of the world, he beavered away at his skills on the bass. Now he had a goal to achieve, however many hours, days and years it would take.

Sting's mother had by then accepted that there was nothing she could do to stop her son doing what he wanted but it was clear that the great divide between Sting and his parents would never be properly bridged again.

Besides all this musical activity, upward social mobility also dominated Sting's mind at that time. He was realistic enough to realise that becoming a pop star might be just a pipe dream, so he did not give up his academic aspirations. His O-Levels were safe but unspectacular, with passes in English language and literature, geography, maths and art.

At home, Sting still felt that he had to fight to get any attention from his father. When he won the junior 100 yards race at the county athletics championships, he rushed home and proudly told Ernie Sumner, 'Look what I won!'

His father replied, 'Yeah?' and looked out of the window without saying another word. Sting so desperately wanted him to say he was proud of his son, but he never did.

Many years later, Sting explained, 'In his generation you didn't show your feelings or even hug your children. I grew up thinking that was the way to behave.'

He promised himself that if he ever had children he would never treat them in such a negative fashion.

THREE

GEORDIE TALES

'Money has always been a catalyst
to help me find something other
than the need to earn a buck.'
                                        - STING

IT IS EASY TO BE RETROSPECTIVELY ASTUTE and say that Sting knew his
ship would come in one day. Naturally, by the time he reached his
mid-teens he was into girls and music, in that order. He saw himself
as the Casanova/Jack Bruce of North Shields. His ambition to leave
the area was still burning a hole in his heart but there were other
priorities on the horizon. Girls smiled at him in the streets and he was
starting to get a reputation as a local heart-throb.

'One day it dawned on me that a lot of my friends were coming
round to drool over Gordon,' recalls his sister Angela. 'I think
Gordon noticed it — he couldn't fail to really.'

At home, Sting's parents were fighting more and more frequently.
They were stretched to financial breaking point by having to bring up
their large family and, ultimately, took it out on each other. Sting tried
to keep out of the family house as much as possible. A handful of his
friends had single parents and he was starting to envy them. It seemed

much more peaceful at their homes than at his own where kids and adults spent much of their time throwing objects and abuse at each other.

The fury of his family life continued to make Sting feel an overwhelming sense of isolation in that he could never actually talk to his parents because of their non-stop aggression towards each other. There never seemed to be time for him or his brother and sisters. He continued to wonder why people ever got married and had families.

Sting started to find solace in sexual encounters which provided an escape from his unhappy home life. There were numerous one-night stands, when he would meet a girl in a local pub, take her down to the beach and fumble about before attempting intercourse and then disappear off home, often too shy to acknowledge the girl in the street the following day.

All of this macho behaviour was actually a front for an extremely intense teenager given to bouts of depression and moodiness. His male friends couldn't really get a handle on him but girls found his vulnerability intriguing. They often initiated a date by providing the perfect shoulder for him to cry on. They seemed to understand him better. He was undoubtedly a complex person but he began to realise that sympathy was the perfect emotion to elicit when picking up pretty girls.

He frequently played intense mind games when he first met a girl. The ultimate objective, of course, was to experience some sort of sexual encounter but he enjoyed the chase more than anything else. He certainly wasn't offhand about sex but, in the AIDS-free environment of the late sixties, girls were just as keen on sexual experimentation as boys.

Even Sting was quite shocked by the forwardness of some of the girls he met. Ironically, his social life had now gone virtually full circle, back to the kids from the nearby local secondary modern, partly because he lived so far from his grammar school but also because he hated most of the pupils there. However, Sting rapidly became frustrated by the type of girls he encountered because they did not seem especially appreciative of his unique brand of mind games which continued to give the impression that he was an extremely intense young man.

Sting tried to abandon those pretensions and simply go for any girl just so long as she had a great face and body. He knew full well that the macho environment he lived in did not really allow for girls to appreciate intellectualism.

He lost his virginity at the age of fifteen to a pretty brunette of the same age who took a fancy to him in a local café and persuaded him to take her to an isolated spot for sex. She saw it as a necessary part of her development before she got locked down by marriage and children. Sting was surprised that any girl could be so casual about making love and, interestingly, he was completely unsatisfied by the encounter.

Eventually, however, Sting got into the habit of expecting sex just like all his other mates but there was a downside to these numerous one-night stands. Condoms were not encouraged. The genuine intensity he started out with seemed to have disappeared momentarily, to be replaced by a callous disregard for the welfare of the girls.

On a number of occasions, 'pregnant' girls confronted Sting about their suspicions and, despite his insistence that he was not a 'bang 'em and leave 'em' merchant, bottles of gin would be purchased with the express purpose of bringing on a late period to extinguish any pregnancy fears.

Despite all these sexual encounters, he was still desperate to find a girlfriend to whom he could actually relate. He felt he needed a middle-class girl with an intellectual capability on a par with his own beliefs and interests. His relationships with his first two full-time girlfriends were especially significant because they seemed to change him from a destructive to a creative personality.

The first was a beautiful local girl who drew envious glances on every street corner, a bit like his mother had done only a couple of years earlier. This girl was a goddess who provided sex on tap but not a lot else. She was madly in love with Sting and worshipped the very ground he stood on. She was loyal, faithful and totally in awe of him, but she was not very bright and Sting grew increasingly frustrated by the long silences between their conversations.

In a desperate attempt to re-educate his girlfriend Sting would constantly try to make her read books like *Howard's End* by E M Forster, but next day she would come back and say she'd read the first page and thought it was boring. Her favourite publications were frothy teen magazines like *Jackie* and *Boyfriend*. Sting felt so irritated by her at times that he wanted to drop her, but her good looks and insatiable appetite for sex made him continue the relationship.

Then the inevitable occurred and she got pregnant. Despite his snooty attitude towards her lack of obvious intelligence, Sting was very considerate. He didn't know what to do but for once he did not try to force his own advice on her. She was too far gone even to mention bottles of gin. This was the real thing and it was terrifying for both teenagers. Abortion was not even mentioned. She actually seemed determined to have the child. Then, more than three months into the pregnancy, she tragically miscarried. Not surprisingly, she went to pieces.

In the months after she lost the baby, Sting kept the relationship going out of sorrow rather than genuine love. He was becoming less and less patient with her even though he felt responsible for what had happened. Eventually, he reacted in the only way he could handle, by running off with another girl. This time he was convinced he had found someone who was his intellectual equal.

Caroline had actually read books like the works of Jean-Paul Sartre, and Sting was infatuated. This was the sort of girl he had been looking for throughout his adolescence.

Meanwhile, his ex-girlfriend, still nursing a broken heart following the miscarriage and the break-up of her relationship with Sting, desperately pleaded with him to go back to her. Shortly afterwards, her mother contracted cancer of the throat and died. Sting tried to be sympathetic and was genuinely torn apart. However, he had now found a new girl to play mind games with.

The first girlfriend went to work in a mental hospital but was so cut up by the death of her mother and the miscarriage that the despair she witnessed there proved too much for her to cope with and, just a year after splitting with Sting, she committed suicide.

Sting was shattered when he heard the news. He couldn't forgive himself for what had happened and was convinced it was all his fault. Yet he knew that if he had stayed with her he would, eventually, have destroyed her life because of his own inbuilt ambition to escape the North East.

The new affair with Caroline went on for three years but then ended so disastrously that Sting is haunted by what happened to this day. Caroline left him for someone else. This had never happened to Sting before; he had always done that to others and was now getting a taste of his own medicine, made all the more painful because he even knew the man she had run off with. It was all so humiliating but, in the back of his mind, he felt he deserved it. That traditional Catholic emotion of guilt was never far away.

Years later, Sting reflected on the way he had felt during those days when he wrote songs like 'The Bed's Too Big Without You'. He always managed to return to those emotions whenever he had to write a song about despair. It was as if he was using those past experiences to gain a foothold in whatever song he was trying to create at the time.

Sting planned to go to university when he left school in the summer of 1969 — if his A-Level grades were good enough. During the holidays he got himself a job as a bus conductor in Newcastle. He enjoyed his new role of strutting up and down the aisle with a smile and a joke for everyone, especially the prettiest girls. There were also dramatic scenes with drunks and fare dodgers. Like everything else at the time, he looked on the job as a learning experience.

When his A-Level results finally came, however, he had managed only mediocre passes in geography, English and economics. His disappointing results meant that only a handful of colleges would take him, including two Coventry-based ones. After a few weeks of trying to sort out his grant and hopping between both places in an effort to decide which one to join, Sting threw in the towel and went back home to the North East. He wanted to do something that really interested him and going to college in Coventry was not on his agenda. His love of music had never faded and he had continued to practise but he didn't know anyone who even vaguely shared his obsession.

Sting was actually very jealous of all his friends who had left school and found jobs. They had the freedom to do as they pleased in the evenings and at weekends. They had the money for flashy clothes and motorcycles while he was still wandering around worrying about his studies. 'I was lost. Totally lost. I decided that it just wasn't for me. I thought that leaving school meant getting rid of the uniform. I thought it meant freedom. It was more of the same in a different uniform. So I decided to leave.'

It was ironic. All those grandiose thoughts of breaking free from Geordie-land had been overtaken by the need to get home. He was back living at the family house with no visible means of supporting his interest in music.

During that difficult first year following his departure from school, Sting worked on building sites in between lining up for the dole. Eventually, he decided to try for something more respectable, got out his only suit and headed for an interview as an executive officer with the Inland Revenue. He got the position but lasted only a few months before the tedium turned him into yet another angry young man.

Next, he applied for a place at the Northern Counties Teacher Training College on the outskirts of Newcastle and was accepted for the 1971 autumn term on the English Bachelor of Education course. Eventually, he moved to the easier Teacher's Certificate in English and Music course.

Sting was in two minds about the entire teaching profession. He loathed schools and their institutionalisation of children but he had a genuine feeling for teaching and helping others not to make the same mistakes as he had.

At the time, Sting hung out at the Wheatsheaf in Newcastle, a pub used mainly by trad jazz musicians for informal sessions. There was a resident rhythm section and the bass player, Ernie, would sometimes let Sting sit in on the bass while he went for a quick drink.

'He had this big double bass. I used to get up, play two numbers and get blisters that wouldn't go away for three weeks. Eventually I got the hang of it and learned to play,' recalls Sting.

One night, Ernie didn't show up and the band asked Sting to sit in. He had brought along his crummy electric bass. 'The band jumped into the modern world that night. It was the first time they'd ever played with an instrument that worked on electricity. They went crazy.'

Not long after this, Sting met someone at teacher training college who would probably prove the biggest single influence on his life and future stardom.

Gerry Richardson was born in Leeds in 1950 and was always destined to be a musician. He sang in choirs and was encouraged to play piano by school teachers who were active in the local jazz scene themselves. At Northern Counties he was in the year above Sting, studying English.

The North East — and Newcastle in particular — had gained a reputation as a hotbed for bands in the early to mid-1970s. Newcastle pub music, with a history that took in Lindisfarne and The Animals, was predominantly guitar music, with hard-driving blues and long-haired, instrumental panache.

The up-and-coming New Wave movement seemed to have all but passed the city by. Many blamed the endless pub and club venues which effectively dampened down the upsurge of musical energy at the time. Others reckoned the new talent existed all right but that there was no back-up of agents/managers/promoters to help to extract any youthful promise.

Gerry Richardson was a keyboards player in a jazz band when his female singer told him about a bass player called Gordon Sumner whom she had spotted playing James Taylor ballads at a local folk club.

'I went along and thought he was all right,' explains Gerry. 'But, frankly, I didn't give a toss about Sting's bass playing until we got talking and I discovered he knew a drummer who owned a van and a PA. That's what I really wanted so I sacked my bassist and drummer and we formed this new line-up called Earthrise.'

At that stage, Sting was rather reluctant to sing and his only vocal performance for the group came when he belted out a cover version of the old Ashton, Gardner and Dyke hit 'Resurrection Shuffle'. None the less, Sting and Gerry became close friends and were forever trying to impress audiences with flashy jazz techniques, despite the band's dreadful horn section.

Sometimes Gerry filled in with a better known, traditional jazz band called Phoenix and, eventually, Sting was offered a chance to join that group as well. The more grown-up Phoenix band had a house rule that every member should be known by a nickname. When young Gordon Sumner turned up for his first day wearing a black and yellow hooped sweatshirt, trombonist Gordon Soloman thought he looked like a wasp. Then a thought came to him. 'Ah, let's call you Sting.' The name stuck. Young Gordon was delighted as he'd always rather hated his own name.

Soon Sting was conjuring up bass lines from New Orleans jazz masters like Satchmo and Kid Ory. The learning experience had moved on to a new, more exciting pasture. Rapidly, he began to get noticed. Another well-respected local jazz outfit called The River City Jazzmen tried to poach him. Then the Newcastle Big Band persuaded him to turn up for a rehearsal but the band's founder and conductor Andy Hudson was not overimpressed. 'To begin with he couldn't really read music,' explains Hudson.

Then the group's sax player Nigel Stanger walked over to Hudson and sniped, 'I can't play with that guy. Get rid of him.'

However, Hudson decided to ignore Stanger on the basis that Sting could only get better. 'Sting had a quality of enthusiasm which was instantly recognisable. He would nick the parts and take them home to study. Another thing about him was the reliability factor. He was never late. That's important. Geniuses who turned up late were no good to me.'

These days, Andy Hudson describes himself as having been the band's 'fixer as we did not have a manager'. He explains away the fact that he got a bigger percentage of each fee because: 'I had to run it. I was the leader. I fronted it and played the keyboards occasionally.' The group had the reputation of being different from everyone else, partly because they had a penchant for starting with one tune and then suddenly sliding into a different number. The music ranged from 'Johnny Dankworth to Average White Band and we never played a tune the same way twice'. Hudson went on, 'We were just a bunch of enthusiastic musicians really. We all hung out at the Newcastle Theatre bar. It was a nice artistic environment.

'The band was really just a residual thing after university. We were as rough as badgers' arseholes when I think back on it. But what the band lacked in skill they more than made up for in enthusiasm. You could say we were on the fringe of The Animals in the sixties. Sting first appeared on the scene when we were having problems with the resident bass player. At the time I let anyone sit in and have a go.'

Within only three or four weeks of joining the band, Sting was beginning to make his perfectionist opinions known. 'He started saying that one of the musicians was a bit rough,' explains Hudson. 'Things turned round that fast because he was so determined to succeed.'

Sting also rapidly adopted a showbusiness stance on certain aspects of the band's existence. Hudson went on, 'We would do the odd bit of comedy and he quickly entered into the spirit of things.'

However, the band did not always get a good reception. One time they were hired by the South Shields Operatic Society, despite having warned them that their kind of music might not be to operatic society tastes. The band were booed off the stage within twenty minutes of appearing 'because they all wanted Glen Miller songs'. Explains Andy Hudson, 'We could have busked it but it would have been like the Blues Brothers in a Country and Western bar.'

At this time, Sting shared a flat with Gerry Richardson and another friend called Tim Archer in the Heaton district of Newcastle. Remembers Andy Hudson, 'It was scruffy batchelordom. Smelly socks. Mess everywhere. Cups and plates littered around the place.'

At teacher training college, Sting had his pick of the girls as there was a ratio of seven to one in favour of female students at the time. He soon got back into the habit of having noncommittal sexual relationships.

Meanwhile, the Newcastle Big Band became the focus of attention most lunchtimes at the city's University Theatre bar and Sting soon found himself playing everything from Duke Ellington to The Beatles' 'Yesterday'. One day, so many people turned up to see the band at one of their regular appearances at the local university that the management decided to cancel them for the following week because they could not cope with the crowds.

Hudson was so infuriated that he and the band decided to perform in the university car park rather than disappoint their fans. Sting hooked up the PA system to the battery of his rusting old Citroën and the group played on, much to the delight of a remarkably big crowd of more than one thousand, until the police turned up and ordered them off the premises just as the band broke into their own rendition of The Beatles' 'Hey Jude'.

Sting never forgot the buzz he got from performing to that crowd. It made everything worthwhile and he wanted more of it.

FOUR

THE ROOKIE

*'I tried to model myself on people like
Cleo Laine and Flora Purim.'*
- STING

FROM 1971 TO 1974, STING BEHAVED like some sort of musical lost soul. He wandered between groups like the Big Band, Phoenix and Earthrise. Throughout, he continued to train as a teacher. He needed direction but had settled purely for survival.

The Newcastle Big Band even cut an album, simply called *Newcastle Big Band*. One side was recorded live at the University Theatre and the other at the Pau Jazz festival in south-west France. Only two thousand copies were pressed and these sold at gigs. Once it had sold out it was not re-pressed and has since become a collector's item.

Sting became a highly active member of the Musicians' Union, supporting Andy Hudson's campaign to take the Newcastle branch out of the hands of the employers, the professional band leaders. For the first time he came into contact with local politics and it interested him immensely. He felt great empathy for his

33

fellow working-class citizens and wanted to do something to improve their lot.

Sting also attended classes to improve his bass technique and was determined to learn how to play the guitar to perfection. Most lunchtimes, he and Gerry would slip away from lectures at teacher training college and go to the music room for a jam.

However, playing with groups like the Big Band did not exactly improve or widen his musical scope. As Sting later explained, 'It was a lovely time for me because I was young and energetic and I could kid myself I was playing with serious musicians. But I wasn't! There was this heavy trip about having the dots written out in front of you whereas it was really an exercise in how much beer you could drink. They all had jobs behind desks and their one delinquency was music.'

Sting could also see his own musical limitations and he was already feeling the urge to write his own songs instead of performing poor imitations of other people's compositions.

At college, Sting became further involved in political activities and proudly declared himself to be a Marxist. It was an interesting about-turn after all those earlier yearnings at grammar school to be middle-class, cultured and rich. However, this was no passing phase. He read all the relevant literature and went out on regular forays against the fascist National Front when they put up an election candidate at South Shields in 1974. Sting even volunteered to drive a bus for the college Socialist Society. Most significant of all, he started to take part in pro-IRA demonstrations, such as the one outside Durham prison against the force-feeding of the Price sisters, convicted IRA terrorists who were on hunger strike at the time. Sting's anger was caught in full flight on the front page of *Red Weekly* in a photograph showing him with a Trotskyite beard and surrounded by placards reading, 'Stop force feeding! Political status now!'

At the time, Sting was fervently anti-establishment and his activities on behalf of the Marxist Party automatically placed him on a list of left-wing subversives that was compiled by British security services. 'Every person who demonstrated outside Durham was vetted by the security services and having his photo on the front page of *Red Weekly* would simply have reaffirmed their interest in characters like Sting,' explained a British intelligence source.

At that time, Britain was in a state of constant alert as the IRA stepped up its bombing campaign on the mainland. British security services were assigned the task of assembling files on every single member of groups like the Marxists who showed considerable sympathy to the IRA cause.

In Sting's case, his open membership of the Marxists and his willingness to explore other people's beliefs were to bring him into contact with some even more ominous powers. Even to this day, he continues to describe himself as a socialist but he now scorns the street politics he used to take part in. Long before the downfall of communism, he dismissed Marxism as 'unworkable'.

In the early to mid-seventies, however, he felt very strongly about the situation in Northern Ireland. 'I know that if I'd been born in Andersonstown or the Bogside I'd be a member of the IRA: a) for my own protection; b) because I'm that sort of person; c) because there is a historical and current situation which is intolerable. However, I abhor terrorism. But that potential is in all of us though,' he says.

Back in the real world, Sting was supplementing his income by working as a glass collector in Julie's Nightclub in Newcastle, which consisted of one large basement room painted in brown and beige, with a small stage. Julie's was a very cliquey establishment often frequented by Newcastle's local mafia and the entrance fee was seven and six, increasing to one pound after ten p.m.

The resident DJ at the time was John Harker who was to become a lifelong friend. John recalls, 'Sting would come in before the club opened for the evening, collect any glasses left over from the night before and then sit on his own on the stage and strum on his guitar. I walked in one night and saw him there and he was actually pretending to himself that there was an audience out there listening to him.'

Harker never forgot Sting's penchant for 'weird clothing. Lots of really horribly coloured tank tops'. He also explains, 'Everyone thought Sting was a bit of a strange one in those days. After all, how many people do you know who would sit on a stage in an empty nightclub and fantasise that they were playing to a packed audience?'

In 1974, Sting moved into a modest flat in the district of Jesmond, a student/middle-class area of east Newcastle. His friend and musical collaborator, Gerry Richardson, had left college a year earlier to work in Bristol. Richardson joined a local band, only to return to Newcastle just as Sting was taking the last of his teacher training exams. The two old friends met up and decided to start a completely new group that would revolve around what they considered to be the perfect combination of jazz and rock.

Determined to keep their standards as high as possible, Gerry and Sting turned to older local musicians such as guitarist John Hedley and drummer Ronnie Pearson, formerly with Back Door. Sting was to share lead vocals with Ronnie.

At first Ronnie Pearson and John Hedley were slow on the uptake and kept putting Sting and Gerry off. 'Then one day they snookered us and organised a session at a college where we both taught,' explained Ronnie. 'We couldn't get out of it.'

That first gig featured a lot of cover material from groups like The Crusaders and a reasonably large crowd turned up, although most of them were Ronnie Pearson's pupils at the very same college.

The new band was called Last Exit and kicked off with a regular Wednesday night spot in a tiny upstairs room at a pub called the Gosforth Hotel. If the group themselves didn't show up by six p.m. they couldn't get in because the place was so crowded. Soon Last Exit progressed to playing Chick Corea and Stevie Wonder cover versions and audiences were amazed at their speed and dexterity. They also provided an unpredictable mixture of soul material, such as Fleetwood Mac's 'I Need Your Love So Bad' and Bill Withers's 'Friend Of Mine'. There were also numerous melodic compositions by Sting and Gerry Richardson.

Two of the first people to see Sting perform were his parents, Audrey and Ernie. Years later, Audrey recalled, 'The first time I heard him speak it was so embarrassing. Sting sang 'Resurrection Shuffle' and I could have crawled under the table. He sounded so gawky. Who would have dreamed that voice would make him his fortune?'

Ernie commented dryly, 'I'm old-fashioned about music and Audrey says he had a squawky voice then. I think it would have been better if he'd been an electrician in the shipyards. That wouldn't have caused this fuss.' It would remain just as difficult for Sting to get praise from his father for the rest of his life. Ernie Sumner's reaction haunted Sting because he meant every word he said. Ernie didn't like to make a song and dance about anything. He was the last father on earth who would have wanted his son to be a rock'n'roll star.

However, other things were also bothering Sting at the time. He was having all sorts of strange experiences and ideas while he taught at high schools as part of his training. One song he chewed over, literally for years, before it emerged as a Police hit was 'Don't Stand So Close To Me'. Sting had wanted to write about sexuality in the classroom because of the way he felt when he taught a number of fifteen-year-old girls who clearly had crushes on him. The problem was that he had fancied them as well. He did not know how he managed to keep his hands off those budding Lolitas. One teacher at a school where he worked commented, 'The song is very revealing. I think that he was more at ease with the boys than the girls here. He was certainly a bit wary of the girls.'

Eventually, Last Exit's regular gigs at the Gosforth and the University Theatre bar became events of the week for local music fans. Despite the cramped conditions, the group managed some superb funk sounds and Sting's own composition, an impassioned love song called 'I Burn For You', regularly left the audience gasping in admiration.

His voice was definitely unusual and even Sting now admits, 'I had a naturally high voice with a high range and I tried to model myself on people like Cleo Laine and Flora Purim. I never tried to disguise that high voice. I never felt embarrassed about it. I used to love voices like that. McCartney has that kind of voice. I loved him. It just cuts through everything — slices through the whole band.'

In the autumn of 1974, Sting began working as a full-time teacher with five to nine year olds at St Paul's First School in Cramlington, a new town just north of Newcastle. He was the only member of Last

Exit holding down a full-time day job. He also moved into a slightly larger flat in Tynemouth, with Gerry Richardson.

Sting got that first job at St Paul's, thanks to head teacher Sister Agnes and she remembers him fondly to this day. 'He had a tremendous gift for talking to young children. He didn't talk to them, but more with them.' However, Sting was no ordinary teacher. Sister Agnes explains, 'At break he could often be found strumming his guitar in the assembly hall or playing the piano. The children loved him.'

Sting himself doesn't particularly rate his abilities as a teacher and even admits, 'The kids in my class were nine or ten years old. You might laugh but they were real delinquents. I loved them though I'm not sure they ever learned anything from me but I'm sure they had a good time. I never gave a fuck about teaching them maths or logarithms. I just wanted them to enjoy themselves while they still had time.'

Despite this, he also remains convinced that being a teacher was the best possible training for his eventual transition into a rock'n'roll star. 'Learning to stand up in front of people and not being an asshole, although I might seem to be one. Self-confidence in front of people. Entertaining, I suppose. I think the phenomenon in the classroom isn't teaching. It's learning. I think what you have to do is create an atmosphere where people can feel happy and want to learn things and I think rock'n'roll is similar.

'I learnt timing, rapport, how to talk to kids without making them think you're a jerk. The trouble was that a lot of them had never really been talked with. Well, the job of a teacher is to be human.'

Every Sunday lunchtime, Last Exit did a free-for-all gig at the Playhouse in the centre of Newcastle. Manager/founder Andy Hudson was always trying to push things along and he organised the regular appearance in such a way that each of the members netted a very useful thirty pounds each week.

Sound engineer, Dave Wood, became very attached to the group during this period. He helped to organise transport for the twenty to thirty hardcore fans of Last Exit whenever the band was playing anywhere outside Newcastle. He explains, 'We used to pick up the speakers and amp and stick them in the back of the van for the lads. I suppose we were unofficial roadies in a way.'

Dave Wood particularly remembers Sting because he was considerably younger than the other group members. 'His voice didn't seem to be the greatest but he had a lot of style and confidence on stage,' he recalls.

Last Exit certainly made a few bob on the pub, club and university circuit. Occasional TV shows, plus packed-out regular Sunday lunchtime gigs often brought in around two hundred pounds, which was good money in those days.

Last Exit even got invited to appear at the San Sebastian Jazz Festival in Spain. Musical megastars like Oscar Petersen, Ella Fitzgerald and Dizzy Gillespie were heading the bill.

Last Exit were actually relegated to playing in a small square surrounded by tiny tapas bars but it was better than nothing. As Dave Wood recalls, 'Everyone got merrily pissed. But Sting didn't join in with the others much. He seemed almost aloof.'

Drummer Ronnie Pearson sets the scene in Spain perfectly, 'We all went by ferry and then drove down to Spain but Sting flew by plane because he was teaching right up until the last minute. It was typical of him to travel alone.'

In a café at Bilbao Airport, Sting found himself sitting opposite British actor, Denholm Elliott. The two did not know each other at that time, but their paths were to cross again just a few years later when they starred in a film together.

At the San Sebastian festival, Sting and the rest of Last Exit drove around in their beaten-up old Bedford van and were put up at various houses dotted around the area. Sting stayed with a family who ran a book shop and turned out to be Basques. One night they took the band to a supper in the mountains where they burnt a forty-foot effigy of General Franco. Andy Hudson also remembers how one member of the band fell in love with the beautiful daughter of a Basque martyr, but he is too tactful to say who it was.

Last Exit stayed on in Spain for three weeks and managed to make enough money to afford decent beds on a ferry back to Britain. It was Sting's first ever trip abroad and it had a profound effect on the young singer. He promised himself that he would try to travel more in the future.

To this day, Andy Hudson still marvels at Sting's professionalism back then. 'There was a song called 'Whispering Voices' which Sting wrote which should have been a hit, it was so brilliantly constructed. Sting performed it with such commitment that all of us were deeply impressed.'

According to Hudson, Gerry Richardson was a different proposition: 'Gerry takes life too seriously. He is probably the most talented person I've ever met but his psyche won't let it out, while someone like Sting was the solid, quick-as-a-flash, do-it-as-you-can type of musician.'

Last Exit drummer Ronnie Pearson looks back on those days with great sentimentality but he also acknowledges, 'I should have known what Sting was up to but I didn't. Sting had a plan from day one. I am just a daft bloody musician who should have known better.'

Ronnie then recalled an intriguing incident when Sting went on a Newcastle radio programme. He explains, 'Sting was actually dressed up for the interview with a jumper that had all the holes arranged in the right places. He had planned the whole thing. He wanted to look the part even though it was a radio interview and no one could see him. That was when I realised something was going on.' Ronnie had insisted on continuing to call Sting 'Gordon' long after the star had adopted his nickname. 'I believe he actually encouraged everyone to call him Sting because he wanted to be a star.'

Frequently, Ronnie or one of the other lads in the band would call round at the flat that Sting shared with Gerry Richardson to ask them out for a pint. 'But more often than not they would refuse to come out because they preferred to stay at home and write songs,' explains Ronnie. 'They'd come back the next day with new compositions, some of which were wonderful.'

At the time, Newcastle had a very large organised-crime problem. Notorious 'families' would come down from the Scottish Borders like packs of wolves. There were about a hundred and fifty of them and every now and then the Northumberland police would chase them down to Newcastle where the city police would have to deal with them for a while before they, in turn, chased them back. Eventually, they settled in the city, bringing their own personal 'family' crime wave with them. Every nightclub in Newcastle seemed to be paying protection money to one or other of these 'families' or was actually owned by them. One night when Sting, Dave Wood and other members of Last Exit were in the Go Go — which featured a particularly tasteless representation of the New York skyline across one entire wall of the club — they heard fire engines in the distance and rushed out to find that the nearby Key Club had burnt to the ground after being torched by vindictive gangsters.

'The gang thing was very heavy at the time,' recalls Dave Wood. 'There was a powerful local mafia and no one ever dared cross them.'

In fact, that same gang warfare inspired the movie *Stormy Monday* in which Sting himself was to star twelve years later.

Also around this time, lead guitarist John Hedley had a dispute with the management of Last Exit and was replaced by quietly spoken Terry Ellis. Ronnie and Sting were both still sharing the vocals at this stage but it was becoming clear that Sting was the more forceful of the two.

Ronnie Pearson inevitably became more and more concerned about how he was being eased out of the singing by the ever-enthusiastic Sting. Terry Ellis explains, 'I actually thought Ronnie was a better singer. Sting's voice seemed very high-pitched at the time but he was forever leaping in with the vocals ahead of everyone else.'

A couple of years later, Terry Ellis saw Sting in Torquay when he was doing a summer season with Cilla Black and Sting was appearing in one of The Police's first gigs. Ellis revealed, 'Sting was already considerably more confident. We had a chat but I could tell he was more interested in his career than anything we had to talk about. I don't think he asked me one question.'

FIVE

SINKING SHIP

*'Pain and anguish stimulate creativity. I think
feeling good and having a nice time is a
pretty bland commodity.'*
- STING

AT TWENTY-THREE YEARS OF AGE, Sting was not the handsome, self-assured character he is today. He stood with a slight stoop. His hair was lank and greasy. In his scruffy beard crumbs of that day's breakfast could often be seen.

Despite all this, he was a walking lump of defiance compared with the other members of Last Exit. His determination and underlying toughness covered up the insecurity created by being told by many that he was not quite good enough, even though Sting was certain he knew better.

Just before Christmas 1974, Last Exit landed a gig at the University Theatre Christmas show, entitled *Rock Nativity*, a musical written by veteran pop writer Tony Hatch. The part of the Virgin Mary was played by a dark-haired, twenty-seven-year-old actress called Frances Tomelty, daughter of veteran film actor Joseph Tomelty.

Initially, Frances found Sting to be introverted, arrogant and rather

43

self-obsessed, while he was intrigued by her soft Irish accent and calmness. There was a spark between them but she was not exactly lighting up the sky. In any case, as she later admitted, she preferred the lead guitarist. However, at the first-night party for the Christmas show — held just after they met — Sting made a point of chatting Frances up.

A few days after that first encounter backstage at the university, Sting persuaded Frances to let him go back to her digs to play her some of his latest compositions. It was a corny line but it apparently worked. Frances recalls, 'The deal was that I'd make the cheese on toast while he'd serenade me with his guitar.'

Sting later conceded, 'Music was very much part of the seduction process. It still works with a large group of people. Serenade all these birds and they want to deliver their bodies to you.'

Frances wasn't just 'any bird', though. She was a feisty girl born in the rough, tough streets of Andersonstown, Northern Ireland. She was more interested in discussing the IRA, the UDA and the British Army than Sting's favourite melodies. But then Sting was already very knowledgeable about 'the movement' so he was delighted that they had so much in common.

When the *Rock Nativity* run ended, Frances returned to London for a play she was scheduled to appear in. Sting was heartbroken and decided to start commuting between north and south at weekends. Sometimes he had to travel to places like Edinburgh or Sheffield as Frances toured with the new play. Back in London, Frances also had a part in a children's TV series called *No Place To Hide*.

Throughout all this, Sting still managed to keep most of his commitments to Last Exit who were now being hired regularly to support bigger bands passing through the North East, groups like Osibisa, Zzebra, Coloseum and a bizarre project entitled *Tubular Bells* by Mike Oldfield, which featured a guitarist called Andy Summers. However, Andy did not meet Sting at that time.

A month after starting the relationship, Sting asked self-assured Frances what on earth she saw in him. 'I'm just a two-bit teacher from Newcastle,' he said.

Frances replied, 'That's not how I see you', to which Sting hit back, 'That's not how I see me either.'

Despite that remark, Frances found the young Sting to be very sheltered, young for his age and very inexperienced with girls despite his bragging to the contrary. 'I just hoped he'd grow into the man he became,' she later commented.

Last Exit entered the North East heat of *Melody Maker*'s rock contest and completely blew it when some of the band members failed to show up. They also auditioned for a Tyne-Tees TV show called *The Geordie Scene*, which packaged a star name with a local band. However, the show's producers insisted that Last Exit's music was too varied to work in the programme's format.

Sting continued to perform with Last Exit at their regular Wednesday-night gig at the Gosforth Hotel. Beer mugs clinked and conversation clattered from all directions until everyone realised the band had gone quiet as Sting murmured into the mike with a passion which had the entire audience of about a hundred hardened drinkers speechless with emotion, 'You and I are lovers ... I burn for you.' That sensuous, glowing song, with its slow crescendo, remained everyone's favourite.

Record companies regularly came up to the North East to see the band and went away again completely confused. Ronnie Pearson explains, 'They could not make out what kind of music we did. We could not be pigeon holed.'

Last Exit continued as before but frequently found themselves at the centre of some problem or other. At one small club just outside Gateshead, they faced a bunch of aggressive miners and Sting made the fatal mistake of taking on the audience when he didn't get the response he wanted. Ronnie Pearson explains, 'They all had love and hate tattoos and Sting started needling them. You just do not do that in certain places. I heard them saying they were going to get us after the show.'

Then a friendly policeman turned up because some of the vans outside the club were illegally parked. 'Suddenly, Sting let loose with his own version of *The Laughing Policeman* and the whole place started laughing hysterically. The tough nuts at the front forgot all about their threats and we all got home in one piece.'

In the middle of all this, Last Exit were also trying to apply themselves to the serious business of recording demo tapes for distribution around various record companies. Between February 1975 and January 1976, they spent a lot of time at Dave Wood's Impulse Studio in Wallsend, just a few hundred yards from Sting's old family home.

On 18 November 1975, they even recorded a single of Gerry's 'Whispering Voices', sung by Sting, and followed that with a nine-track album on cassette because it was cheaper to produce than vinyl. The title of the album was *First From Last Exit* and the songs included Sting's 'We Got Something', 'Carrion Prince', 'On This Train', 'Oh My God', 'Truth Kills' and 'Savage Beast', with Gerry's 'I Got It Made' and 'Whispering Voices'. They also included an instrumental from guitarist Terry Ellis who had earlier taken over from John Hedley.

Studio boss Dave Wood says he recognised certain elements of those tracks in Sting's later multi-million-selling material for The Police and later as a solo artist. As recently as early 1995, Wood met up with Gerry Richardson and mentioned the similarities. 'Gerry was very subdued when I talked about it,' explains Dave Wood.

Drummer Ronnie Pearson is only slightly more philosophical about the tracks' similarities to what Sting has done since. He says, 'Listen to that tape of demos and then listen to what he's doing today and you'll find traces of a lot of stuff which he and Gerry wrote back then.' However, Ronnie insists he is not bitter about Sting's echoing of those old tracks. 'It's funny really. I didn't feel that close to Sting or anyone at that time we were together in Last Exit. It is only in recent years I realise I was closer to Sting. I am proud of what he has done.' He then added thoughtfully, 'Sometimes I hear some of his stuff now and think "Shit, that's my idea." But so what? That's just the way it goes.'

The use of elements of Last Exit music by Sting — which is not surprising as he was the band's main writer — later in his career has caused a certain amount of bitterness among some of the other group members. When studio boss, Dave Wood, announced a few years back that he intended to turn all those original demo tapes into an album entitled something along the lines of *Sting — The Early Days*, he was threatened with legal action by Virgin Records who owned the rights to all Sting's early material.

Wood was so shaken by the reaction that, when Sting visited Newcastle in the early nineties, he approached the singer in a car park and offered to give him the originals so that he 'had some copies for himself'.

Impulse Studio owner, Dave Wood, was also responsible for introducing Sting to reggae after Wood's father returned from a holiday in Barbados with a pile of records. Dave found a song called 'Put On Your Wings And Fly' and encouraged Last Exit to record it in the hope that they might be one of the first groups on the reggae bandwagon.

However, Gerry and Sting argued over who should sing it. In the end, Gerry did it in a duet with Ronnie and the honest appraisal from Dave Wood is that 'it was awful'. Some of the other band members just did not like reggae and Ronnie Pearson even refused to play one song written by Sting called 'Let Me Do It To You'.

Back on the domestic front, Sting was still courting actress Frances Tomelty and insisting he was a teacher who just happened to play with a band occasionally. He loved to explain to her how different he was from all the other hardline teachers at the school where he worked. He made a point of turning orderly classroom procedure upside down by bringing the children boxes of musical instruments and singing with them in class.

Frances believed she had found a very special man in Sting, even though he was a couple of years younger than her. She also happened to be pregnant.

On 1 May 1976, they were married at St Oswin's Roman Catholic Church in Front Street, Tynemouth. While the serenity of a church seemed a little hypocritical, considering he had not been religious for a number of years, Sting believed he would not have felt married if they had not done it in church.

Sting was relieved when Frances announced that there was no way she could settle in Newcastle. He needed that push finally to escape after so many years of thinking over it but doing absolutely nothing about fleeing south.

Gerry Richardson believes this was a turning point in Sting's development. 'I think Frances pushed him like fuck ... although he has always been an incredibly competitive bloke — try playing Scrabble with him.'

Just before the wedding, Ernie Sumner — concerned at what he considered to be a serious romance at an age when his son should be having fun — turned to Sting and said, 'Go to sea and don't ever get married.' It was a sad reflection on his own attitude to marriage.

Ironically, soon after Sting's marriage to Frances he did go to sea as a musician for the P&O Line. He got an Equity actors' union card after Ronnie Pearson helped him to fill in the application form by pretending all their gigs had been appearances in theatres.

The infamous sea cruise on the good ship *Orianna* — which, sadly, sank off the coast of East Africa in the early 1990s, after a chequered history which included being hijacked by Arab terrorists — is still fondly remembered by the other members of Last Exit who made the trip. The fact that Sting had been married only a short time did not even merit a mention from them.

Ronnie Pearson takes up the story, 'Sting and Gerry kept nagging me about getting them on a cruise so one day I said to them, "All right, lads but you gorra understand that it'll be foxtrots, waltzes and quick steps. There'll be no room for any rock 'n' roll." '

'We'll do it! We'll do it!' came the enthusiastic reply. Sting insisted to Ronnie that he was in dire need of a holiday. Whether this was in response to his recent marriage or not we shall never know.

Next day, Ronnie contacted one of his friends at the P&O Line and convinced them he had a great band on offer. A few weeks later they turned up in Southampton to board the *Orianna*. It was 17 July 1976.

'I remember the first night we got on board,' recalls Ronnie. 'Sting was sitting in the dining room when he was offered some cheese from the cheese board and took the whole bloody lump. He didn't have a clue about manners in those days. I even said to him, "Sting, you're only supposed to take as much as you want." He barked back at me, "That's how much I want." ' Unfortunately, Ronnie and his merry men proved to be, in his own words, 'hopeless'. After only two days on board, Ronnie was pulled into the ship's musical director's office and warned that, 'Unless you lot start playing middle-of-the-road stuff, we'll drop you off at the next port.'

Luckily, the next evening the group were playing on the back deck where the audience was quite a lot younger. Ronnie explains, 'We started playing a bit of rock'n'roll and then this guy came up and said he thought we were marvellous. He turned out to be the captain. Word got back to the musical director and from that moment on we were allowed to look after the young people.'

By all accounts, Sting and his two compatriots had a riotous time throughout the two-week cruise. At every port they got off the ship and toured the local bars and clubs. The pay was one hundred pounds a week, which was good money in those days. Ronnie Pearson still works as a musician on cruises to this day.

However, Gerry Richardson had a slightly less nostalgic recollection of the cruise: 'The problem was that Ronnie organised it and anything he did he wanted to be brilliant, whereas I just wanted to keep people happy and Sting wanted a holiday. It was a ghastly compromise'.

The cruise itself actually opened up some bitter wounds between Sting and Gerry Richardson. The two men were becoming increasingly competitive about who should write and perform their songs. Only a short time before the cruise, Gerry had broken a plate over Sting's head and then Sting poured a bowl of hot soup over Gerry during a furious clash at the flat in Tynemouth. It was a similar sort of creative tension that later flared up between Sting and the other members of The Police.

One hot summer's day, Sting, Frances and Terry Ellis drove in Sting's battered old grey Citroën Dyane down to the beach at Marsden because Sting had just purchased a new snorkel and wanted to try it out. They also took a small rubber dinghy. Frances packed a modest lunch of sandwiches and coffee in a basket and off they headed.

Terry Ellis never forgot that day because the heavily pregnant Frances was left to fend for herself while Sting behaved like a kid with a new toy as he spent hours swimming around the rocks that bordered the beach. 'They didn't seem that close, considering they were married, and Sting just spent the whole time talking shop,' recalls Ellis.

A few weeks later, Sting's Citroën burst into flames while they were hurtling down the M1. Luckily, the car was insured and the money they claimed actually helped them to find a decent flat to rent. As Ronnie Pearson put it, 'If you dropped Sting on his head he would be OK.'

Meanwhile Last Exit was struggling along and there was a genuine fear that the group might end up as old men still playing at dive halls if they weren't careful. Frances — taking a break from acting — actually turned to helping the band at this stage. She even advised Sting on how to perform on stage. 'When I first saw Last Exit, he used to look around a lot. He thought he was drawing the audience in, but I knew it diffused concentration and made him look nervy and awkward. I said, "Be still." ' Sting took his wife's advice and started to get noticed.

Frances also took the group's latest demos on another tour of London record companies. 'It's quite soul-destroying for a band to do that themselves. "Listen. This is my art." It might have been an advantage to have me there able to joke and flirt with the A and R men — and very pregnant, too.'

In the inevitable power struggles that followed within Last Exit, the band leadership switched from Gerry to Sting. Years later Sting confessed, 'I'm a usurper. Should I hide my light under a bushel? I ain't that sort of person.'

Gerry has since rationalised his resentment about what happened with Sting. 'To get on we had to shove Sting to the front. I knew Sting was going to be a star. He developed this incredible relationship with the audience. He was bright, he wrote songs, had a brilliant voice. And, of course, there's this incredible charm. Everyone who knows him likes him.'

Sting concedes that the undercurrents were ominous. 'Gerry was always over my shoulder. I love him dearly, but I'm very much into rivalry and we are still rivals.'

Living together in that flat actually caused the sparks to fly more than anything else. Sting always seemed more capable of conjuring up a song or two with little effort, while Gerry found it a struggle.

When the group performed, it was Sting's songs that got the audience singing along. One of his most renowned was a composition called 'Don't Give Up The Day Job'. Sting believes it summed up his situation at the time. 'That was the most overt example of my crass desires.'

That song was actually a self-mocking piece which Sting composed just days after he had finally taken the plunge and quit teaching. It was the summer of 1976 and unemployment was creeping up and up. With Frances about to give birth, Sting had taken a startling risk. As he later explained, 'Frances was already into that style of life. Anyway it was a relief. I'd had two jobs for two years and I was fucking knackered.'

At the time, the Sex Pistols had just been launched in London and Sting felt inspired by them — for all the wrong reasons. 'They were destroying something which had held me back. I was older, a much more sophisticated musician than Johnny Rotten or Sid Vicious, but I could relate to that anti-establishment feeling. The energy and aggression — hatred!'

Thanks to the Last Exit songs he later adapted for The Police, including 'The Bed's Too Big Without You' and 'So Lonely', which began life as Exit's 'Fool In Love', there are subtle clues about Sting's musical tendencies at that time. Some of his main artistic influences in 1976 are worth mentioning because they provide an insight into his bleak, dark sense of humour. The fate of executed American killer Gary Gilmore, the book *Lolita*, which Sting has read at least three times, and a Ted Hughes poem called 'Truth Kills

Everyone' all had a profound effect. He was also very interested in learning the classical Spanish guitar and paid Last Exit guitarist Terry Ellis five pounds an hour to teach him.

Meanwhile, Last Exit were close to being discovered. Carol Wilson of Virgin Music Publishing took such a shine to the band that she persuaded a battalion of company executives, including boss Richard Branson, to travel up to Newcastle to see them support Alan Price at the City Hall. Unfortunately, it was a disastrous performance because the band didn't do an efficient sound check and failed to have enough mikes on the drums, with the result that they sounded like amateurs.

The Virgin contingent left Newcastle very unimpressed, but Carol Wilson still asked Last Exit to come down to London and record some tracks at a studio. Ronnie Pearson said, 'We hired a van. I was driving. We got about ten miles outside Durham and the van broke down.'

The AA came to the rescue and, eventually, the group found themselves staying in a scruffy hotel in Paddington, West London, in the middle of the capital's red-light district. They were even told by the record company that they would have to pay for the hotel themselves.

Last Exit recorded eleven tracks in one day at the Pathway Studios on behalf of Virgin Records. It was a remarkable achievement in such a short space of time. However, the group were very disillusioned by the attitude of Virgin. Ronnie Pearson explains, 'We did the whole thing on our own. No one from Virgin even bothered to show up.'

Then Virgin hauled all the members of Last Exit into a meeting at their London offices. Ronnie recalls, 'They just shouted at us "This is no good. You gotta come down and live here. We'll find you a squat." '

Ronnie was appalled. 'I could not stand the thought of it. We told them that we could always fly down or take a train or whatever. There was no reason for us to live in London. That was my thinking anyway.'

None the less, Virgin still offered Sting a publishing deal on the rights to his compositions and everything he was planning to write in the future. Frances was the first person to read the Virgin contract when it arrived in the post at the tiny flat where she and Sting had moved after their wedding. She claims that neither of them fully understood its significance but they signed it anyway.

Sting insists he didn't appreciate that he had just accepted the publishing royalty of 50 per cent with five annual 'options', one of those phrases which perhaps doesn't stand out so much in a contract as it does in conversation. Later, Sting explained, 'I assumed that it meant "mutual options", that I had as much freedom to pull out as they did. That was my stupidity. It wasn't a great deal but I was so excited that I took it. I thought, "I'm a real songwriter." It was like a trophy that proved I was a songwriter. I could talk to people about *my publishers*. It was another great thrill.'

Sting was on 50 per cent when many major writer/performers are on 80–90 per cent. It was to be a contract that would haunt Sting for many years and lead to a bitter feud between the singer and the famous entrepreneur Richard Branson.

At the time, however, Sting and the other members of Last Exit were just pleased that success seemed to be on the horizon. Carol Wilson at Virgin booked the band a showcase gig at Dingwalls club in London and they were given good reviews by the music press. Virgin gave them more time to record some more demos at Pathway Studios.

Their deal gave them new confidence and the group finally agreed to move to London, despite the problems of uprooting themselves. A highly complimentary piece about Last Exit appeared in the Newcastle *Journal* column written by Andy Bone in late 1976. The article was headlined 'LAST EXIT TAKE THE ROAD SOUTH TO FAME'.

It read, 'It's not surprising to see one of our local bands, Last Exit, packing their bags and seeking fame and fortune in London. The rock group have gone as far as they can in the North with their vaguely jazz funk approach. In London they are likely to be truly appreciated. The gigs are there and so are the deals. Already there are murmurings of likely recording contracts. I caught the band making their last appearance at the Gosforth Hotel after playing twice weekly there for two years.'

Melody Maker gave them their first ever national mention following one of those rare trips to appear in London. Sting recalls, 'I was thrilled because there was a sentence about us in a review of another band. I remember thinking, "At last, we're a tiny microcosm in the rock business, at last we've been recognised." I've still got the review.'

Last Exit actually announced their departure for London during a gig at St Mary's Teacher Training College. In the audience that night was Curved Air drummer, Stewart Copeland, who was winding down after an earlier energetic performance with his group. As he watched a confident Sting leading the audience, an idea for a new group began to germinate in Copeland's head. It was clear to him that this was a young man in an old band — 'a vibrant force surrounded by fuddy duddies'.

Copeland later recalled, 'I remember thinking, "I wish they'd get on with it." I had the feeling it was the people around Sting who were holding him back.'

By the time Frances gave birth to the couple's first child on 23 November 1976, neither she nor Sting had a clue what the future held for them. Joseph was named after Frances's father but, as Sting later commented, 'The constitution we set our marriage on was very flexible. I said, "Right. We'll have this kid but I don't ever want to say to him I gave up the best years of my life for you, because it was said to me." I wanted to carry on living my life to my standards — and both of us were like this!'

Nothing and no one was going to get in the way of Sting. His mind was set on stardom.

SIX

LUCKY BREAK

*'I am a strange creature. I'm essentially
introverted and, yet given an opportunity,
I become very much larger than life.'*
                                    - STING

STING'S PLANS TO SET UP LAST EXIT on the London club circuit were
ruined when all the other band members, except Gerry Richardson,
changed their minds about moving south. 'I'd left my steady teaching
job and there they were — the professional musicians — scared to
actually make the move,' explained Sting years later.

He even wrote the other Last Exit members a letter, saying: 'I'm
totally committed to Last Exit but I'm committed to the Last Exit who
said they wanted to make it, who said they were coming to London.
Come down or the group's finished.' No one but Gerry Richardson
had the courage to make that full-time commitment.

Sting recalls, 'I suppose it was a bit of a pipe dream, that the whole
band would move their families and their lives to London. But I was
still very disappointed.'

By a strange twist of fate, a few weeks later, in January 1977,
Curved Air drummer Stewart Copeland found himself back in

Newcastle so he called local rock critic Phil Sutcliffe and asked him if he knew where Last Exit might be appearing. Sutcliffe took him to see the band at the Newcastle Polytechnic. Years later Stewart recalled, 'It was a terrible gig and the numbers were all seven minutes long and very intense. But they went down a storm just because of Sting. Because of his raps with the audience. Because of his singing. Because of his presence. Sting had then what he has now.'

Stewart asked Sutcliffe for Sting's phone number and he called him up that evening from his hotel. 'I'm thinking of getting a band together and I want you to come and join us,' Copeland said to Sting. Sting could not believe his ears. The invitation had come completely out of the blue. He did not hesitate to say yes. Stewart was astounded at how easy it was to persuade the young singer to join him. He did not realise that Sting had already planned to move to London with Frances later that month.

Sting was deeply impressed by Stewart Copeland's credentials. Not only had he been a member of Curved Air but he had worked inside the music industry for many years and clearly knew the right people.

*   *   *

Stewart Armstrong Copeland was born in Virginia on 16 July 1952. His mother was an archaeologist. His father, Miles Copeland Jr, was a highly rated jazz trumpeter who had played in the Woody Herman band before the war, specialising in Glen Miller tunes.

When the war came Miles joined US army intelligence, moved to Washington DC and then switched to the CIA. The family eventually travelled all over the world with their father in his capacity as a CIA operative. Those connections later helped The Police to overcome all sorts of obstacles while travelling the world.

Miles Jr quit the CIA in 1956 and opened his own agency providing an information service to large American corporations such as Gulf Oil, Mobil Oil, National Cash and Pan Am. However, he always remained in touch with his old contacts.

Stewart started playing the drums when he was thirteen, in various groups formed by the children in the Beruit community where he lived at the time. Then he was sent to Millfield, an expensive private school in southern England.

Stewart eventually joined Curved Air as a tour manager before landing the job of new drummer after the group had all but broken up. That didn't last long, though, because Stewart was unhappy about the way Curved Air needed to do everything very commercially because they spent so much money on their albums. 'Every album we made had to be a hundred thousand seller just to break even. Consequently, we couldn't take any chances.'

In the end it was only natural that he should progress to forming a band like The Police.

*   *   *

Back in Newcastle, Sting and Frances loaded two-month-old baby Joe and everything they owned into their battered car and headed for London. Life in the smoke wasn't easy for Sting and his young family. Initially, they found themselves sleeping on the floor of Frances's showbusiness agent friend Pippa Markham who handled both their careers.

In the time-honoured tradition of struggling musicians, Sting went on the dole. 'It was a frightening and humiliating experience when I had a wife and child to support,' recalls Sting. 'I hated having to go to the dole office to pick up my money. They all acted as if it was coming out of their own pockets.'

Sting kept a diary of his thoughts and life at this time when he found himself saddled with a young family while living on less money than could support most single people. At one stage he wrote:

My tired mind is in turmoil. Please God help me and what is going to happen to us? I went to the dole — feel all the usual nausea — the sickening queue.

A few weeks later he sounded even more desperate:

*Money, or lack of it, has raised its ugly head again — Joe is so
innocent and vulnerable — God please help us.*

As the months went by, Sting found himself struggling desperately to
find the rent and food for Frances and baby Joe.

He had long since signed a contract with Virgin Music but all he
earned for the first two years was two hundred pounds. All his dreams
of wealth and fame seemed further away than ever before. In
desperation he wrote in the diary:

I must support my wife and child — keep them safe and happy.

A few weeks later he sounded as if he was contemplating the ultimate
escape from his problems:

*What we are doing here is either heroic or stupid. No money,
nowhere to live and neither of us has a job. Could this be the end?*

Sting wavered between empathy and anger towards his young family
during those difficult and painful times. At one bleak moment, he
even conceded to one friend, 'I never wanted to be a father, never
planned a child. A lot of the time it wasn't terribly logical.'

Meanwhile, up in Newcastle the rest of Last Exit were so riddled
with guilt over their non-appearance in London that they eventually
turned up to perform in a few pubs in the capital. However, Terry
Ellis and Ronnie Pearson continued to refuse to move down
permanently. They disbanded at the beginning of 1977.

To this day, Terry Ellis remains somewhat bitter over the situation
but it has nothing to do with Sting's subsequent success. He is still
angry because Sting took a PA with him to London. 'We all bought
that PA but after Sting took it to London we never saw it again. I
could have done with getting some money from it as we were all
pretty broke at the time,' he explains. If true, this story may reflect

Sting's anger about the band's change of mind over their move to London.

Terry and the rest of the band did form a Last Exit Mark Two, but it soon faded out. He still insists he never thought Sting would make it, especially as 'he was forever telling us "I'm not a musician, I'm an actor." '

Like other members of the group, Ellis has since noticed that many elements of Last Exit's compositions have 'popped up' in The Police and Sting's later solo work, which may not be surprising given Sting's writing prowess, even during the Last Exit days.

At least Sting already had a new band to fall back on. Without such a safety valve, Gerry Richardson was penniless and had to fight his way into the London music scene where he eventually became musical director for Billy Ocean before moving back to the North East. These days, Richardson is reluctant to blame Sting for what happened. 'I can never feel that angry with Sting for deserting me, so to speak. It was a close relationship and the split did just about kill me. But he had moved down with his wife and baby and he had to jump in any direction he thought it might happen.'

Even Sting concedes that he 'fucked Gerry up. Not deliberately, but I fucked him up. I was very saddened because I never meant to ... there's a history of that with me. People get burnt and I'm not that apologetic about it. I know it happens — musically and socially. I've always said that ambition is stronger than friendship and people have been shocked by that, but I actually believe it. I'm not justifying it morally; I'm just saying I think that.'

It must be remembered, of course, that Sting wasn't exactly first-choice lead singer for Stewart Copeland's new band, The Police. The drummer had spent months trying to find someone through the music business grapevine and had even advertised in the music press without success. Sting was his last hope.

Shortly after getting Sting on board, Copeland introduced a young Corsican called Henry Padovani as lead guitarist. He had played in a number of unknown groups but his biggest claim to fame was that he hung out with the Flaming Groovies and that was how he had met

Copeland during his days with Curved Air.

Henry went with Stewart to all the hippest London clubs like The Roxy. One night they saw the Damned and even dropped some acid together. A few weeks later, Henry was offered a job fronting a new punk outfit called London. Copeland's response was to persuade him to join The Police instead.

On 12 January 1977, Stewart, Sting and Henry had their first rehearsal together at Stewart's spacious two-storey flat in Mayfair. Sting was impressed. It wasn't until a few days later that he discovered Stewart was squatting there.

The threesome immediately began rehearsing ten songs written by Stewart. Sting was not all that impressed by the end of that first session. He considered Stewart's ideas to be weak, although he was impressed by Stewart the man. 'I saw something of myself in Stewart. He's very egocentric. Very, very energetic. Very determined. Very intelligent. He was an opportunist, like me.'

Stewart's memory of that first session provides an interesting insight into Sting as he was then. 'Sting was a typical provincial boy. He thought he was going to get ripped off by everyone. He wasn't at all sure about the music.'

Meanwhile Henry Padovani had a few problems of his own when it came to playing his guitar. Explained Copeland, 'He knew a few chords and he was really enthusiastic and when he'd had his hair cut and stuff he looked the part. I mean, he could play guitar better than I could.' But then, Copeland was the drummer.

Sting — a perfectionist even in those far-off days — quickly spotted the deficiencies. 'Henry was deadweight. I couldn't write guitar parts for him because he couldn't play the way I liked. He had feel and spirit, but for what I wanted he was wrong.'

However, Stewart stuck with Henry for the time being and the group decided to cut a single before they made any live appearances. They knew they had little chance of getting a major recording label interested but there might be possibilities within the highly active, independent-label punk scene that was thriving in London at the time.

Then in walked Stewart Copeland's brother Miles. He'd already set up a company which dealt with the business end of punk, managing bands and getting records released. He'd also been largely responsible for getting Stewart into the business.

Miles Copeland was as savvy as Stewart and Sting were determined. He could see the punk era sweeping previously unworkable acts towards fame and he wanted a big slice of the action. 'Punk was like a light bulb going on in my head; an escape from the morass I'd got myself into,' explains Miles Copeland now.

A lot of punk purists claimed that Miles was a chameleon-like, music-biz entrepreneur who was as fickle about music as a politician is about honesty. Miles, on the other hand, saw himself as a tough guy who had been through the crummiest end of the recording industry and had come out the other end. He wasn't keen on helping his baby brother too much. He quietly advised Stewart at first, but insisted on not getting directly involved with The Police. Eventually, Stewart, who was still living in the squat in central London at the time, borrowed a hundred and fifty pounds from a friend and booked a recording session at Pathway Studios where Last Exit had made their demo tapes for Virgin a few months earlier.

They recorded one of Stewart's songs, called 'Fall Out', on 12 February 1977. The B-side was a tune called 'Nothing Achieved', written by Stewart and his other brother, Ian, another musician.

While Stewart arranged to have the record mixed and pressed and organised the design of the cover, he encountered American punk singer Cherry Vanilla who had arrived in England with only one of her band members because she hadn't been able to afford to bring anyone else for her tour. Stewart immediately offered himself, Sting and their equipment if The Police could go on as her supporting act and be paid fifteen pounds a night. She agreed.

The Police's live debut occurred at the Newport Stowaway Club in Wales and lasted all of forty minutes. The set was mainly made up of Stewart's songs, including 'Kids To Blame', which he had written and recorded with Curved Air, plus a couple of numbers by Sting.

Shortly after that, the band did a gig at the Nashville Rooms in West Kensington, London. As they stepped out in front of the predominantly punk audience they soon realised that they would have to play to the crowd. 'Here's a punk song for you, you assholes,' announced Sting to the delighted crowd. Back in Newcastle his words would have provoked a riot. Here in punk-infested London, the audience lapped it up. In actual fact, Sting really seemed full of contempt for the crowd that evening. He explains, 'I was reactionary but that was just because I wasn't sure where we stood with all these punk bands.'

Around this time, Sting first encountered Boomtown Rats lead singer Bob Geldof, who explains, 'We kept bumping into each other. They were making interesting music. It sounded like aggressive reggae and it definitely did not fit in with the punk sounds of the time.'

A few months later, Geldof was at the Camden Music Machine in London, where The Police were appearing. He goes on, 'The stage was seventeen feet from the floor and there were only about fifteen to twenty people. My group was at number six at the time and we watched this three-piece with some interest. I liked the vibe and the sound. Then I went to meet them backstage and Sting was very defensive. In those days he was rather aggressive. I think he was embarrassed because there were so few people in the audience.'

Miles Copeland continued to keep a close eye on The Police, but still held back from getting directly involved. He did not particularly approve of Sting's non-stop pretence of being a punk and actually ignored Sting a lot of the time in those early days. Miles considered him something of a charlatan because he was trying to pretend to be something he clearly was not.

The problem was that The Police were no one's idea of a true punk band and Stewart's former membership of Curved Air was frequently mentioned as hard evidence of that fact. A lot of music business people refused to accept that he could move from old-fashioned seventies rock to New Wave in one leap.

Those first Police gigs were not exactly show stoppers and Stewart Copeland began to find himself ostracised by many of his one-time pals in the rock'n'roll business because they thought the group was trying to pull some huge confidence trick over punk.

There was also another big problem — Henry Padovani's guitar playing seemed doomed never to fit in with the group. Henry's most useful role in the band was to paint graffiti on walls across London, promoting the group.

However, Stewart was the leader of the band in those early days and he even made a point of telling Sting: 'Don't let's go for chart hits which don't really mean anything. Let's go for one group of people and really hit them hard. Let's put everything into one objective — sound — and then we can get a small following which is dedicated rather than a following which is dependent on whether or not we get airplay and will leave us if we don't.'

It all sounded more like a business management plan than the young, drug-orientated leader of a new rock band, but Stewart knew exactly what he was doing and he had Miles encouraging him every step of the way.

In those early, stagnant days Stewart had his work cut out holding on to Sting. Gerry Richardson tried to recruit him for Billy Ocean's backing band after he became Ocean's musical director. He offered Sting ninety pounds a week — a tempting sum compared to the pittance he was earning with The Police at the time.

Stewart even sensed that Sting's commitment to The Police was less than wholehearted. 'He didn't identify with the group. His attitude was "Convince me — keep me in the band." ' So, every day, Copeland called Sting and made sure he always had something to tell him. 'I've just got the photos back from the session,' or 'I've just finished the record sleeve, why don't you come over and have a look at it,' or 'We've got a gig'. Everyone else at that lowly end of the music business was lucky if they got one call a week.

There was another problem looming — Sting's attitude to Henry Padovani. Sting did not rate him as a guitarist, nor did they like each other on a personal basis in those days. Stewart knew that one of them would have to go and he was well aware that the more talented Sting was eventually going to be pilfered by another group if he did not sort out the situation.

Then Mike Howlett, former bass player with the well-known band Gong, asked Sting if he would join him in a new group called Strontium 90 who were to play a one-off gig at a Gong reunion in Paris. Stewart was worried until Howlett persuaded him to play the drums in the group. However, Howlett had no interest in hiring Henry Padovani because he had already recruited a brilliant guitarist called Andy Summers ...

*   *   *

Andrew James Summers was born in Poulton-le-Fylde, near Blackpool, on 31 December 1942. He was a wartime baby whose father was in the RAF. When Andy was two, the family moved south to Bournemouth where his father ran a restaurant.

By the time he was sixteen, Andy was playing guitar with keyboard wizard Zoot Money at a Bournemouth jazz club called The Blue Note. He was superb at copying any classic songs but audiences tended to be astonished by his presence on the stage because he looked nearer twelve than sixteen.

By 1963 Andy was playing major gigs with Zoot Money, including a regular appearance at the Flamingo Club in London's Soho. Home was a bedsit in Finchley and Andy even changed his surname to Somers for the following few years.

Throughout all of this, Andy remained a clean-cut-looking guy despite the onset of psychedelia and wild parties with the likes of Paul McCartney, Jimi Hendrix and the Moody Blues. Andy experimented with LSD after encountering The Animals when they returned from a US tour with dozens of acid tabs. He even lost his girlfriend to Animals leader Eric Burden during an acid trip. He remained with Zoot Money in a variety of bands and they were eventually signed to CBS records, releasing one of the all-time cult classics, 'Running Through The Fields'.

Andy freely admits to sleeping with dozens of groupies in those days, and was even featured in a book written by supergroupie Jenny Fabian who described Andy's genitals as 'perfectly formed'.

Shortly afterwards — in the spring of 1968 — he split with Zoot Money and joined Soft Machine, one of the most avant-garde bands to emerge from the psychedelic movement. However, that didn't work out and Andy soon left to rejoin Zoot Money who'd just split with Eric Burden and the reformed Animals.

Andy then married an American girl called Robin Lane who had inspired Neil Young to write one of his greatest songs, 'Cinnamon Girl'. He dropped out of rock music completely to study classical music at a Californian college for the following three years. Struggling to survive financially, he broke up with his wife and drifted back into the rock business. For a while, he even shared an apartment with *Starsky and Hutch* star Paul Michael Glaser in Los Angeles. He also toyed with acting but then decided to return to London in a bid to reignite his musical career.

In 1973, he married his girlfriend Kate and managed to get a job as a backing musician for Neil Sedaka. Various jobs followed, including touring with David Essex, before he joined Kevin Coyne who was emerging from the club circuit at the time.

Andy was still nothing more than a highly respected session musician but he was prepared to try virtually anything and, in 1975, appeared in a touring version of *Tubular Bells* which happened to appear in Newcastle where the supporting band was Last Exit, featuring Sting.

Andy recalls that group as being 'lousy', while Sting insists Last Exit blew them off the stage.

Two years later, Andy met up with Sting and Stewart when they were rehearsing for the Strontium 90 concert at the Virtual Earth Studios in Swiss Cottage. The concert went ahead but Andy rejoined the Kevin Coyne Band afterwards, while Stewart, Sting and Henry Padovani continued their awkward alliance. However, fate would eventually reunite them.

SEVEN

PUNK WARS

*'Musically, I thought Stewart's
ideas were shit. But the energy, the
dynamism of the guy really affected me.'*
- STING

THE ATMOSPHERE WAS TENSE as The Police warmed up in front of the predominantly punk crowd at New Wave emporium The Marquee in London. Stewart Copeland and his two fellow band members knew full well that their punk status was marginal and they feared they were about to be found out. In the audience, Andy Summers watched with interest. 'This is as phoney as hell,' he thought to himself. 'They'll be lucky if they get outta here alive.'

However, he had to confess that they had something going for them. Sting seemed larger than life and Stewart was an undoubtedly good drummer. 'I could see the potential in them, but it just wasn't being realised,' explained Andy years later.

Back at The Marquee that night, Stewart became painfully aware that Sting was far from happy with Henry when he muttered bitterly to the drummer, 'I'd forgotten the guitar had six strings and there's more than three chords you can play on it'.

A few days later, Sting received a call from Andy Summers. 'I should join the group because the three of us could be really strong,' Andy barked.

Sting mumbled back, 'You may be right.' But he was unwilling to be the one to tell Stewart that Henry should go and so he told Andy that they would have to talk further about it another time.

That same day an extraordinary coincidence occurred that was to reshape the lives of all three men and, eventually, bring them untold fortunes.

Andy Summers was getting off the tube at Oxford Circus when he bumped into Stewart Copeland. They greeted each other warmly and went for a coffee.

'You need to sack the rhythm guitarist and get a new one — me,' insisted Andy to Stewart in no uncertain terms. He was lecturing Stewart as if he had already joined the band.

Stewart was far from confident as he told Andy, 'We haven't got anything going for us. The record company is me!' Knowing that Andy was used to playing in proper 'grown-up' bands, he went on, 'And even if you did join us we'd break up within a month because you wouldn't be able to handle humping your own equipment into gig after gig.'

The truth was that Stewart was very afraid of letting such an experienced musician into the band. He was making up excuses. 'I told him that Sting's feet were really bad. I was starting to say anything because I didn't believe him. I just didn't believe he was prepared to chuck in the salary he was getting from Kevin Coyne.'

None the less, thirty minutes later Andy joined The Police and phoned up the Kevin Coyne management to cancel his weekly retainer. He didn't seem to care that he was risking his credibility. Andy just wanted in and he was convinced The Police would make it to the big time. He made only one condition: that The Police remained a trio. That meant Henry would have to go.

Sting had no problem with his departure but Stewart retained a certain fondness for Henry whom he considered a good friend and soulmate.

Reluctant actually to confront Henry, the group even made a number of appearances as a four-piece outfit. Their first gig, at the Camden Music Machine in London, was a disaster. Not surprisingly, Henry and Andy did not hit it off. Henry later explained, 'Andy was the ultimate guitar player. "Do this! You can't? Oh ...," I felt like the young fox being made to listen to the old wolf.' That was putting it politely.

The bitterness between the two guitarists reached a peak at the Mont de Marsan punk music festival near Bordeaux in France in early August 1977. Arguments about amps ensued and Henry was so pissed off by the end of the gig that he refused to talk to the rest of the band and went off in a huff with a girlfriend.

Just a week or so later, a recording session under the supervision of producer/songwriter/performer John Cale turned into a slanging match because neither Andy nor Sting liked being given directions. Henry Padovani could sense the end was near.

That evening of 12 August, he got a call from Stewart saying it was all over and Henry headed back to his family home in Corsica for a much deserved holiday. He got back into the music business a few months later but never fully recovered from his experiences with The Police.

Meanwhile, Stewart's sharp-eyed businessman brother Miles was still keeping his distance from the band. He also happened to be deeply unimpressed by Andy Summers. 'The guy's got short hair and bell bottoms,' he told his brother Stewart angrily, completely ignoring Andy's musical talent.

Not surprisingly, Andy sensed Miles' disapproval. 'That immediately made me not want to have anything to do with him. I thought that Stewart was being over-influenced by his elder brother.'

However, Sting was delighted by the recruitment of Andy who took on an entirely fresh persona once he joined The Police. Andy was the consummate professional and he insisted that the group rehearsed every song each night for the following week.

The new trio made its debut at Birmingham's Rebecca Club on

18 August 1977. Sting realised for the first time that they had got it right. They really seemed to gel together as a band, although there were still numerous obstacles to overcome.

The biggest problem was one of image. Punk fans and clubs alike knew The Police were not in any way related to their style of music. Bookings dried up and British rock fans and promoters were equally confused by the group's identity. Then the band decided to hire a full-time manager and picked Laurence Impey, a school friend of Stewart's from Millfield. Miles Copeland took a back seat.

One time, they thought they had been booked as a support band for a gig in Holland. They piled their guitars and one amp into Andy Summer's Citroën Deux Chevaux, only to get to Rotterdam and discover no appearances were scheduled for them.

Then they managed to link up as support to a band in Paris and headed for the French capital. On 20 September 1977 they played the Nashville in Paris. However, things went from bad to worse as they could not afford accommodation and ended up sleeping in their car in the city's red-light district after the gig.

That was when Sting noticed the first of numerous prostitutes on the streets who were to inspire one of his greatest compositions. 'It was the first time I'd seen prostitution on the streets and those birds were actually beautiful. I had a tune going round in my head and I imagined being in love with one of those girls. I mean, they do have fellas. How would I feel?'

> *Roxanne*
> *You don't have to put on the red light*
> *Those days are over*
> *You don't have to sell your body to the night*
> *Roxanne*

'It's a beautiful name and there's such a rich mythology behind it. Roxanne was Alexander the Great's wife and Cyrano de Bergerac's girlfriend. It has an emotive quality about it,' added Sting.

However, the riches that 'Roxanne' and other tunes were to bring to the band were still a long way off. For the time being, The Police had to survive on virtually no income. Sting was turning to Frances more and more for support. She was the breadwinner in the house and that meant taking just about every acting job that was offered. One part in a TV serial called *The Survivors* conveniently called for a mother and baby so little Joe found himself earning a crust as well.

Sting eventually began moonlighting as a model, thanks to agent Pippa Markham who had first put the family up when they came to London. His first assignment was to appear in a cinema advertisement for men's necklaces, and other occasional work followed. A commercial for Brutus Jeans saw him in a figure-hugging pair of trousers featuring bulges in all the right places. Sting later recalled, 'There was this really randy chick flashing her tits at me for six hours of filming. It nearly drove me mad.'

Then came a commercial for Triumph Bras which saw him cavorting in the near nude with *Absolutely Fabulous* star Joanna Lumley. As Sting later disclosed, 'I got to grope Joanna Lumley's tits.'

Lumley — then famous as the star of TV's *New Avengers* — got into a rumpus with Sting when she complained to the commercial's director that he was taking his role 'too seriously'. In truth, Sting found himself mesmerised by Lumley whom he considered to be a 'very classy actress'. He also kept thinking about those skin-tight black leather suits that Lumley wore for her role in *The New Avengers*.

Not long after this, Sting auditioned for a Wrigley's chewing gum commercial. The director made it clear that he felt Sting was not punky enough until Sting leapt on to a table and started spitting in all directions. Minutes later he was told he had the job. Then the advertising agency behind the commercial said they were looking for a group also to appear in the advertisement. Naturally, Sting offered them The Police.

However, there was one condition — all of the group had to be blond. Sting had already bleached his hair by this stage; Stewart was actually red-headed but game for anything; Andy was not so keen but found himself outvoted.

It has long since been acknowledged that the blond look helped enormously to transform the group's image into something more exciting and interesting. However, the new blond look did not exactly win The Police the deepest respect from their fellow musicians. Many sniggered behind their backs because they felt that it was yet another reason why the group could never be considered a serious rock'n' roll band.

The trio were still struggling financially and were delighted when they pocketed their first reasonable pay cheques after agreeing to play on an album being assembled by German electronic jazz funk king Eberhard Schoener in Munich.

On 10 November 1977, the group returned to London after three weeks in Germany. They expected to find lots of new equipment and gigs lined up but after a month there was still not a gig or recording contract. All The Police had achieved was four weeks of free rehearsals, during which they managed to fine-tune their performances significantly.

Another two months of rehearsals followed, but absolutely no gigs. People in the industry started to ask what had happened to The Police. 'One day we just decided "Fuck these guys" and we loaded our equipment into our cars and just pissed off,' recalls Stewart today.

Throughout all of this, Sting, spurred on by the arrival of Andy in the band, had been writing furiously. 'There was constant pressure on me. I was coming up with new songs all the time.'

After getting rid of their management, the group decided to record an album and release it themselves. They figured that an album would make better business sense than a single and even worked out that they needed to sell five thousand to cover their costs. It seemed a realistic target. Even so, they didn't have anywhere near enough money to cover those costs so Stewart went to his brother Miles for help. Miles reluctantly agreed to lend them enough to pay the studio bills. He was hesitant not only because he didn't like showing favouritism to his brother, but because he still had deep reservations about the group itself.

Before they could get the project underway, Christmas interrupted proceedings. Sting, by now living in a small basement flat in Leinster Square, Bayswater, threw a New Year's Eve party featuring Stewart's hi-fi and reggae collection.

In the first week of January 1978, Sting returned to Newcastle for a Last Exit reunion at a jam-packed University Theatre. It was his first gig in over two months and he started to wonder if, perhaps, his move south had been one big and ghastly mistake. Then he looked at the faces of the other band members and realised that he wanted more than just to be in a friendly band rolling around the North East from gig to gig. He wanted stardom and wealth and he felt that The Police were on the verge of getting it.

Within a week of returning from Newcastle, Sting was back with The Police, recording songs for a low-cost album at the Surrey Sound Studios in Leatherhead, Surrey. The studio was the brainchild of Nigel Gray MD, who had dropped his medical career for one in rock'n'roll. It was the only place The Police could afford to rent.

Miles Copeland, although not officially on board as manager, ended up doing all the negotiations for the studio on behalf of the band. Initially, he offered Nigel Gray two thousand pounds on completion of recording or a percentage of sales of the album if he was prepared to wait. Gray settled for the two thousand but spent many months trying to squeeze the money out of Miles.

The band decided the album should be called *Outlandos d'Amour*. Occasionally, Miles would drop in at the studio to keep an eye on his investment. The first time he came down to Leatherhead, the group had just completed 'Be My Girl'. Miles hated it and started yelling at the group that it sounded like Curved Air from five years earlier.

However, Miles's next visit was greeted by the sound of 'Roxanne'. He was blown away by the song and grabbed a copy of it, promising to use it to get the band a proper record deal.

Miles took the tape to A&M Records where one of his other bands, Squeeze, had already been given a good deal. Copeland persuaded them to release 'Roxanne' as a single. The band were elated when they heard the good news. Their indifferent attitude towards Miles instantly disappeared. Even Sting admits, 'It was Miles masterminding our initial deal with the record company that gave us our freedom of movement. Once we got going we were unstoppable.'

The deal cut by Miles Copeland was equally unstoppable. He actually gave the single to A&M Records without demanding any advance on the basis that he believed sales would be so high and the group would earn much more from royalties. They eventually made millions from that record alone. Miles Copeland had taken an extraordinary risk and proved himself to be a superb manager and negotiator in the process.

Miles's new-found enthusiasm for the band soon got them a host of live gigs. They supported the American group Spirit on three British dates in March that year. However, Miles had still not given complete commitment to The Police. It was a gradual process, with him taking over more and more of the everyday functions of the band.

Miles had already built up an impressive stable of successful bands, including such names as Wishbone Ash, Renaissance, The Climax Blues Band and Al Stewart. Just three years earlier, however, in 1975, the bubble had burst and he had been forced into liquidation. 'I learned then that reaching the top is not nearly so difficult as staying there,' he later explained. 'The greatest pitfall is that you have a few hits and think you have made it forever and that you can relax.'

Miles has always remained very modest about the part he played in launching The Police. 'I just happened to get them started. If I hadn't been there they would still have made it.'

At last the identity of The Police was starting to take shape. The recording of *Outlandos* continued in two-day spurts throughout the first half of 1978. When people first heard the album, the adoption of so-called white reggae led to criticisms from within the music industry. Sting, however, considered that he had done nothing more than adapt reggae to his own sounds. 'It was in my mind that you could set the two forms alongside each other and it would sound good; the pace would suddenly change. Then, as we progressed, the two styles merged,' explained Sting years later.

'Roxanne' was actually released on 7 April 1978 and received favourable reviews but little radio play, partly because programmers were reluctant to use a love song about a prostitute.

Sting's opinion on his masterpiece is interesting. 'I felt very strongly about "Roxanne" because that was a serious song about a real relationship. There was no talk about fucking in it. It wasn't a smutty song in any sense of the word. It was a real song with real lyrics and they wouldn't play it on the grounds that it was about a prostitute. But write a silly song about fucking that hasn't got the word fucking in it and you've got a hit. It gets a bit depressing.'

Sting was so enthused by recording 'Roxanne' that he felt inspired enough to write 'Can't Stand Losing You'. A&M Records were still so uncertain about the band as a whole that they tried to remix the track before its release, only to admit later that they were wrong and put out the original version.

Another visit to Eberhard Schoener in Munich followed but this time Sting's vocals took over the German's project. Schoener later even claimed that he taught Sting how to sing but there is no doubt that Sting knew what he was doing long before this.

Back in England, in June, 'Roxanne' had still not got beyond the fringes of the top forty and it seemed as if the group was going to continue to struggle. Despite this slow start, the song was said to be Mick Jagger's favourite record and Miles Copeland began to get calls from the Rod Stewart and Rolling Stones offices from people wanting to go to the band's gigs.

In July 1978, a sound engineer called Kim Turner joined The Police to look after their output and act as their tour manager. The result was that the quality of their sound became transformed virtually overnight.

Kim was the brother of Martin Turner, the bass player with Wishbone Ash, the first band that Miles Copeland ever managed.

When Kim was just fifteen he had joined another of Miles' bands, Cat Iron, as their drummer. The group's tour manager at the time was Stewart Copeland. Kim eventually took over as tour manager for some of Miles's other acts and became one of the family.

In those early days of the development of The Police, Last Exit's one-time manager Andy Hudson regularly came down to London in his daytime capacity as director of the Newcastle Festival and he would sometimes stay with Sting and Frances plus baby Joe at the small, damp basement flat in Leinster Square, Bayswater, where they had moved to almost six months after arriving in London.

'It was a tiny little flat', recalls Hudson, 'and I slept on the sofa a couple of times. One thing I remember significantly was that Frances had a bit of a problem with me because I had quite a reputation for being a drink and drugs merchant at the time.'

Frances did not approve of Andy Hudson's lifestyle and she told him so in no uncertain terms.

'I remember one day chatting to Frances about fidelity and she pointed out she was a staunch Catholic and that she was sure Sting would never sleep with other women.'

Hudson was astounded by Frances's sweeping statement and told her, 'But you've got to be realistic. A pop star on the road is highly likely to sleep with the occasional woman.'

Frances looked appalled at the very prospect and cut Hudson stone dead. 'That'll never happen,' she snapped at him.

Hudson now reflects, 'We agreed to differ on that particular point but you have to remember it was the seventies and shags were a-plenty. I would say that Frances definitely was not too keen on that element of the pop business.'

Andy Hudson has had relatively little to do with Sting since those days and one of the main reasons for this is Miles Copeland. He explains, 'I felt Miles, in some way, seemed to resent my role in Sting's beginnings and if I ever tried to contact Sting it usually had to be through Miles so I considered it was a waste of time.'

Hudson — now owner of a successful video production company

— was even commissioned by Miles to shoot a special concert given by Sting in Newcastle in the early nineties, but it was not an easy experience. Hudson explains, 'We were not allowed to do anything out of the ordinary because Miles was in charge. I think he quite enjoys breathing down people's necks.'

However, Hudson got the last laugh on Miles after the concert because Miles insisted on buying all the footage of the concert from Andy's company. 'He wants to put them out on a record one day,' reckons Hudson. 'But I was delighted because we screwed him for some more money and that's what hurts Miles the most.'

Hudson's take on Sting's relationship with Miles Copeland is interesting. 'Sting and Miles seem to get on as people. There is no pretence between them. It is a fact of life that as you move on to superstardom it is difficult to exist without a manager like Miles because he protects Sting's arse and makes all the decisions Sting doesn't want to face.'

Hudson believes that Miles 'has a sinister strength. He puts across the air of someone you would not want to double cross. He doesn't actually say, "My father was a CIA chief in the Middle East and I could have you knocked off " but then he doesn't have to because there is already something there lurking in his persona. I have spent a lot of years in this business and I know that heavies aren't necessarily physically large people. Characters like Miles have implicit strength.'

Hudson does concede that Miles has become one of the finest managers in the rock'n'roll business. 'He is very, very good at what he does. He drives a hard bargain and resents paying for anything, like all legendary managers.'

On one rare occasion, following Sting's elevation to rock superstar status, Andy Hudson did get a call from Last Exit drummer Ronnie Pearson, saying that Sting wanted him to call him. The two men arranged a working breakfast at Sting's north London house.

'He was remarkably easy to talk to considering his stardom but I was off to a meeting and he had a game of tennis arranged so I didn't stay for long,' explains Hudson. 'But I have to be honest about it and say that I have spent much of my life trying to avoid celebrities.' Then a reflective Hudson added, 'I miss the old Sting. I found him a pleasant human being to be with.'

Back in the summer of 1978 success was still proving elusive for The Police, so Sting remained determined to keep all his options open. He had hankered after a career in acting ever since meeting Frances and he took The Police's slow development as an opportunity to start auditioning for television and film roles.

His first movie part was in *Quadrophenia*, a version of The Who's concept album set in the heyday of the Mods. Sting got the role of Ace Face, a Mod gang leader, and filming began in September that year.

However, A&M Records had by no means given up on The Police. They were convinced that 'Roxanne' deserved to be a success and on the back of that decided to release 'Can't Stand Losing You' on 14 August 1978. Again there were good reviews and no airplay. This time it was the suicide angle that upset programme controllers. The record sleeve, featuring Sting dangling from a noose, didn't help either.

Despite all this, A&M Records optioned the right to release *Outlandos* and paid out the handsome sum of ten thousand pounds to the band on delivery of the album. It might not collectively even have covered their debts, but at least it was a beginning, a step in the right direction.

Miles Copeland, however, was far from satisfied. He was managing a band with two failed singles and little else to show for all their combined efforts. On returning from a trip to America he confronted the band with an outrageous proposition. He had a crazy plan and he wanted them to listen to it.

EIGHT

TRICKS AND TREATS

> *'It's difficult being a normal dad because
> I can't come home every night.'*
> - STING

THE BIGGEST SELLING SINGLE OF 1978 was 'You're The One That I Want' by John Travolta and Olivia Newton John. That year, three popes were elected at the Vatican but only one survived and The Police found themselves embroiled in an audacious plan to invade another country.

The first they knew about it was when Miles Copeland greeted them with the immortal line, 'We're going to the States, guys.' It was early October 1978.

'Great. But who's booked us?' came the bemused reply.

'No one. We're gonna find a few clubs and start slowly and build on it.'

Sting sat back in astonishment as he heard the details of Miles's audacious plan. Even he — the ultimate risk taker — was stunned by the idea of landing in America without a proper tour being organised.

Then Miles explained that The Police would never get the venues unless they did it his way. He knew all about the club scene, having just returned from a loss-making US tour with Squeeze.

Miles's initial plan was that The Police should go to the States and play a series of club dates around the East Coast. It was against all the rules for promoting British bands in America, but Miles had been studying the form closely and he reckoned it could work.

Miles was also being aided by his other brother, Ian, who had been working all that year organising tours for southern rock bands.

On 20 October 1978, Sting, Stewart and Andy found themselves carrying their own instruments as they lined up for tickets on Freddie Laker's Skytrain. At London's Gatwick Airport, at exactly the same time, was their rival group The Boomtown Rats, led by the inimitable Bob Geldof.

Geldof recalls, 'We were number one with 'Rat Trap' at the time and we were travelling club class and cruising through the airport when we saw these three guys queuing up at the Freddie Laker check-in desk. They had their guitars in their hands because Laker was like a bus and you had to take your own stuff on the plane.'

Sting looked very irritated when he saw Geldof marching towards him.

'What's happening, man?'

'We're going to America,' replied Sting.

'Where you playing?' asked the friendly Irishman.

'We don't know,' came the terse reply.

'What?' said an incredulous Geldof.

'We're just going over to see what happens.'

In fact, Miles Copeland had already managed to book the band an opening gig at CBGB's club in New York at midnight on the night they arrived in the Big Apple. The Laker Skytrain turned up at JFK at 11p.m. After clearing Customs, the group jumped into yellow cabs at the airport and went straight to the gig.

Sting had never been to America before and was struck by the steaming streets full of bums on every sidewalk. 'Man, this is incredible, it's like Hades!'

CBGB's club was even worse. The band stumbled onstage in a

daze, suffering from severe jetlag. 'But we tore the place up,' recalls Sting. 'We really thought, "Fuck it, we've got to survive here." '

However the tensions that would eventually come to dominate The Police burst to the surface after that exhausting début gig. Sting and Stewart were so pumped up by their performance and the great response of the audience that they had a fight in the dressing room afterwards.

The basis of the row was that Sting thought Stewart had been playing too fast on the drums and Stewart reckoned Sting had slowed his bass playing down to a snail's pace.

As the two grappled on the ground, there was a chanting noise from the stage out front. The crowd were pleading for an encore. Just as Sting had begun to throttle Stewart, both of them froze in mid-air. They couldn't believe their ears. Then they leapt up. 'Let's go for it,' screamed Sting as they rushed back on the stage.

Ten minutes later, they were back on the floor fighting when there was a call for a further encore and they repeated the entire operation all over again.

'That was our first night in America,' recalls Sting.

Looking back on that night, Sting is proud of the mobility and adaptability of the band. 'We were tough. We carried our own gear, we drove hundreds and hundreds of miles, we slept in the same bed in grotty motels. We gave our blood and guts. It was like being at war. We were out there fighting a war — and we won!'

The tour eventually consisted of twenty-three gigs in twenty-seven days and took in such exotic sounding locations as Poughkeepsie, Willmantic, Swissvale and Centerville as well as Philadelphia, Boston, Detroit, Cleveland, Toronto, Buffalo and Washington. Transport between gigs was provided by a van driven by Ian Copeland, which had been bought by Miles for a few hundred bucks during a visit to the States earlier that year. The tour grossed the grand sum of 7,142 dollars, but Miles still came out on top because he restricted each of the band members to expenses of just twenty dollars a day.

The trio felt as though they were pioneering New Wave music and the radio stations started to play 'Roxanne'. Audiences seemed to take them more seriously than they had back in Britain.

Most important of all, they played together continuously for four weeks and it helped them more than anything to fine tune the band.

Around this time, Geldof and The Police both happened to be in Los Angeles, so the Boomtown Rats singer headed for a Police gig at the infamous Whisky A Go Go on Sunset Boulevard.

'It was my turn to be jealous and irritated. They had become overnight celebs in the States. This time when I met Sting he was far more relaxed and he knew exactly where he was going.'

For Sting, the trip to the States was a complete eye-opener. Not only had he never been across the Atlantic before, but he found the schedule punishing. Often the group would travel literally hundreds of miles to find that less than half a dozen people had turned up to see them. Sting said, 'Getting it up for three people was quite an experience. We did it though; we were very good for three people. But we all knew the potential. That's what kept us going. Touring America was on the way up. We had reached the nadir well before that — six months of not working at all.'

The road crew on that trip consisted of lone Brit Kim Turner. A&M Records were upset that Miles had even attempted the tour as he had no support whatsoever from them. But the Copelands weren't interested in record company money. They just wanted 'Roxanne' to be properly promoted.

This was a do-it-yourself tour in every sense of the word. Everyone hammered up stickers advertising the group's appearances and all concerned mucked in when it came to carrying gear.

And it worked. 'Roxanne' began to get lots of airplay on the East Coast and by the time the group returned to New York in the middle of November, the single was rising up the charts.

Shortly after The Police returned to Britain, A&M released *Outlandos d'Amour*. The reviews were moderate, sales were steady, and their low budget approach meant they recouped their costs almost instantly.

However, The Police still could not command a British tour

themselves. Shortly after returning from the States they took the support slot to Alberto Y Los Trios Paranoias, a satirical British band.

On the first night of the tour, at Bath University, an audience of more than a thousand showed up and most of them were there because of 'Roxanne' and 'Can't Stand Losing You'. The band were surprised that the records had actually made such an impact in the UK. The reaction throughout the following dozen gigs was exactly the same. The Albertos were stunned by the way their support group had, in effect, stolen their thunder and it was a significant breakthrough for The Police.

However, there were still only small amounts of money dribbling through to the trio. On that tour they had accepted a deal for fifty pounds a night between them and out of that had to come the ten pounds a night for using the Albertos' PA.

Transport was a Ford Transit and Kim Turner stepped in as lone roadie once again. Bed and breakfasts at two pounds a night provided accommodation but the fuel bill was ten pounds per day.

Immediately after Christmas, The Police played an impromptu performance at the Electric Ballroom in London and then the band agreed to play more concerts for Eberhard Schoener in Munich.

A few weeks after their return from Germany they were back at Surrey Sound working on their second album, *Regatta de Blanc*. This time the costs rose to approximately eight thousand pounds but that was easily covered by the profits from *Outlandos* so the band and Miles could keep their independence from A&M Records who would have preferred to pay the bills and exert some control over the group.

Speed was of the essence for The Police and Miles maintained pressure on the trio not to waste any valuable studio time. Despite all this, one of the first songs written for the album by Sting was 'Message In A Bottle'. He had had the riff in his head for quite some time before putting pen to paper and it inspired Stewart Copeland to produce one of his finest ever performances on the drums.

Meanwhile, Sting, Frances and Joseph were occasionally reunited as one family at their basement flat in Leinster Square, Bayswater. It was hard for all concerned because Sting would come home exhausted after rehearsals or touring and was finding it increasingly difficult to come to terms with the sharp contrasts in his life.

One morning Sting was just walking up the steps from the front door of the flat when his eyes locked on to an attractive willowy blonde with one of the sexiest mouths he had ever seen. They smiled at each other and continued to do so occasionally over the following few months. That girl's name was Trudie Styler and she was eventually to play a huge role in Sting's life, although neither of them realised it at the time.

She was then a struggling actress working as a bunny mother — supervising bunny girls — in a London nightclub to make ends meet. Her duties included passing suggestive notes between wealthy Arabs and the girls. She also compered a rather racy floor show in Arabic. 'I wore a bow on my bum and it was demeaning,' Trudie explained many years later. 'But I was hungry and I had to pay the mortgage.'

Trudie was intrigued by the young blond guy living in the basement flat next door. He had a wicked smile and she certainly found him attractive. He looked familiar. Maybe he was a rock star? However, Sting was hardly at the top of her list of priorities at the time.

Even then Trudie had a tough streak in her. She was not prepared to slum it just because there was no straight acting work around, so she would work wherever there was money. However, she did not take to being bossed around. Once, when she worked as a temporary secretary, she spat in her boss's tea because he had insulted her. Working in a club at least gave her some freedom.

On the musical front, 'Message In A Bottle' seemed tailor-made to be a hit single. All the rest of the tracks on *Regatta de Blanc*, like 'Walking On The Moon', followed with ease and the entire album was completed in just one month of studio time.

By the spring of 1979, The Police were finally close to taking the music scene by storm but it had certainly been a hard slog. As Miles Copeland now explains, 'The nucleus was developed to a point where it would reach critical mass and explode.'

The band hit the road and stayed on it for the next sixteen months. For

Sting it was a weird and wonderful time. On his rare visits home to Frances and Joseph, he was an enthusiastic parent but found it difficult to relax because he was so wrapped up in the success of The Police.

His long absences started to create a barrier between his home and work lives. He found it difficult to relate to toddlers and teething problems and then, a few hours later, find himself at the centre of major adulation from thousands of fans. It was a crazy, mixed-up life but it was the path he had chosen and he was not about to blow his career for anyone or anything.

The Police's first ever TV appearance was on BBC 2's *The Old Grey Whistle Test* in October 1978. This was marred when Sting managed to spray a can of aerosol in his own face and had to go on stage in dark glasses which belonged to Stewart. He looked absolutely ridiculous and even now acknowledges, 'Stewart had a much bigger head than me and they kept slipping off my face.' None the less, Sting was fairly chuffed by his appearance on *TOGWT* because some of his mates back in Newcastle actually saw him 'on the telly'.

Two more important TV appearances soon followed, with Tyne-Tees Television's *Alright Now* and the BBC's *Rock Goes To College* series which featured a concert The Police performed at Hatfield College.

Alright Now producer Gavin Taylor first encountered Sting backstage at the show and went on to become a long-standing friend who has made numerous TV programmes with him since. 'Sting was very raw then,' says Taylor. 'The group were somewhat awkward.'

Alright Now was presented by Den Hegarty, then lead singer with rock group The Darts. Guests on the show included Billy Connolly and Micky Most and some of the programme was filmed at Newcastle's Club A Go Go where legends like Jimi Hendrix and Eric Burden had performed in the past.

Meanwhile, Miles Copeland decided that The Police must return to America soon in order to sustain the interest that was now being shown in them. First 'Roxanne', then *Outlandos* had sprung into the charts and transformed The Police from no-hopers to contenders and Miles had arranged a further thirty dates across the country. This time it was in planes and cars instead of one battered van, but Miles yet again refused to take an advance from A&M Records on the basis that they would promote the band more heavily if they did not spend so much on other aspects of the tour. He was absolutely correct.

A&M Records also began to sense that British interest in the band was picking up and re-released 'Roxanne' on 12 April 1979. When the band returned for a short break from America, 'Roxanne' was already in the top thirty and they were booked to appear on *Top Of The Pops*. That, in turn, helped the song climb the charts to number twelve.

The Police did not tour Britain again until June of that year and by then demand for tickets had escalated so much that many venues changed from clubs to larger halls.

'Can't Stand Losing You' was re-released in August and this time reached number two, only to find itself thwarted by Bob Geldof's Boomtown Rats. It was a bizarre situation because it actually felt as if the group were doing an exact repeat of 1978, thanks to those re-releases. However, they accepted the wise words of Miles Copeland who assured them that his strategy was paying off at last. In fact, few members of the public even realised that either record was a re-release.

For Sting, appearing on BBC's *Top Of The Pops* was a mind-blowing experience. In accordance with the programme's rules, he was obliged to mime along to 'Roxanne' so he swung his mike-stand around two feet from his right ear in a blatantly honest send up of the programme's sugary sweet set-up.

Sales of the band's first album eventually exceeded a hundred thousand copies and The Police went to Europe for a series of headlining concerts. Then they returned to Britain in late August to top the bill at the annual three-day Reading Festival in front of twenty thousand people. In the space of less than a year a struggling band had turned into a headline act.

As Andy Summers explains, 'We'd really started to pick up speed then. We could all feel it. There was something new happening every day and we'd have to work on it together. There was this tremendous thrust.'

Another British tour was launched just after the Reading Festival and Sting now discovered that, with all this newly acquired fame, came a certain amount of personal danger.

During an appearance in a theatre in Oxford, fifty skinheads broke through the crowds and knocked over an old lady and a doorman before ploughing their way through the audience to the front of the stage yelling, 'Sieg heil, Sieg heil'. The mob then started taunting Sting. He looked at them disdainfully and then started shouting at them. 'Come on, you're on stage, let's see you work.'

The skinheads looked completely bemused. Sting started playing and made them join in. He later told a friend, 'It was like dancing with bears'. All that training in the bars and clubs of the North East was at last coming in handy, as well as his old experiences as a teacher.

Sting's film debut *Quadrophenia* opened around this time and Sting became labelled as a type of Mod thanks to his performance in the moderately successful movie. His role received a lot of publicity because of his new-found fame as a rock star, but the reality was that he was on screen for 'long enough to make an impact but not long enough to blow it'.

However, that didn't matter to the film's producers. Sting became the face advertising the film on posters, the TV and the front page of newspapers and magazines. Suddenly he developed a magical ability to be photogenic.

It still bemuses Sting to this day. 'It started when I was about twenty-five, I think. I decided that I could impose beauty on myself. As a result of a feeling that it should be. It's a strange thing to talk about. But there is an expression I have. Seductive. Serious.'

Sting's modesty was already fast disappearing and he rapidly became renowned as someone who would flick his fingers through his hair, suck in his cheeks slightly and make a face at the camera. It was the Sting look.

The mass media recognised it instantly and he became the centre of their attention, especially in the scandal-hungry tabloids. The rest of the band were shoved into the background as Sting's handsome features dominated any reference to the group. Many speculated that this media mass hysteria would make Stewart and Andy bitter with jealousy but nothing could have been further from the truth during those early days of fame and fortune. They were more than happy to let 'heart-throb' Sting get all the attention while they got on with their lives in relative peace and tranquillity.

Sting even appeared on the BBC's *Juke Box Jury* show and he made another film appearance, in something called *Radio On*, which was also released to reasonable reviews, although the movie never got beyond the art-house circuit. Sting was paid just twenty pounds for his three-minute spot as a garage attendant in *Radio On*. Much of the scene consisted of him sitting in a caravan doorway strumming acoustic guitar and singing Eddie Cochran's 'Three Steps To Heaven'.

He also landed a part in the Sex Pistols film *The Great Rock 'N' Roll Swindle* but his role was edited out before the piece reached the screen.

This performance involved Sting French-kissing Sex Pistols member Paul Cook. Miles Copeland was horrified when he heard about it and begged Sting not to do the movie but he went ahead with it anyway.

Back in the late seventies two men kissing was still considered very daring and many believed that Sting would face a public backlash and a dip in sales if the scene had been shown.

On the other side of the Atlantic the initial burst of enthusiasm for The Police, and for Sting in particular, had cooled down. During a third tour which lasted two months that autumn, they evoked nothing more than mild interest. Some inside the music business were saying that Miles had blown it by overexposing his band. At one concert, in West Virginia, The Police played to just five people even though they were number one in Britain with both the album and single on that very same day.

However, they did at least have one captive audience Stateside — the inmates of Terminal Island Prison, where four thousand dollars were raised to buy musical instruments for inmates thanks to the group's appearance.

The Police roadshow rolled on. No sooner had they finished their American tour than they were being whisked to Paris to start the first in a series of European dates. They even crammed in another dozen British shows before Christmas. Over the previous six months, Sting had managed to see his wife and son for only a few days. It was a difficult way to keep a family together but Miles Copeland was adamant that the group's exposure should continue at a hellfire pace. He also believed he had stumbled upon another market that none of the trio had even considered up until this point — teenyboppers between eleven and fifteen. The Police were starting to be mooted as the unlikely successors to the Bay City Rollers and David Cassidy.

Sting and the rest of the group happily played along. Miles was in charge. 'He was a great catalyst. It was infectious and gave us confidence. Colonel Parker was to Elvis what Miles was to us,' says Sting now.

A date at the Queen's Hall in Leeds provoked scenes of mass hysteria as security men dragged more than eighty unconscious teenage girls from where they had collapsed in the screaming crowds. Sting was stunned by this reaction and the young age of the audience. He was particularly astounded by the way those young girls were looking at him. He just didn't know how to handle it.

He now explains, 'We saw it just as it was about to happen. As it started to come over the hill I thought "Yeah!" and went for it. When we were rehearsing for months on end without a gig we never thought about it. We just wanted to be a group making top ten records. To a lot of people teenyboppers are a subspecies not even to be entertained. I don't agree. If you can transcend the screaming you can take a generation with you into something else. It's a real challenge.'

In London they travelled between two gigs in Hammersmith in an armoured personnel carrier to save them from the screaming pubescent girls, although it has to be said that Miles Copeland dreamed up that particular method of transport as a clever publicity stunt.

Sting started to love the attention but fear the aftermath. As the band's frontman and heart-throb, he was the one who got stalked in the street or asked for a kiss by complete strangers who were not averse to slipping their phone numbers and sexy notes into his pocket.

Thanks to the newspaper headlines, at home in their cramped basement flat in Bayswater Frances was well aware of her husband's new role as a sex symbol. All efforts to have a normal life with Frances and Joe were proving virtually impossible. No sooner had Sting turned around after an exhausting tour than he was off again, back to the screaming crowds, the groupies and the drugs that gradually became an essential part of his life at the time.

During 1979, The Police sold five million singles and two million albums. A few of their fans were so deluded by the status of their idols that they actually imagined the band were real policemen. A&M Records got a letter from Eldon Griffiths MP, parliamentary consultant to the Police Federation, saying they had received hundreds of applications to join the Police Fan Club and asking if the group would be available to play at the Federation's Annual Ball — or so the story goes ...

However, tension was also beginning to appear. After their vastly successful appearance at the Hammersmith Odeon in December 1979, a home movie clip shot by film buff Stewart showed a very tense Sting eating and holding his fork very badly. Suddenly, for no apparent reason, he lashed out at everyone sitting at the table with him. 'What the fuck is going on?' he screamed. No one reacted. Sting was already starting to show the stresses and strains of being a rock icon.

Stewart later explained, 'There was tension all the time and it was too much like sibling rivalry. It was vicious but we lived off it to a certain extent.'

Sting revealed one startling fact that seemed to sum up the feelings between the band members. 'Stewart built his cymbal so he couldn't see me on stage. It was quite funny. We were always having fist fights. It was nasty stuff.'

Indeed it was and Andy Summers filmed many of the fights on Stewart's home movie camera for everyone to see later.

Even Sting and Miles had their problems. When Miles told one journalist that Police's worldwide touring made the band become more socially aware, 'especially Sting', the singer was outraged. He hit back at Miles, 'That's crap. I was educated by the radio more than anything else. That is nonsense.'

Tension had become the lifeblood of The Police but it wasn't making anyone particularly happy.

NINE

CASUALTIES OF WAR

*'Tension breeds excitement — and that
is what it's all about.'*
- MILES COPELAND

STING WAS IN A DAZE. Stardom had swept him off his feet and refused to put him down again. He hardly saw his young wife and child. Everything revolved around The Police. It was consuming his entire life and for the present he was lapping up every moment of it. There was no denying he enjoyed the fame and attention. He became immersed in his own hype. He was slipping into megastar mode and there was a danger that the real world might soon disappear from sight.

With The Police taking off and records in the charts, Sting was at last able to write something less gloomy in his diary:

This is as far as I've ever got. The deep-pile carpets, the cane furniture and the Parker pen.

Meanwhile Miles Copeland was meticulously planning the band's next move. His aim was global. He wanted The Police to conquer the world, with Sting at the forefront. 'Most groups wait until their career is over before they go outside the States and Europe,' declared Miles at the time. 'I say the energy of The Police is now. Let's take them to the rest of the world when they're at their most impressive.'

Miles had visited a few Third World countries to test the water and the response he received was incredibly enthusiastic. In some places, like Egypt and India, they knew they would lose money on the actual gigs but Miles believed the marketing of the group would more than make up for any short-term losses.

In an often-quoted remark Sting joked before they set off, 'We'll be able to find some interesting ethnic music to rip off.' He had meant it to be a humorous comment following criticism of the band for their heavy reggae influence, but many took it as a serious insult.

Miles's secret agenda for the tour was to build it up into such a success that it would gain The Police a foothold in world music domination only matched by the Beatles in their heyday.

The tour started in Japan in February 1980, where the group, and rock music in general, already had a keen following. Unknown territory in Hong Kong followed, where they played in front of just fifty people in a club. That didn't matter to Sting, as he later explained in his own inimitable fashion. 'You have to stay hungry at the same time as you've earned a massive fortune. That is why the band are doing things that are strange — like playing to fifty people in Hong Kong.'

As befitted the son of a CIA agent, Miles Copeland had perfectly sound logical reasons for setting up such a vast tour. 'I believe in free enterprise capitalism. For instance, we walk into a new country, Greece say, and find we have the number one album which means fifty to sixty thousand. You take all the countries in the world outside the United States and that gets to be pretty heavy money. In India now they're screaming out for Police products.'

Then The Police moved on to Australia and New Zealand where Sting contracted laryngitis, forcing the band to postpone their concerts for a week.

The health scare was all the more surprising when one considers the extraordinary level of fitness that Sting had attained over the previous eighteen months. He had developed a pulse rate as steady as that of an Olympic athlete thanks to a daily, rigorous, keep-fit routine which included running three miles, sixty strenuous sit-ups and an hour of agonising muscle exercises and arm-wrestling contests with his bodyguard.

It seemed as if Sting was deliberately avoiding the traditional pitfalls that had befallen so many rock stars in the past.

While there was no doubting his physical health, Sting was also hiding a secret from doctors that would have shocked them. He had developed a fondness for drugs — particularly cannabis and cocaine.

At every gig the band played, drug dealers were available at the flick of a finger. While Miles Copeland maintained a very disapproving stance about drugs, the band itself was more relaxed and, in some cases, even insistent that a plentiful supply of cocaine and hash be available.

Sting convinced himself that he needed drugs to enhance his performance on stage and to cope with the fans whom he found terrifying. 'In Dublin once, leaving a club one night after an awards ceremony, I was jumped on. It was dark and I didn't know where the car was. Suddenly, all these girls came out of nowhere. In seconds my hat, scarf and jacket had gone and I was standing there with my shirt in tatters. It was like being eaten alive by pretty piranhas. After I had been rescued I decided I needed a minder. Also, there are people who just wanted to pick fights with you, simply because of who you are. It's not that I can't look after myself — I can. But I don't want to have to. I've got too much to lose. If I break a finger, I can't work. It's as simple as that.'

With all these fears in mind, Sting hired a huge bodyguard called Larry Burnett, a six-foot two-inch New Yorker built like a brick outhouse. 'Larry is the ultimate deterrent. He's like a shark — an incredibly efficient creature. His reflexes are practically electronic. I mean, who would pick a fight with Jaws?'

Sting was finding it very hard to come to terms with all his fame and newfound wealth, especially because of his working-class background and Marxist leanings. There were often times when he just wanted to be left alone with his thoughts. Paranoia and guilt prevailed, often much accentuated by the constant supply of drugs on offer at every venue.

It was around this time that Sting sank to probably his lowest point. He considered his existence to be a living hell and sometimes wondered if it would all be easier if he ended it there and then. Getting out of life seemed a reasonable option. It was a drastic measure but he felt he had to stop the torment he had created for himself and those around him. Stardom was proving far from enjoyable and his interest in drugs was making it all the worse. The women were simply making his deep-set Catholic guilt even more painful. Every time another girl threw herself at him, he felt so bad about Frances and Joe.

He said to one friend that he felt confused by the lifestyle he was leading. He tried to use his songs as an outlet for his frustration and guilt, even admitting, 'My songs are metaphors for loneliness. Everybody feels lonely. Who do they think I am. Maybe they've been fooled by "the cool". I suppose that's it. I've succeeded in fooling them. Jesus Christ! I feel lonely making love to my wife. It's like we're all here but we're totally isolated. No matter how close you are to one person or a hundred, you're always totally isolated.'

It was very intense stuff but Sting had already become a man at war with himself and no amount of one-night stands were going to help to ease the tension and guilt he was suffering. It seems that there were dozens of women in those first few years of Police success. Cut off from his family, Sting had developed another life, although it wasn't exactly making him content.

The Police's world tour had a profound effect on Sting, especially the trip to India. He later explained, 'I saw a lot of poverty and what we call degradation. I didn't see despair. If you walked through Moss Side in Manchester you'd see more real despair.'

Sting considered the gig played by the band in Bombay one of the finest moments in his life. 'They'd never seen a rock concert so there was no element of ritual, no preconceptions. It was organised by the Time and Talents Club of Bombay which is a group of old ladies who put on charitable jumble sales.' The group actually performed for free and helped to raise five thousand pounds in aid of sick children.

The concert sparked enormous media interest around the world. In India most people had never even heard of The Police but they were soon learning about them from every newspaper and TV channel across the nation.

When the group began the soundcheck before the concert, the crowd lining up outside thought it had already started and police with batons had to calm them down, much to the consternation of the band members. Finally dozens of VIPs, including the Chief of Police, the Lord Mayor and a number of high profile Hindus, turned up to see the band. To prevent any further problems, the Indian police decided to open the gates to the arena and allow everyone to come in free of charge.

Sting could hardly believe his eyes when he walked calmly on stage. Everyone was sitting down as if they were about to attend a Mozart concert. 'Look, this is essentially dance music so please get up,' said Sting over the mike to his vast audience. Everyone obeyed and soon the weird and wonderful crowd were dancing. More police baton charges followed and Sting began to comment pompously to the crowd that: 'If you give a man a baton he's got to hit someone'.

Throughout the entire tour a TV documentary entitled *The Police in The East* was being shot by husband and wife filming team Derek and Kate Burbridge. The Burbridges were particularly interested in the reaction of people to Sting — i.e. the adoration and reverence. The documentary proved beyond doubt that he was the epicentre of the group. His moodiness, his meanness, his vicious tongue were all there for everyone to see.

Stewart Copeland was also secretly filming everything with his own home movie camera. He was well aware of the tension that had been gradually creeping in throughout that year and he had no hesitation in catching highly personal moments on film, including numerous explosions between the band members.

In Cairo, the world tour almost ground to a disastrous halt when Sting nearly landed in jail.

Sting takes up the story:

During the gig there was this guy in plain clothes throwing people back into their seats. I yelled at him, "Fuck off! Who invited you?" He still wouldn't go away and started threatening me so I said "See him? Fill him in" and all these kids piled into him. Well, he was the head of the Cairo police and I was in one of my moods.

Afterwards, Miles came back ashen-faced and said, "Ummm, he demands an apology". I said "Fuck off" and Miles said "Sting, please, please". Then this guy came into the room and stood there waiting, just looking at me. His honour had been damaged. I couldn't do it so I got my bag and walked out. He followed me all the way to the car, breathing down my neck so I realised I'd have to apologise otherwise I'd be in prison. I turned around and literally choked on the words. I could not. Then Miles jumped in and said, "What Sting means is that he's terribly, terribly sorry". The guy said, "You're a man of honour. I accept your apology" and walked away. That's the kind of person I am. I cannot accept somebody else's ascendency and power.

Greece, Italy and Spain followed and seemed tame in comparison. The entire trip was rounded off with a homecoming gig for Sting in Newcastle.

It was a nice idea to put Sting back in his home territory but, unfortunately, the band were so exhausted from their gruelling world tour that the concert did not really live up to expectations, which left Sting particularly disappointed. 'We went on stage to polite applause and I almost walked off. It could have been good. It should have been good.' But it wasn't.

Last Exit manager Andy Hudson recalls meeting Sting, Frances and Joe when the singer jetted back to London for a brief break following the Indian leg of the world tour. 'I was living in Muswell

Hill, north London at the time and Sting just showed up at my house one Saturday. He seemed completely wiped out with exhaustion,' says Hudson.

In fact, Sting was so desperate to try to return to some semblance of normality that he insisted on going to the local fish and chip shop with Hudson where they picked up four helpings of sheer stodge and returned to Hudson's house to eat it all in the back garden. 'Sting had changed a lot since the last time I had seen him. His hair was bleached blond and he seemed distant. I actually felt a bit sorry for him,' reflects Hudson.

Even on the road Sting kept up his daily journal. He was also obsessed with writing a screenplay. It wasn't so much a matter of getting it made into a film as yet another way to prove to himself that he could do anything he set his heart on.

He would also regularly fiddle around with his portable synthesiser so that it would play orchestral pieces.

As the tours extended and The Police's popularity reached saturation point, Sting became particularly disillusioned with the lack of privacy. 'One of the great things about America used to be that I could be quite anonymous. We could just get on with the show, be famous for an hour and then vanish into the hinterland.'

However, Sting was continually fascinated that the type of audiences they were attracting consisted of fifty per cent girls and fifty per cent boys. 'I think that's a lot healthier than any bias either way. It's a much nicer situation.'

That word 'nice' seemed to be a key ingredient for the image of the band, despite the bleached blond hair and Andy Summer's occasional snarls.

Even then, Sting was rather proud of the fact that he had a full and open appreciation of the commercial aspects of the music industry. He explained at the time, 'I have a commercial brain as well, which enjoys selling millions of units. That really appeals to me, the fact you can have your finger on the pulse of a nation for a few weeks and literally have everyone whistling your song.'

Miles Copeland was the epitome of that sort of attitude. 'The thing you have to understand about Miles,' says Sting, 'is that he has this very *laissez-faire*, rightist attitude in which he sees rock'n'roll as bringing freedom to all these obscure places we've gone and played in.'

Despite the sudden wealth, Sting made a real point of telling anyone who would listen where his politics still came from. 'I'm a socialist and I care passionately about politics but I just find that pop songs are not a good medium for political thought.'

He then made a fascinating proclamation about the Beatles to writer David Hepworth. 'I think The Beatles were perhaps the most important political force in entertainment of the Sixties and yet they never wrote a political song. They just created a lifestyle that changed the world.

'I think The Beatles, in a very roundabout way, were responsible for America losing the Vietnam war. In that they created a total opposite to the "my country is right" attitude — they created the atmosphere that allowed hippies to happen.'

On the tour circuit, Sting's ambition to match The Beatles in terms of appeal seemed to be succeeding admirably. At the Glasgow Apollo, police had to charge at fans three times in order to stop a riot occurring. The Police limousine was chased through the streets of the Scottish city as girls banged on the roof. Sting described it later as 'madness' but it was what he and the other members of the band had set out to achieve.

Sting had to admit at the time, 'To maintain normality under those circumstances is pretty difficult. We try as best we can to be accessible for autographs and things but sometimes you can't because of the size of it. It's gotten out of control.'

In June 1980, both Sting and Andy Summers moved to Ireland for tax reasons. By this stage Sting had also already bought a house near Hampstead Heath in north London.

The large house he purchased in Ireland was about as far west as you can get. It was the sort of place where the phone only works when it feels like it and then only if you wind it up and shout. At first Sting kept finding buckets of shrimps in the hallway, left by generous neighbours. The house itself was filled with surprisingly dull furniture inherited from the previous owners, but there were also Harry and Mary from across the road who agreed to help to take care of the house and garden while Sting was away. One of the biggest problems at this time was the sheer scale of the success that The Police had attained. It meant continued separation from Frances and Joseph. They considered themselves lucky if they saw each other for more than two weeks out of every three months.

Whenever Sting did manage to get to Ireland there was always an entourage in tow, including Larry the bodyguard and a personal exercise trainer who sometimes doubled as a housemaid if Sting needed someone to make the tea.

Sting's fitness continued to be a virtual obsession. He was particularly proud when a doctor gave him a medical check and pronounced him superbly fit. Sting himself reckoned he was fitter than he had been since the age of seventeen.

Having so much instant wealth was certainly an interesting prospect, but, as he explained at the time, most of his millions were still on paper rather than in his hand. 'I haven't really got the money. We've sold five, six million albums and I get twenty pence each. It's a lot of money but I haven't got it yet. I don't have expensive tastes. Next year I'll be rich and that's when the rot could set in.'

The group's productivity, and especially Sting's output, ground to a halt around this time. That summer had been set aside for writing and recording their third album but only one new song had been brought into the band's live act throughout the world tour. 'Driven To Tears' had been written by Sting as a reaction to 'watching the Third World die on television every night. You know, reading a colour supplement over a cup of coffee on Sunday morning and seeing a picture of a child well on the way to a horrible death.'

Significantly, Sting's concern for the Third World was becoming apparent even before he had been alerted to the plight of rainforests.

In the short term, Sting was in desperate need of a break to recharge his batteries and get to know his family again. He had bought the beautiful Georgian house in Ireland on the advice of his accountant who suggested that the move might save him hundreds of thousands of pounds in tax thanks to the loopholes for artists that existed in Ireland. Frances had also been keen to move back to what she considered to be her homeland.

On arrival in Ireland, Sting took his phone off the hook, refused to see anyone other than Frances and Joseph and tried to unwind while thinking up some new songs for the group's third album.

While all this was going on, the group received some heavy critical flak from within the music business and among their fans for repackaging their previous singles and putting them out as a 'limited edition' of fifty-eight thousand at £5.99 in May. Miles claimed it was essential 'to have some product out there' but the trio admitted it was a dreadful error of judgement to expect fans to shell out money for a third version of 'Roxanne'. It was an unfortunate example of The Police being drawn into thoughtless business practices.

The furore over the singles set marked a definite deterioration in the band's relationship, with Miles Copeland regularly being found in the middle of numerous problematical situations.

One big blow-up occurred when Stewart started arguing with Miles because the manager was intending to start a Belgian tour earlier than planned even though the band was still recording their next album *Zenyatta Mondatta*. In the end they completed the album at 4 a.m. and then set off to Belgium on the first leg of their new world tour.

Sting was particularly unwilling to go back on the road after his much needed rest in Ireland with Frances and Joseph. 'I was keen to record *Zenyatta* because I'd written a lot of songs for it, but when it came to going back on the road I had to be virtually dragged out of the house.'

The key to the problem lay partly in the control which Miles now had over the band. He was the fourth member of The Police. He earned a quarter of everything the band earned and he made the decisions when it came to all aspects of the day-to-day running of The Police. The problem was that the trio were often so wrapped up in performing and recording aspects that they sometimes failed to get involved in dates for tours and other such logistical problems.

When The Police interrupted their tight recording schedule to do a major charity gig called Regatta De Bowl at the Milton Keynes Bowl, Miles alienated himself from the press by trying to get all photographers to sign a contract giving him a percentage of the money from pictures of The Police.

As *Sounds* music paper said at the time, 'Is this how the manager of a successful band should behave? We don't remember him trying to stop people photographing The Police before they were successful. When you consider the role photographers have played in making his band successful, it fair makes you puke doesn't it?'

Not surprisingly, few photographers agreed to sign Miles's three-page contracts and it would be fair to say that the scheme definitely backfired.

Miles even negotiated down the fee of producer Nigel Gray so that, in the end, the band's third album, *Zenyatta,* cost just thirty-five thousand pounds to produce — incredibly cheap considering it was a guaranteed million-seller.

The relationship between Sting and Stewart had always been volatile, to say the least, but during this period they took to bear wrestling and using arm-locks. It was a kind of pressure valve for the two of them. However, there was always a slight note of seriousness when the physical side of things got out of hand, which was frequently.

While Sting was the stronger of the two physically, Stewart knew precisely how to hit below the belt. 'If I wanted to reduce Sting to a screaming maniac, all I had to do was call one of his songs a pop tune. It worked every time.'

Sting managed to get his own back on Stewart once. Stewart explained, 'He once got me screaming and shouting for about a day when he told me people in discos couldn't dance to our records. That one got to me. After all, that's the whole point of being what I am, a rhythmist. What I pride myself on is the dance-ability of our music.'

To the outside world it might all sound rather childish, but to The Police it was deadly serious.

TEN

Cool as Ice

*'As soon as the group is no longer useful
I'll drop it like a stone. I'm out for
myself—and the other two know it.'*
- STING

THE SEPTEMBER RELEASE OF 'Don't Stand Too Close To Me' brought instant sales of virtually half a million in its first week; the release of the *Zenyatta Mondatta* album a few weeks later provided the group with their second double number one.

The critics had a field day, describing the album as everything from 'a grade D failure' (*Melody Maker*) to writer Julie Burchill asking in *NME*, 'Where is Cherry Vanilla now The Police need her?'

Andy later admitted that the album had been 'a bit of a cock-up' because the band had rushed it out.

The public perception of Sting continued to be one of an aloof, slightly moody individual. Jean Rook of the *Daily Express* summed it up when she described him thus, 'A private meeting is like being locked in your car, with the windows shut, with a good-looking scorpion. Sting is polite, cold-eyed, intelligent, brilliant and ruthless.'

In London, Sting found himself with a rare night off and went to see Frances play her most important role so far, as Lady Macbeth in an Old Vic production starring Peter O'Toole. Unfortunately, the production — and especially O'Toole's performance — was savaged by the critics, although Frances escaped any personal attacks.

The play had received a mountain of publicity before it even opened because of the supposed curse on *Macbeth* which many speculated might affect temperamental O'Toole. The first piece of supposed bad luck occurred when an actress called Trudie Styler, who was playing one of the witches, was rushed to hospital with a burst appendix only hours after being given the role.

Happily, she recovered and later encountered Sting backstage after rehearsals one evening. The two immediately recognised each other from when they had been neighbours in Bayswater two years earlier. Frances thought nothing of it but Sting could not get Trudie out of his mind.

When Frances suggested that Trudie should come and visit them the next time they were all in Ireland, Sting was delighted. He knew he shouldn't be having those sort of thoughts about another woman but he really couldn't help himself.

At that time, Sting was certainly feeling confused about exactly where his marriage to Frances was heading. She was very much her own person and would often openly criticise Sting. It wasn't so much a clash of egos as a relationship founded on complete and utter frankness. The problem was that the incredible success of The Police had cocooned Sting into a life where no one disagreed with him about anything. Coming home to a mountain of criticism from Frances was sometimes difficult to handle.

In his heart of hearts, Sting genuinely believed that he was much better off having married before he became famous so that he could keep his feet on the ground. Frances was often a hard task mistress and he, in turn, was starting to wonder why he should put up with her. However, she had something he wanted very badly — the ability to act.

The acting bug was gnawing at him all through that period. It was almost as if he wanted to prove he could be even more successful than

Frances. It sometimes angered her that her husband seemed so obsessed with breaking into her career.

For the rest of that year, The Police tried to press further ahead in America. On each trip the venues were slightly bigger. *Zenyatta* was better received than *Regatta* and by the end of that year 'De Do Do Do De Da Da Da' was their first hit single in the States since 'Roxanne'. Miles set up his own record company in Los Angeles and signed several British and American acts, such as The Stranglers, Sector 27, Magazine and Oingo Boingo.

Just before Christmas 1980, the band headed south for Argentina. They were virtually unknown in South America but the idea was to spread the word.

They stayed at the Sheraton in Buenos Aires. Sting had Frances and Joe in tow and Stewart had his wife Sonja with him, but Andy Summers was alone after splitting with his wife Kate. Journalist Gordon Blair was the only writer allowed to accompany the band on that leg of its tour.

It was shortly before the Falklands War and tensions were a little high in Argentina but the group couldn't walk around anyway because they were mobbed everywhere they went.

Writer Blair explains, 'I had a few drinks with Sting one evening. He kept talking about the importance of having his family with him. It was almost as if he was expecting me to ask him about marital problems. Frances seemed aloof but there was no sign of any problems between them.'

Sting made a particularly big fuss of Joe. They swam in the pool together as the wives drank gin and tonic in the sun.

Blair says it was fairly obvious that drugs were being kept out of sight from him and his beady-eyed photographer. 'Andy Summers said, "You should see the things we get up to in the dressing room — groupies, drugs, etc." Then he saw Miles and clammed up.'

The afternoon before their gig, Blair and his photographer drove out into the country to do a photo session with the band. The idea was to dress them up as gauchos. Miles was delighted with such a good photo opportunity. 'The shoot went very well although the band were obviously getting a little tense as the time for the gig approached.'

When they actually got to the stadium that evening, it was chaos.

Blair takes up the story. 'There were about two thousand kids packed into this hall. It was more like a school hall. The military were walking around armed.' As soon as The Police got on stage the real hysteria began.

They had never seen anything like this. Everyone was on their feet, dancing. The soldiers started slapping people around, hitting them to make them stay down. The kids then tried to get up again each time. I was in the wings standing besides Miles and even he was shocked.

The band looked at each other as they watched the soldiers and Sting shook his head and bounced over to the wings and said to Miles, "I don't fucking like what's going on here. I don't like what's happening."

He then went back on the stage. But the crowd was so enthusiastic about The Police that they couldn't help themselves. One young girl kept leaping up from her seat. She was smashed down by a fat policeman. He hit her and she fell back in tears.

At that point, Andy Summers went to the front of the stage and swung his leg at the same policeman hitting him on the shoulder. He then swung at him again and hit him, straight in his face with his foot.

The hall then went silent. No one said a word. They sat down and there was this hiss of shock. What had he done? No one could believe it. The band kept playing. The real police looked up, incredulous that foreigners should abuse their policemen this way.

I looked at Sting and his jaw had dropped and he glanced over at Andy who had gone towards the side and was looking at Miles who had his head in his hands. Sting then said to Andy, "You're obviously going to be here over Christmas. What shall we send you in prison?"

Everyone was looking at Andy, who was playing on.

Meanwhile the policeman he had kicked had moved round to the side and was shouting and swearing at them up on the stage. Other policemen came in and ushered him away.

Minutes later, after the end of the concert, plain clothes officers went backstage. There was shouting and screaming and Miles rolled his eyes and said, "Here we go."

The interpreter was trying to calm things down. But the cops were very angry. We headed for the dressing room which was a spartan college dressing room with metal lockers all round. I got downstairs with the band the moment they came offstage.

We stood to the side and Miles started on Andy and so did Sting. "What the fuck were you playing at? You do not do these things." Andy replied, "I'm not having children abused that way. I am not having it."

Next thing the cops burst in dressed in raincoats. Five plus one in uniform. There was also the interpreter and tour operator. One of the cops in the raincoats grabbed Andy Summers by the throat and pulled him off the ground about four inches and then threw him against the lockers and his head hit the back of the lockers.

Everybody froze. My photographer went to take some pix and was prevented by the police. Meanwhile Andy was continually banged against the lockers. Miles shouted at the interpreter, "For God's sake sort this out!" It was chaos.

"There must be a way to sort this out," screamed Miles.

"Yes," replied the interpreter. "We have to pay some money."

I never found out what they paid. But everyone calmed down. Sting and Stewart were told to get back to the hotel. Andy was detained. He sat on the bench against the lockers, shaking like a leaf, while everyone else was still shouting and arguing in different languages.

Then the police went to the door and came in with another suited man who came in with the cop who had been kicked by Andy earlier. Miles then told Andy "You have to apologise, publicly." They got their own photographer in the room and insisted both men shake hands and smile so that a story about how Andy had apologised could be leaked to the press. After the photo was taken, everyone left. It was on the front page of the local paper the following day to show the local kids that you cannot get away with doing this. The police disappeared as quickly as they came in. Only myself, Andy and the photographer were left in the room. Andy was shaking and crying. I said to him, "Come on mate, it's over, finished, it's done."

We drove Andy back to the hotel because they hadn't even left him with any transport. I then turned to Andy and said, "That's over. It's finished. Let's the three of us go and have a drink. You don't want to sit on your own."

Andy just sat there shaking in the back of the car, "I can't do it. I just gotta go to my room and be alone."

Miles later told Gordon Blair, 'You chose the right gig to come to, didn't you?'

The following day it was all just light-hearted banter. Sting even said to Andy, 'Oh, are you still here? We thought you'd been banged up.'

On 22 December 1980, the band came home and played three quick shows, including a couple of gigs in a five-thousand capacity tent on Tooting Common in South London. There were no seats and it was unbearably overcrowded. A lot of people fainted and there were numerous injuries. The band got a lot of press criticism but no one was really to blame as it was just an experiment that went wrong.

Daily Mail rock critic Simon Kinnersley wrote, 'This was a disgrace. Fans paid five pounds to queue for 45 minutes in the mud to get in and waited another two hours before The Police deigned to appear. Even when they did arrive most of the fans couldn't see them because the stage was not high enough above the audience. The idea of appearing in a circus tent might work in July, but in December it was a disaster.'

After the final Tooting concert, a party was held for The Police at the Holiday Inn in Chelsea. Sting was the first to fall into the pool and promptly pulled Frances in too. Andy Summers then stripped down to his underpants and dived in, followed by dozens of other guests.

Back at home in Ireland with his family, Sting felt utterly exhausted after the gruelling tour and recording schedule. It had been made worse by the excessive amounts of cannabis and cocaine he had consumed over the previous twelve months. He was fidgety and impatient with almost everyone.

The yuletide break proved all too brief for Sting. No sooner had he started to regain a handle on family life than he was flying off to America for what Miles classified as 'The Big One' — a sell-out concert at New York's Madison Square Garden, one of the most prestigious stadiums in the world.

Miles was particularly hyped up by the event because The Police were the first so-called New Wave band to be allowed to play at the Garden.

Sting was ecstatic about the reception at the Garden but he was also completely wiped out with exhaustion. The Police had tours of Japan, Australia and Europe already fixed up, which would repeat what they had already done just a year earlier. This time, however, they missed out on the rest days in exotic locations. They even recorded Spanish and Japanese versions of 'De Do Do Do'. This was a punishing pace which few would find easy to keep up.

The band needed to stop being The Police for a moment and unwind and enjoy the financial security they had finally achieved. They also needed to discover themselves as individuals once again. The bickering and bitterness that had started to come through that year were apparent for everyone to see and some started to wonder how much longer the band could hold things together. They had just spent two years on a non-stop roller coaster ride across the world as the ultimate rock stars. Something had to give. The energy that had carried them through everything could not last forever.

In March 1981, they cancelled the European leg of their latest world tour. Sting breathed a sigh of relief. He knew the cracks were beginning to appear and that everyone needed a break from each other.

Sting was in a reflective mood at the time. 'We're all workaholics but I've realised this is as far as you can push a group in one go. We need a break from the pressures — mental, personal, fatigue in every form. I need it more than the others, I think.'

However, winding down Police business did not mean a break in work commitments for Sting. He had five movie offers on the table at that time and he'd picked the leading role in *Artemis 81* as the perfect platform for his up and coming other great talent.

Sting was paid peanuts to play the role in *Artemis 81*. He had turned down the main villain part in the latest Bond film, *For Your Eyes Only* 'because it was too camp'. He preferred the more arty role in *Artemis 81*.

In one saucy scene in *Artemis 81*, Sting washed in a lake and bared his bottom. Photos of the sequence were in big demand among the tabloids.

Sting was also writing for other performers, such as Grace Jones. He even recorded a version of Bob Dylan's 'I Shall Be Released' for a TV film soundtrack. It was clear that there was life beyond The Police and Sting started to wonder if he hadn't put too many of his eggs into one basket.

ELEVEN

CLOSE ENCOUNTERS

*'I can't say I've sinned because I've failed
to be monogamous. As chemicals in a relationship
become acclimatised, the chemical reaction between
two people lessens and you have to shake it up.'*

— STING

STING WAS LEARNING TO PLAY the press like a concert virtuoso. In 1981, already labelled rock's number one heart-throb, he gave an extraordinary interview to an attractive young female journalist in which he talked in explicit detail about his love life.

'If God's got anything better than sex to offer he's certainly keeping it to himself,' he told twenty-two-year-old Arabella Campbell-McNair-Wilson, before admitting he had a penchant for making love on dining room tables. 'There's a certain sacrificial element in it,' he explained for an article that would eventually end up between the obscure pages of *Interview* magazine.

However, the most intriguing aspect came when he insisted that he had to make love at least once a night. This must have come as a surprise to Frances as he was spending at least six months of the year away from home touring at the time.

In the same interview, Sting revealed that he liked 'dressing up' for sex and added, 'Sex should be theatrical. I like my partner to look good.'

The truth was that Sting had become fairly self-obsessed and that meant he was not shy about taking his pick of any available women, wherever he might encounter them. He was also consuming large quantities of alcohol and drugs at the time which tended to loosen any inhibitions. During one particularly active week on tour in the US Sting managed to sleep with five women. He even admitted to friends that he felt it was 'cool' to be promiscuous.

With the cracks between The Police widening on a daily basis, Sting clearly saw the day ahead when he would no longer be in the band. He had grown edgy towards Andy and Stewart who, he believed, were leaning on him too much to come up with the goods for the band.

'I know for a fact when we're approaching an album, Stewart and Andy are thinking "We'll write a few songs, OK, but Sting will write the album." And I know I've got to do it, but is it there? I do resent that, even though there'd be terrible trouble if they did suddenly come up with the best songs, just hell!

'I'm sure if I saw the potential in one of their compositions as a single I'd accept it. The thing is once the hit is written I believe it doesn't belong to me any more and stands on its own two feet. I haven't felt that with anything of Andy's or Stewart's yet though, and after all it's me who has to sing the fucker.'

The potential threat to group harmony was obvious. Sting was openly baiting the other two band members and he was growing increasingly restless. Stewart and Andy were finding it difficult to get Sting to use their compositions because he couldn't identify with them.

Sting piled on the tension by continuing to make his thoughts public. 'Andy isn't a writer of melodies. It's very separate from musicianship and it's very hard for a marvellous technical musician to take. I mean, I'm not a great musician but I do rate myself as a songwriter.'

The other two tried to rationalise it but there was another motive lurking in the distance — cash. Sting believed he was worthy of a bigger share of the musical royalties.

When the group headlined at the Gateshead Stadium in 1981, they were supported by U2 and the newly hip Channel Four TV programme *The Tube* was there to film local boy Sting's every move, which included sprinting round the famous athletic track with Jools Holland and long-distance runner Brendan Foster.

The Tube itself was a raw, chaotic programme which went out live at 5:30 p.m. every Friday. Producer Gavin Taylor takes up the story. 'All the big groups would travel up on a Thursday night and stay overnight at the biggest hotel in Newcastle. The taxi drivers loved it, the hotels loved it and British Rail and British Airways were just as keen because all the flights and trains were always fully booked.'

The show's staff would visit local nightclubs and hand out free tickets to more than two hundred youngsters who made up the live audience each week.

Eventually, *The Tube* drew a cult following and all round the country the nation's under-thirties would watch it in the pub before they went home or as they were getting ready to go out on a Friday evening. *The Tube* was recognised as being the perfect platform for record sales because people would actually watch the programme and then go out and buy the tracks they had just heard on the show.

The Tube also had a reputation for being very daring — which meant troublesome — in the eyes of TV executives. Once it was actually shut down by Channel Four just before going on air when co-presenter Jools Holland did a live promotion slot during children's hour and told viewers to 'get down, you groover fuckers'. And no one ever forgot how comic Rik Mayall walked on stage in front of millions with a mouthful of vegetable soup and pretended to vomit on the audience.

Sting's first appearance on *The Tube* was relatively trouble free but his next visit to the programme caused quite a furore. He was interviewed by presenter Paula Yates and members of the production team immediately noticed that Yates was flirting with Sting. She later told crew member John Harker that Sting and Marty Pellow from Wet

Wet Wet Wet were the only two rock stars she had interviewed for the show 'who I'd really like to bonk'.

At one stage, just after interviewing Sting, Paula turned to Harker and some of the crew on *The Tube* and said, 'I think I've just creamed my knickers, lads.'

Towards the end of his appearance on *The Tube,* Paula actually made an offer to Sting that few men would be able to refuse. She wanted to stay the night with him in a hotel suite at the luxurious Gosforth Park Hotel in the centre of Newcastle.

Says one member of the crew who was present, 'Paula couldn't keep her hands off Sting. She was scheming like crazy and told us openly that she was planning to fuck him.'

Sting played the situation down very carefully. He couldn't resist returning some of Paula's flirting but he simply wasn't that interested in Paula physically.

'Paula's short and a bit stocky. She just wasn't Sting's type really,' explained the crew member.

However, Paula Yates would not give up and after the show she even tried to insist that Sting should go in her car to the airport where he was scheduled to fly out that evening. 'She told me she planned to seduce him in the limo and then persuade him to stay the night in her hotel suite.' Somehow Sting escaped unscathed. In any case, he was great friends with Paula's rock star husband Bob Geldof and for years afterwards the two men cracked jokes about Paula's crush on Sting.

*   *   *

The way in which Sting came up with ideas for certain songs in some ways resembled the way that a good Hollywood screenwriter or novelist is inspired to brilliance.

'Walking On The Moon' came about when Sting was lying drunk in a Munich motel room, slumped on a bed, when a riff came into his head. Sting got up and started walking round the room singing, 'Walking round the room, ya ya, walking round the room'. In the cold light of day he remembered what had happened and wrote the riff

down. However, 'Walking Round The Room' sounded like a silly title
so he dreamed up 'Walking On The Moon'.

The majority of Sting's compositions came from looking inside
himself but his own intensity sometimes led to misinterpretations of
his music. 'De Do Do Do' turned out to be probably his most
misunderstood song because many believed it to be a meaningless
tune that simply cashed in on the commercial viability of The Police
at the time.

Sting insists, 'I wanted to write about the perversity of words; their
dangers. Of course it was a self-indictment too. I'm clever with
words.' He was baffled and hurt by accusations that he had written
a bubble gum classic. He genuinely had not intended to give
that impression.

Such compositions were really a convenient camouflage for a mind
in constant torment. In 1981, Sting explained, 'The whole thing about
being a writer is that with every traumatic experience part of you is
thinking, "I can use this." I've had bad times in my life. Loneliness
hits me a lot. And I glorify in it! Without it I wouldn't have written
'So Lonely' or 'Message In A Bottle' or 'The Bed's Too Big Without
You'. I thank God for the times I was down, the awful reactionary
school I went to which I fought so hard. I'm praying for something to
fight against now...'

                    *   *   *

Around this time, Sting did make an extraordinary prophesy that was
eventually to haunt his first marriage. It was the first time he
acknowledged that maybe his marriage wasn't forever. 'This is scary.
Do you know I even cynically think about the day that Frances and I
might break up. I love her dearly. I mean I'm devoted to her and yet I
can see how useful alienation is.

'If you're determined to be an artist you have to be hungry and
my life now is too easy. I'm full. The artist in me is looking for
death, for destruction. Artists are perverse. They're not normal.
They ain't. I'm not normal.'

Sting had clearly become painfully aware of a whole range of emotions that dominated his life. He continued, 'The songs on *Outlandos* are all me, me, me. "I Feel So Lonely", "Roxanne", "I Won't Share You With Another Boy", "I Was Born In The Fifties". With *Zenyatta* I think I stopped writing about me and turned to what's happening outside.'

What Sting seemed to be trying to say was that, to begin with, he could only write about himself and what he was thinking. It took three best-selling albums before he could start to consider the outside world as a subject for his songs. The inner turmoil he felt as a teenager was coming back. Being part of a trio did not really suit his mentality. He wanted to be alone again.

To make matters worse, creating a song was primarily a solitary labour. Sting would spend days alone in a room making a tune work to perfection and then find himself expected to perform it with the rest of the band. Yet in his mind it was his song, not theirs.

Girls were the other big problem. Sting might have resisted Paula Yates but he had succumbed to many women, although he tried to be as discreet as possible about his sexual adventures.

Andy Summers — also married with a young child back in London — was much more open about his conquests. He couldn't resist the females he encountered during Police's adventures around the world. 'A lot of women are very interested in me very fast and they are ready to go to bed with me at the slightest provocation,' explained Andy at the height of Police's popularity. 'The meaningful one-night stand is something that has become a permanent feature of life in the modern world. One-night stands don't have to be tacky and nasty. To be really honest, they are one of the rewards. What does any man want when it comes down to it? He wants a few things — power, money, sex and security. There is not much else beyond those things. I think all men are promiscuous by nature but I think they want a double standard. They want to sleep around all over the place and have a woman at home doing nothing.'

It was clear from what Andy Summers said at the time that wine, women and song were very much a part of the day-to-day life on the road with The Police.

Clearly, the priorities among The Police had changed enormously since they had started. Andy Summers's role was crucial because of his superb guitar skills but he was really the odd one out when it came to the complete trio. Stewart was recognised as the founder and in some ways the father figure, even though Andy was considerably older than both of his fellow Police members.

Sting considered Andy to be the laid-back one. 'We needed someone easy-going in the group. With another Stewart Copeland or another Sting we wouldn't have lasted long.'

In reality, both Sting and Stewart were hard task masters and Andy Summers was starting to feel the strain. When the band recorded 'Driven To Tears' for the *Zenyatta* album, Sting and Andy almost came to blows. Sting explains, 'I wouldn't let Andy out of the studio until he got it. I put him in a really bad mood. "Look, this has to destroy all guitar solos! Just fuckin' play like you hate me!" Then it was great. Everything about it is wrong and it's perfect.'

Andy commented, 'Sting knows his strengths and when he decides to turn on the power sometimes you have to deal with him.'

Arguments between Sting and the other band members continued with alarming frequency, particularly with Stewart, whose self-confidence spilled over like volcanic lava. Initially, the rows would centre around music but, gradually, differences arose on a more personal level.

Sting summed it up when the band were at their peak. 'That energy of Stewart's behind you all the time has to be controlled. "Wait! Wait!" He explodes with it. On stage he's not that responsible a performer that he knows exactly what he's doing. It's great and it's a drawback. He gives everything too much and too often. It's the drummer's problem. They're all mad.'

Then Sting admitted, 'Anyway, it comes back to rivalry between me and Stewart. He's at the back and he wants to be at the front. What's so fascinating about him is he's a lead guitarist in the guise of a drummer. And, of course, I'm a lead guitarist with a bass. So when Stewart's good he's great and when he's bad he's fucking awful. The best drummers are orchestral. They play the song without losing the pulse. That's what I need from him, the pulse, not the flash.'

Eventually, Sting's harsh words had the desired effect on Stewart Copeland and he conceded, 'You can't be an upfront drummer. Sting's voice and songs make The Police what it is. I know I'm red hot and all that, but The Police would probably have been pretty successful with just some drummer who could hold the beat.'

However, one thing no one could argue over was Sting's voice. Producer Nigel Gray summed it up when he said, 'There's nobody in the world can tell Sting how to sing. He records vocals first time after one run through. Wind the track back a couple of times for harmonies and that's it. His voice is the best I've ever recorded, just the character of it. Not many bands have a singer you know. There's usually just someone who belts out the vocals.'

None the less, Sting's 'artistic temperament' and overpowering public persona did not prevent him from getting some highly critical responses from other rock stars.

Singer Elvis Costello slammed into Sting when he said, 'Somebody should clip Sting round the head and tell him to stop singing in that ridiculous Jamaican accent. They make great records, they can all play, they're all pretty and I can't stand them.'

During media interviews, Sting had a way of dealing with journalists that won him some cynical admiration from his colleagues in The Police. Stewart Copeland invented a special word to sum up the way that his lead singer manipulated the media — Stingola. 'It works like this. A journalist comes on the road with the band to write a feature. I talk to him for hours. Andy talks to him for hours and Sting never says a word — except that, just once, he walks through the room where I'm busy bending this guy's ear and he says "Where's the toilet?" And that's the headline!'

Sting admitted to manipulating the media deliberately. One time he set his sights on *New Musical Express* writer Paul Morley who accompanied the band on their trip to Bombay.

Sting explains, 'I'd twigged that Paul was very influential on that paper after he'd slagged off our first album. It was my job to get in there and win him over. When we did the interview he was really into my game, but he just went overboard.' The vast three-page article written by Morley focused almost entirely on Sting and created a big rift with Andy and Stewart.

'They were furious,' admits Sting. 'Livid. At me. They thought I engineered all that publicity. I did in a way but I was just doing my job. I'm the frontman off stage as well as on. They had to put up with it. I had no sympathy with them when they got like that.'

Stewart and Andy got so fed-up with what they saw as Sting's huge ego that Miles Copeland had to intervene and issue edicts through their press agent that Andy and Stewart would do most of the talking from then on. However, Sting soon started to feel ignored and more trouble brewed.

A classic flare-up occurred when the band did a photo session with Alan Ballard for *The Sun*. Sting takes up the story, 'He said to me, "Sting, could you come forward a bit?" So I do. [Fierce American tones] "I don't like this. We get too much of Sting out in front." So I stand humbly behind Stewart.

'I didn't want to play that game. I couldn't stand the feeling that there's this jockeying for position going on. It was pathetic.'

Stewart let his feelings be known in one interview when he admitted, 'I don't care if Sting is Superman. That doesn't make him better than me!'

The band's founder member later also conceded, 'It's true he can be dangerous to be around. He has a tendency to eat people because he has such an incredibly high output of everything it takes. I mean, look at the guy. The talent, the voice, the intelligence, the personality, the looks. It all adds up and unless you have a high opinion of yourself it can be very trying on your self-esteem to work with him day after day.'

Then Stewart made a very incisive comment, 'I have my musical ability and my ability to enjoy myself. In some ways I'm probably better at that than Sting. I find it easier to smile than he does. I manage to keep my pecker up most of the time.'

The biggest indication of how the rivalry between the band

members had become well known both inside the music industry and among their most ardent fans came when Stewart received one fan letter that said, 'I hate Sting and I hate Andy and you're the one that's most handsome.' It almost seemed as if the rift was proving healthy for the band.

When Sting was voted number one in *Smash Hits* magazine's Most Fanciable Person poll and Stewart was fifth, it said it all, even though the band's closest associates were still insisting that Sting was not the boss. 'It's never Sting's group,' said sound specialist/tour manager extraordinaire Kim Turner. 'He would never be where he is without Andy and Stewart. I wouldn't want to see him try and dominate — and the others wouldn't allow him to.'

Stewart, sensing the powerplaying that was painfully apparent to all concerned at the time, insisted, 'Sting didn't take my band off me. The Police is still my band and I'll carry on painting "Police" on walls until someone takes it off me.'

Andy admitted, 'Each of us is out for himself and we've achieved so much because our egos are all very strong. There's a tensile strength in a trio.'

The most remarkable aspect of the tension between the band members was that it had become open warfare. No one was denying it. They actually seemed to be thriving on it.

Sting says, 'I fought tooth and nail for what I wanted. I was very myopic about that. Stewart is a very similar character and there was a lot of conflict between us.'

Stewart was even more blunt, 'Sting can be very abusive and ride roughshod over people's sensibilities.'

However, at the peak of Police success, the rows were still being taken with a pinch of salt, despite the bitter undertones. Sting said, 'I have terrific rows with Stewart. On the other hand I can say to him, "I love you" and he's said the same to me.' Interestingly, Sting added, 'I wouldn't say the same to Andy though I'd probably seek out his company more and he is a very good friend.'

The war of words would continue for some time yet.

TWELVE

THE CORPORATE PLAYER

*'We have always wanted the luxury of being
able to do what we want to do — and you
only get that with financial independence.'*
- MILES COPELAND

AS THE FLAK FLEW among the three members of The Police, Miles Copeland kept a diplomatic distance from the warring factions. He was quietly satisfied that the band had achieved precisely what he wanted. Along the way he had played a huge role in overturning the music industry's traditional work practices.

As the group's manager, Miles tended to stay out of the media spotlight most of the time but he was particularly proud of some of the handful of articles written about him at the time.

'One reporter said I was like "an electrical engineer on speed",' he explains with glee.

The Los Angeles *Times* called him 'the Colonel Tom Parker of the New Wave'. Miles adored the description as it put him on a level with Elvis's legendary manager and Sting continues to use it as a backhanded compliment to this day.

Others who have encountered Miles Copeland describe him as

completely non-materialistic and someone who does not stand on ceremony about who does what. 'If he sees the bog's dirty he'll clean it,' says one associate.

Miles often gave the impression he was rude because he couldn't stand small talk. However, the truth was that he was much more interested in talking about product than the people he worked with. One of his employees, Vermillion Sands, commented, 'Talking to Miles is like talking to your father sometimes. He's like a warlord. You go to him for everything. You should have an argument with him. He has a tremendous sense of rage. I'm not saying he's a violent man; I've never seen him hit a human being, but he's certainly bust up some telephones.'

Despite his clashes with Stewart, Sting remained on very good terms with Miles and had an interesting view on him at the time. 'If Miles had been born in the last century he would have been a Presbyterian minister. A hellfire and damnation preacher.'

Stewart was less clear about his feelings for his brother. 'Miles is a wonderful human being. Or rather he is wonderful, but I'm not sure he's a human being. He might be a robot dropped in by Strategic Air Command at the end of the war.'

Stewart insisted in a backhanded sort of way, 'Yeah, Miles is honest. I don't mean he doesn't sometimes have to tell lies. Everyone in rock 'n' roll does that. But he doesn't steal.'

Miles's lifestyle certainly didn't reflect the millions of pounds he undoubtedly earned from the success of The Police. He didn't drink or smoke and his attitude towards drugs had always been completely puritan. He rarely bought any clothes and usually stuck to modestly priced turtle-neck sweaters and off-the-peg jackets and trousers.

Naturally, the relationship between Miles and Stewart was difficult at times. Stewart commented, 'Like any manager Miles has to be watched very carefully. The way to use him is to talk to him once a week, tell him what's happening and he will advise you very shrewdly about the next move. He's good on overall strategy but bad on important details.'

Miles was well aware of the arguments among the trio and put a lot of the tension down to the group's enormous success. 'The bigger anything gets, the less together it gets in some ways. It's inevitable. The group is going to have to come to terms with that. So am I. If I was going to keep a twenty-four-hour watch on The Police I'd have to hire another ten people and double my commission. The group aren't going to pay me any more so we have to face it. We've always been a bit schlocky. I'm not the kind of guy where every detail is watched, every penny squeezed out of the promoter. He makes an extra three or four hundred dollars, so what? The more he makes, the more I make in the end. The important thing is that we get there.'

Miles caused a ripple of discontent among the staff at his Faulty Records company in London when he gave The Police's senior road crew Christmas bonuses of up to two and a half thousand pounds per man but did not treat his employees anything like so generously.

The most common criticism of Miles was that he spread himself too thinly, although he insisted at the time, 'There are four people keen on the band working hard — Stewart, Sting, Andy and me. Most artists say they want to be successful and a big star, but they don't really want it bad. Stewart and Sting want it bad. I haven't pushed and pushed them. In fact, until 1981 it was me saying, "You gotta take some time off to be with your families." I'd seen how being on the road had destroyed things at home for other bands.'

Miles prided himself on having his 'family' of Stewart, Sting, Kim Turner and road manager Billy Francis, close to him. He also admitted there were some distinct disadvantages, 'We're all close. We fight each other and we fight for each other.'

Miles also conceded that he found that the neverending cycle of worldwide tours gnawed at his enjoyment of life. 'I don't like going on the road except some place new. I hate just travelling. I hate it. I don't like living out of a suitcase, never having a social life, never having a personal life. Basically, you have all this success and you're empty.'

As if to prove his point, Miles continued to encourage all three band members to bring their girlfriends/wives/children on tour because he felt it would keep them more settled and help to improve their confidence on stage. When the group travelled alone women frequently approached all three for sex.

Stewart explains, 'Girls approached us all the time offering themselves. Not just the slags and groupies you get hanging around, but married women too. At times it almost shocks me. I'll be sitting there talking politely with a famous record company executive and his wife when he wanders away and suddenly it comes out. It gets very weird.'

Sting was more reticent about confessing to his encounters with groupie types but would gladly tell anyone who'd listen: 'The only thing that keeps me from drinking gallons of whisky or shooting up is my marriage. I know that without that firm, solid love and trust and affection I would be a mental case.'

Then, talking about Frances, he continued, 'I needed someone who could cope with me, who isn't just an appendage to me. A partner. A sparring partner. Frances will fight back fiercely. I'm closer to her than anybody. She's my ideal, I suppose. I'm very lucky. She's intelligent, thinking and beautiful ...'

However, coping with Sting was proving quite a strain for Frances. As a natural competitor, she also found it hard to see him offered acting work when she was in dire need of a job. She admitted at the time, 'Partly, I feel resentful, not so much for myself as for my whole profession that these opportunities should come to him so easily. All that attention he got from a small role in *Quadrophenia* when really good actors like Phil Daniels were ignored. But another part of me feels very happy that someone I love should be doing so well.' Frances added, 'Then again, Sting is jealous of my successes too.'

The stress and strain of looking after their son Joseph also had a telling effect on Frances's attitude towards her rock-star husband. She had her own work to do but was reluctant to dump Joe at a crèche or with a childminder. It started to dawn on her that not only was she holding down a career but she was also bringing up their child virtually single-handed.

In theory, the tension between Sting and Frances should have eased when he took long breaks between tours and recording sessions. Certainly his determination to get to know his son was not in doubt. 'I'm a very serious father,' insisted Sting at the peak of The Police's success. 'Probably so serious I'll be dreadful at it. At the moment, Joe's very good.'

Whenever he was asked what his father did for a living, Joe would reply, 'My daddy shouts and jumps up and down — but it's too loud for me.'

Confronted with the possibility that Sting might be enticed into bed by other women, Frances once again reiterated that she would not ignore adultery on the part of her handsome rock star husband. 'There's no such thing as an open marriage between us. We're both jealous as hell and utterly monogamous.' Sting insisted he felt the same way, 'It's true. I'm very very jealous, too. I couldn't take that kind of frivolity. I'm old fashioned that way. The whole idea of "Ah, it doesn't matter that much." It does!'

However, Sting did fully appreciate his sex symbol role. 'It's a matter of "I am what I am." If anything, it makes me more attractive. It's real sexuality. We're married men. We've had it. I think that's the point.'

At the time, however, Sting was reluctant to get drawn on exactly how often he got propositioned by women while on tour. He insisted, 'I never trust the reasons behind it. I do like beautiful women around and they are there. But I do not give myself easily. I won't jeopardize my position for a quick fuck. I also like remaining aloof. It's a perversion of mine really; self-imposed isolation which I find very useful.'

They were strong words that Sting would one day live to regret.

It seemed that the pressure was still piling on top of him. He told one writer: 'I feel as if I am being torn apart. It is impossible for me to lead a normal life — and that means that my marriage, which is very important to me, cannot be normal either.

'I have a pressure-cooker existence — and every so often it explodes. People see the glamorous side of things but my life is not easy. I am propelled by rocket fuel and those around me are inclined to get burned. I can't change myself.'

It was almost as if he knew what lay just around the corner.

*   *   *

It was finally agreed that the trio should take three months off to recharge their fast-fading batteries. After the break, the band reunited at George Martin's AIR Studios on the Caribbean island of Montserrat in the second week of June 1981. During his break Sting had decided that the band was still useful to him and he would not walk away from them just yet.

The group's recording sessions lasted just over a month and Hugh Padgham, best known for his producing work with Phil Collins and Hall and Oates, supervised the band. The Police planned to go off on a South American tour and then travel to Canada to mix the upcoming album based on the tracks they had laid down in the Caribbean.

Sting's fear of flying was further fuelled when The Police were caught in a hurricane *en route* from the recording studio in Montserrat to Caracas where they were continuing their world tour.

The flight — in a shabby, two-engined 1943 Dakota — turned into a horrific experience as bits of the plane started to fall off the main body of the aircraft and a door was almost blown off its hinges. Eventually the aircraft hobbled into Caracas.

A few weeks later, Sting acted as best man when Miles Copeland married Mary Pegg in New York. It was a significant development because it confirmed just how close he had become to his manager.

Back in London a few days later, Sting walked right into a storm of protest about the group's latest single 'Invisible Sun'. The BBC banned the video which accompanied the record on the basis that it was a 'political statement' because it showed kids playing in the streets of West Belfast, amoured cars, the British Army, graffiti-covered walls and a funeral.

Sting was infuriated and made his feelings known to anyone who would listen. 'The song is about people who ought to have a choice but, for reasons beyond their control, don't.'

Sting was nothing if not proud about his associations with Ireland and he went on record at the time, 'I married a girl from there and I get very upset by what's happening there. It was originally about Belfast and how people carry on normal life, but since I wrote it conditions that exist in Belfast are happening in other British cities only the kids haven't got a flag to wave.'

In April 1981, a children's book was published with a musical tie-in, entitled *Message In A Bottle*. Some rock business observers were surprised that a band like The Police should be involved in such a 'soft' project but Miles considered it useful exposure for the band during a low-key period.

When *Ghost In The Machine* was released in October 1981, Sting found himself having to do some explaining about the album's title, taken from a book by psychologist Arthur Koestler, which stated that man was becoming much more machine-like. 'What I'm saying is that we shouldn't be like machines. We're much more complex, more creative, more destructive.'

Sting became even more intense about the album in a press kit distributed to journalists at the time of the release. 'I've lost faith in the political process to solve our problems. I think the answer to our problems is in our own heads. I'm disillusioned with order.'

There was little time left to spend with Frances or his young son. Inevitably, he was becoming a stranger in his own home.

Up in Newcastle, Sting's family were also living in the shadow of his fame.

The Sumner family fully appreciated that their Gordon was a genius — and a multi-millionaire to boot. Up until that point, however, they had tended to take all the publicity about him with a pinch of salt and found it difficult to equate the man in the papers with the shy youngster they all knew and loved.

Sting's sister Angela — by now married and working at Newcastle Airport as a ticket supervisor — was particularly close to her brother. She had never doubted that Sting was going to make it but was doubly impressed because he appeared to have remained very non-materialistic about his possessions, despite his immense wealth. In some ways she still looked on him as a mummy's boy who occasionally popped back to the family base for some of Audrey's delicious home cooking. Angela occasionally got pestered for her brother's autograph and personal information about him, but she soon learned to ignore all the interest. 'I don't have young girls queuing up on my doorstep but I have to admit that people think they can have a glimpse of his fame through me,' she said at the time. 'How wrong they are. I can't stress how much of an individual I really am.'

Angela was especially touched by the fact that when she went into hospital for major surgery on her spine in January 1982, a massive bouquet of flowers turned up at the hospital from Sting who was in the middle of a hectic US tour.

However, Angela still found it difficult at times. She was particularly hurt when stories started circulating their Newcastle neighbourhood that Sting was regularly contributing cash to the family. Angela insists to this day, 'As well as working as a ticket sales supervisor at Newcastle Airport, I also have my own clothes-designing business. Recently, I turned up with my husband at a dinner wearing a mink coat. Lots of people asked if Sting had bought it for me. That hurt; my husband had bought me the coat for an anniversary present.' Certainly, there was no way that animal lover Sting would purchase something as politically incorrect as a fur coat for his sister.

On the other hand, Phil Sumner got so fed up with people picking fights with him because of his famous brother that he let his anger rub off on his relationship with Sting and a rift emerged between them. 'He never seemed to have sufficient time for his family and it caused problems,' explains Phil, who was still living in Wallsend and delivering milk round housing estates in Whitley Bay.

Although there were three years between them in age, Phil had virtually identical looks to his famous brother and that caused him a lot of problems on the streets where they grew up. 'I've developed a complex about going out alone. I often used to go to the local pub on my own but now I can't face it,' Phil explained back in September 1983. 'Everyone talks about Sting and I can't always face that alone. It puts me on edge. Some people can be pretty heartless and cruel. To me he's our Gordon — not Sting. He's my brother. Not a god.'

Phil's biggest problem was something he shared with Sting — incredible sensitivity. It was, after all, only natural that he should feel ambivalent about his older brother's success, especially when he was having to get up at 4 a.m. every morning to deliver milk to more than three hundred homes.

In a reflective comment, Phil said at the time, 'I know I'm not musical but I could easily get some record company to put a single out. People would buy it just because I'm Sting's brother. But that's not what I want.'

Earlier, the family had been deeply upset when Sting had told writer Kristine McKenna in 1980: 'I come from a family of losers — I'm the eldest of four — and I've rejected my family as something I don't want to be like. My father delivered milk for a living and my mother was a hairdresser. Those are respectable occupations, but my family failed as a family. I grew up with a pretty piss-poor family life. I lived in Newcastle, and the whole thing for me was escape.'

Phil and the rest of Sting's family were devastated when they read his comments in *Rolling Stone*. It caused an especially bitter rift with Phil.

Three years after that damaging interview Sting tried to win forgiveness for hurting his family by saying, 'Some things I said about my childhood hurt my family deeply. I learned a big lesson there and had to work very hard to repair the damage done by the article. It was purely my own arrogance and lack of thought.'

However, it took a lot longer and some tragic occurrences before Sting was entirely forgiven.

It was the constant prying that really upset Phil and the rest of the family. He explained, 'Guys I don't even known come up to me in the pub and pretend they're mates just to impress their girlfriends.'

Phil also complained bitterly that people in Newcastle 'seem to think I'm loaded because I am Sting's brother'. He explained, 'I'm not at all. I earn enough money to make life comfortable but, despite that, I haven't had a holiday for three years.'

Phil couldn't help having a dig at his brother over his lifestyle. 'He hardly has enough time to see his own children, let alone come up here to visit us. Our Gordon may be laughing all the way to the bank, but I do worry about him. He's worried about going out, even with bodyguards or friends. There must be a lot of lunatics out in America and all it would take would be one nut to take a pot-shot at him and he'd be dead.'

Sting was the one who had got away. Now he was paying the price.

THIRTEEN

The Root of All Evil

'Cocaine is for horses, not for men;
They say it'll kill you, but
they don't say when.'
- TRADITIONAL BLUES

ALL THE DRUGS, SEX AND ROCK 'N' ROLL in the world couldn't help Sting to come to terms with the fact that he was now one of the richest people in Britain. The Police were earning upwards of 10 million dollars a year and huge cheques would turn up on Sting's doormat with alarming regularity.

For the former Marxist it was all a little too much to handle and there were times when he felt immensely confused by the events of the previous five years. 'I can't face the idea of becoming rich even now,' he explained at the time. 'When I look at the accounts it's not mathematics, it's astronomy.'

Yet on other occasions, he would insist that he had loved every minute of his success and enjoyed spending all the money. In a nutshell, he was a very confused young man.

For Sting, wealth remained a mystery even after it arrived. He donated hundreds of thousands of pounds to charity in a bid to offset his guilt at being so rich. His confused political stance made things even more difficult because Britain was at the peak of Thatcherism and Margaret Thatcher had been responsible for introducing tax breaks that encouraged dozens of celebrities to stay in the UK rather than flee to a tax-free bolt-hole.

In Sting's eyes, Margaret Thatcher also represented everything that was wrong with Britain. 'To her, people without money can go to the wall. It's a deliberate economic measure, creating unemployment to keep inflation down. It's a disgrace; it's immoral. She's throwing a generation down the drain, completely wasting their talent and energy.'

In a weird piece of logic, Sting believed that the low taxes he was paying on his huge earnings were entirely justified because the Tories were not building more schools or hospitals. 'She's not feeding the kids who attend them, she's building sites for American nuclear warheads and sending working-class kids to get killed in Belfast. I'm not going to pay for it if I can help it.'

Besides donating a hundred and fifty thousand pounds to youth organisations each year in the early 1980s, Sting and Frances sent numerous cheques to flood and earthquake victims across the world. They also paid a hundred and fifty pounds a year to a scheme which supported the education of a young girl called Achira in Kenya.

Sting felt guilty about his fame and wealth in some ways. Every time he caught himself sipping a glass of Dom Perignon or eating some lavish meal in a vastly overpriced restaurant, he had to stop and remind himself where it all began.

In 1982, Sting helped to raise funds for a number of ultra-left youth training centres in London. He even turned up at an event at a pub called the Governor General in Catford, South London, which was organised by the controversial Workers' Revolutionary Party.

Sting led the judging panel in a Battle of the Bands contest which was held to raise cash for the left wingers. Sting kept a low profile throughout the evening. The youth training group — whose chairwoman is actress Vanessa Redgrave — ran centres for unemployed youngsters in London's Brixton, Edge Hill in Liverpool and Tobago Street, Glasgow. Ms Redgrave also happened to be chairwoman of the Trotskyite WRP youth wing, the Young Socialist Movement.

He also appeared at a charity benefit for Amnesty International, called The Secret Policeman's Ball, which was held at London's Theatre Royal on Drury Lane. Other stars included Eric Clapton, Jeff Beck, Phil Collins and numerous British comedians. Sting sang two songs — 'Roxanne' and 'Message In A Bottle'.

However, the concert was marred by a recurring throat problem which regularly threatened to stop Sting singing permanently. His voice, with its near operatic range, had become a source of much anxiety. He was prepared to try virtually anything to keep it working.

By the time of The Secret Policeman's Other Ball, the following year, Sting was practising something called the Alexander Method which involved the singer lying flat on the floor of his dressing room for twenty minutes while he tried to get his back exactly level with the ground. The theory was if his body relaxed then so would his troublesome larynx.

Sting continued to be a very difficult character to deal with. Record company executive Mike Hales encountered him frequently and believed that much of Sting's aggression and paranoia was brought on by drugs.

'It was a sudden, complete change in Sting's personality. I think cocaine was probably responsible for the way he turned into a rather aggressive person for a while.

'I first saw the change when he stopped at my office for a game of table tennis one afternoon. We had played many times before and it had always been something we did for a laugh but this time I could see him gritting his teeth and taking it really seriously. Even so, I beat him. Then he threw his bat down and snarled, "You're supposed to let me win. I'm the star." '

Hales believes that drug usage also led to much of the tension within the group. 'One time the band did a long, difficult picture session. At the end, I showed the photographs to them and Sting grabbed hold of some prints of him holding a saxophone and scored them over in a frenzy with his ballpoint pen. "No, never," he shouted. "Those must never go out — ever."

'I realised during that picture session just how serious things had become among the three members of The Police.

'Though nearly a hundred pictures had been taken, each member of the group wanted to look better than the other two in any pictures we put out.'

In the end, there was only one photograph that the three of them would agree to have released. All the rest had to be thrown away.

One of the most worrying aspects of all this pressure was that Sting feared he was losing touch with ordinary people, whom he saw as his life blood. 'You have to force yourself to be interested in other people. Because you're so used to being the object of attention, just to have a normal conversation is very difficult. You feel yourself churning out your interview spiel.'

Sting continued seriously to consider the end of The Police. He admitted, 'I'm out for myself and Stewart and Andy know it! As long as the group is useful to my career I'll stay. As soon as it isn't I'll drop it like a stone. The alternative is saying we're all in this for life. All for one, one for all. Fuck that. That's very limited. This is the longest job I've ever had. I want something else. It's not the whole "Police Split!" thing, I'm not seriously suggesting that. But when we next play I'll have to really want it.'

Stewart still firmly believed that Sting 'would be a fucking idiot' to leave the group. 'He's the star of the show. Everyone's running round for him. If he leaves the group it will be for a good reason, and if it's a good reason for him then it's a good reason for me.'

For the moment, the trio somehow held together. The situation was certainly helped by a vast contract for a new album from A&M Records which, in effect, guaranteed them one million pounds up front, irrespective of what they delivered. As Sting put it at the time, 'It's a great temptation to present them with an album of farting — and they'll be legally bound to give us the money.'

In many people's eyes The Police could still get a whole lot better. In America, there was a definite feeling that they had to improve in order to sustain their success. However, that very response to the group was further evidence to Sting that he needed to start planning for the future.

He commented at the time, 'It's fatigue. We're pushing this as far as it will go. It's really starting to tell on me. I'm a bit worried at this juncture. I used to be a glorious amateur and love every minute. My whole week was centred on waiting for Wednesday night when my old band Last Exit played the Gosforth Hotel in Newcastle. But now it's such a pain to get through a show — actual physical pain in my throat I mean. You can hear it.'

Shortly after this, Sting returned to Britain to start work on yet another film project, Dennis Potter's *Brimstone and Treacle,* with Joan Plowright and the late Denholm Elliott.

He landed the part after fellow rock star David Bowie turned down the role. The project had an interesting history, having been originally produced by the BBC, and later picked up for production as a feature film.

Dennis Potter believed that Bowie's decision to drop out was probably a blessing in disguise. 'Sometimes Bowie looks as if he is dead — he's too chilling — whereas Sting has more bottled-up warmth, although he has a slightly arrogant air very necessary for this part.'

The movie was filmed at Shepperton Studios for seven weeks and Sting knew that his first important task was to establish a rapport with co-stars Elliott and Plowright, then married to Lord Olivier.

'What I had to do with them as people, not just actors, was seduce them,' explains Sting, 'convince them that I wanted to learn a trade, that I wasn't just an upstart standing on their toes.'

Bisexual Elliott was so taken with Sting that he later admitted he was turned on watching Sting donning black see-through lacy gloves for one of the film's most disturbing scenes in which he rapes a mentally handicapped girl.

At his home in Ibiza in 1989, Elliott admitted to me, 'Sting was a gorgeous lad. I fancied him like crazy but I usually had a rule not to get involved with any fellow actors.' However, Elliott insisted, 'I thought Sting was giving me the come on. I was probably wrong but I convinced myself that he wanted to go to bed with me.'

For the following few weeks, Denholm Elliott later explained, 'I did everything in my power to lure him into bed but I failed miserably. I wanted him but he ended up being the one who got away.'

In fact, Elliott was so heartbroken by his inability to seduce Sting that he 'rushed into the arms of the next young boy I could seduce'.

Brimstone and Treacle caused an outcry from some quarters when it was released in Britain. One critic, Ivan Waterman, wrote in the *News of the World*, 'It is sick, sensational and bound to anger the parents of every handicapped child. For mothers and fathers of handicapped youngsters this is an all-time low in nightmarish entertainment.'

The actress who played Sting's rape victim — twenty-one-year-old Suzanna Hamilton — says she was not in the least bit bothered by the graphic nature of the film. 'It didn't make any difference to me. In my role I never got to talk to him at all.'

The movie's producer insisted, 'It's a moral piece of work. Anyone who says it is sick isn't looking at it in the right way.'

Some critics did look beyond the sex and gore. *The Mail on Sunday* wrote, 'To stress that incident [the rape] is to misunderstand its motives and intentions. The film, despite some fussy direction, is, in fact, a powerful black comedy which says some profound things about the devil of lust we do know and the God of Love we don't.'

At the time, the after-effects of playing the part of a man possessed by the devil certainly seemed to ricochet Sting's life from one crisis to another.

In January 1982, Sting took off on yet another US tour. The relentless aspect of this took a serious toll on him because he was feeling increasingly bored and restless. He was getting fed up with landing at the same airports, playing at the same venues and staying in the same hotel suites. He had also grown bored with the endless women and the drugs.

On 18 February 1982, The Police flew down to Chile to attend the twenty-third Musical Festival Internacional at Viña Del Mar, a picturesque nineteenth-century town on the Pacific coast. The town is filled with people of British decent because it was once the main port on the Pacific side of South America for the nitrate business which thrived there in the early twentieth century.

Sting and the rest of The Police found themselves in the unlikeliest of surroundings in a country run by a despotic dictator suspected of killing thousands of political opponents.

Explains local recording engineer Herman Rojas, 'The military were firmly in charge. There was a lot of control over the people. It was a strange place for The Police to turn up.'

The Police actually took the festival by storm in more ways than one. The youngsters loved them, but the media derided them and described them as pigs because of the group's habit of spitting on the stage during a performance. This was a legacy left over from the old days when they had tried to be as punk as possible.

At the venue Rojas noticed that Miles Copeland himself had been pushing kids off the stage whenever they tried to clamber up to get closer to their idols and that irritated a lot of locals who believed Miles should not be behaving in such a way.

Rojas encountered the group in the bar of the slightly rundown Hotel O'Higgins where Miles had insisted the band stay because it offered a better room rate. 'I started talking to Sting over a beer and we found we had a lot in common. They had just finished their gig and had completely blown the audience away because they were different from anything we had ever seen before in this country,' recalls Rojas.

Herman Rojas was astounded when Sting put down his beer and joined the other members of the band in a spontaneous jam session using a piano and an acoustic guitar that just happened to be in the bar. Once the word got out that The Police were in the hotel, the real police had to be called to control the crowds that gathered.

A few well-deserved days off in Rio followed at the end of that month before they flew back to Florida to restart the seemingly endless US tour that was to continue until the end of April.

In May 1982, Sting was forced to sell his home in Ireland because of fears for the safety of Frances and Joseph. He was 'freaked out' after being threatened in a pub by an angry local resident. The singer also received an anonymous letter warning him to get out. His house was quietly sold to a local business man for seventy thousand pounds. Sting had bought it for just sixty-two thousand eighteen months earlier.

The full details of the threats to Sting and his family have never been revealed but, according to residents, there was a certain amount of resentment towards him because of fierce anti-British sentiments over the troubles in Northern Ireland. It was ironic when one considers that Sting actually sympathised with the Republican cause.

However, there was another reason why Sting had decided to quit Ireland, which has never before been disclosed. Behind Frances's back, Sting had developed a close friendship with attractive blonde actress Trudie Styler who had been staying just a short distance away at actor Peter O'Toole's house.

To make matters worse, Trudie was one of Frances's best friends at the time. The two women had been through some tough times together during *Macbeth* and Frances had never had any inkling of what was happening between her husband and her friend.

Sting was riddled with guilt about his two-timing behaviour but he reasoned that selling the house in Ireland and getting the family back to London might help to rescue his marriage.

*   *   *

On the album *Ghost In The Machine* the track entitled 'One World' was particularly significant because it marked Sting's first attempt at looking at the world outside his own emotional experiences. 'The sooner we think in terms of one world as opposed to the three that we have artificially created, the better we are going to solve our problems.'

There were other definite messages from Sting in that album, including the track 'Spirits In The Material World', in which he maintained that he had lost faith in the political process to solve the world's problems and that he was disillusioned with order.

Sting's intensity seemed directly linked to his troubled mind and he could not see contentment anywhere on the horizon.

FOURTEEN

PUMPING IRON

*'I think we thrive on arguments. Every day
there's a fresh one. The day we have nothing
to argue about is when we'll break up.'*
- STING

THESE WERE HEADY DAYS for Sting. He was now the focus of the attention he had always craved. There was no doubt in anyone's mind that he was a rock star but he also wanted to be a big-time movie actor. In the middle of all his musical activities, he still managed to complete his role in *Brimstone and Treacle*. During one day's shoot, he injured his hand by accidently sticking it through a plate-glass window. Completely undeterred by the injury, he went on stage for a gig the following night with his arm in a sling and handed over his bass duties to a member of the crew.

On New Year's Eve 1982, the group played a concert in Scotland, then set off for a two-week tour of France, Germany and Scandinavia before moving on to yet another US marathon in Boston on 15 January. The gruelling pace of the previous year was being matched, gig for gig, and the band was soon feeling even more exhausted than they had before they took their break.

141

The Police's North American tour resumed with a show in Miami in the second week of March. Criss-crossing America in a vast convoy of buses, the group played on until late April when they wound things up with a whole series of appearances in the New York State area.

In April 1982 — on the eve of the Meadowlands gig — Frances gave birth to the couple's second child, Fuchsia Katherine. She weighed eight pounds ten ounces. At virtually the same time, Sting moved out of the family's recently purchased home in North London.

Just before the birth, Frances had found out that Sting was dating her friend Trudie Styler behind her back. Obviously, Sting's absence from the birth of Katherine was caused by his bitter marriage break-up with Frances. He issued a tactfully worded statement when he got to the States, proclaiming that he was 'bowled over. A daughter completes the set'.

A few weeks later, rumours of the split between Sting and Frances reached Fleet Street rock music gossip columnist John Blake. He wrote: 'The marriage of rock star Sting and actress Frances Tomelty has run into problems, I am saddened to learn. The pair have argued and spent little time together lately — partly because of Sting's fondness for a 27-year-old blonde actress, who was a friend of his wife's until recently.'

Blake then went on to quote a close friend as saying, 'It is very odd. They both seem to love each other but their marriage is falling apart.'

Behind Blake's exclusive revelations in *The Sun* lay an intriguing power battle between certain members of Sting's family and friends. The story was the direct result of a number of anonymous letters sent to Blake's Fleet Street office. 'The writer insisted that the rumours were true and that I should print something immediately,' explains Blake. 'It was very weird. It felt as if I was being manipulated by someone close to Sting.'

Blake has his own suspicions as to who was behind the letters but, for legal reasons, it would be impossible here to name the people involved.

However, the campaign to bring Sting's adulterous behaviour out in the open suggests that he was in two minds about whether to end his marriage. Shortly afterwards, the couple issued a statement insisting that they were not contemplating divorce but everyone knew it was on the cards.

During the early summer of 1982, Sting started legal proceedings against Virgin Music in a bid to regain control of the publishing rights to his early material, which had been snapped up by the company when he was still with Last Exit. Sting maintained that he had been treated unfairly by the company and that they had taken advantage of him because he was a struggling musician at the time. Details emerged of the Virgin contract which involved a five-year deal giving Sting and Virgin a 50–50 split on income for the first three years and a 60–40 split in Sting's favour for the remaining two years. Prompted by Miles Copeland, Sting sued Virgin.

Despite the pain and anguish she must have felt following the discovery of her husband's affair with Trudie, Frances appeared in the witness box to testify on behalf of her husband. She testified that she had worked to help to make her husband a rock star. She had guided him, nagged him and pushed him as he stumbled from obscurity to fulfilment and eventual worldwide fame.

However, Frances did describe her husband as 'naïve' when it came to the business side of the music world. 'He took his usual attitude of not being interested in anything but singing and playing.'

She told the court how she had hawked Sting's demo tapes round many record companies and had even 'nagged' Sting to seek legal advice before he signed the contract. Frances seemed to sum up the situation perfectly when she said, 'We were a very naïve bunch of people. Just a bunch of idiots really.'

That contract actually gave Virgin fifty per cent of his publishing earnings on the first two albums and forty per cent on a third record.

The case provoked screaming headlines in the press who projected a David and Goliath-style battle between Sting in one corner and Virgin king Richard Branson in the other. The case lasted two weeks before an out-of-court settlement was negotiated, with both parties claiming victory.

Afterwards, Sting was so concerned that people might think he had lost the case against Branson that he felt obliged to explain to reporters why he had taken legal action. 'My songs are like my children,' he explained. 'You want to protect them when they're being abused. I won the case because I will get my songs back.'

Miles was even more blunt and to the point. 'They've earned over five million from him. For years I tried to renegotiate and they never wanted to know. Even though Sting wrote three-quarters of the songs on the first Police album, *Outlandos d'Amour*, at the time Stewart and Andy were earning more from the songwriting. In America they got seventy five per cent and Sting less than fifty per cent.'

What had hurt Sting the most — besides the money — was the knowledge that the company owned the copyright on his songs until fifty years after his death. This would have enabled them to exploit them in any way they wished. A deodorant commercial which used 'Don't Stand So Close To Me' (much to Sting's disgust) was only the beginning.

Under the terms of the settlement between Sting and Virgin, the songs would revert to Sting in 1990. Virgin also agreed to pay him an extra seven-and-a-half per cent royalty on every record he had made up to the time of the court case. That two hundred thousand pounds was to pay his legal costs. Virgin also agreed to collect royalties on the next Police album only in the UK and Ireland.

Sting said ruefully at the time, 'Any kid with a contract should go to a music business lawyer. I didn't spend the necessary six hundred pounds. It's cost me millions and far more in heartbreak'.

Colourful Virgin boss Richard Branson was rather more tactful about the settlement. 'It is a sensible compromise and I'm very pleased it has been resolved. It has been a bit of give and take.'

The end of the case coincided with a brief announcement by Sting's press agent that he was planning to sell the North London house that he had shared with Frances until their split three weeks earlier.

The rift between Sting and Richard Branson has continued to this day. At a concert Sting played at only weeks after the end of the case, he told a stunned audience, 'I'm going to tell you a story about when

I was young and innocent six years ago and I signed a contract to an asshole.' Sting then went on to tell fans that he was particularly upset about how Virgin had allowed his music to be used for that deodorant advertisement.

In contrast, Virgin boss Richard Branson said he was not in the least bit upset by Sting's remarks. 'No action can ever be totally amicable,' he told one reporter.

A few months later, Sting, Stewart and Andy found themselves in the company of Great Train Robber Ronnie Biggs, in a clever stunt organised by Miles Copeland during a tour of Brazil. The idea was to get The Police to 'arrest' Ronnie Biggs. Coming so soon after the much more outrageous Sex Pistols and their *Great Rock 'n' Roll Swindle,* it seemed tame in comparison.

Biggs takes up the story in his own inimitable fashion, 'I got a call from a mate who said that The Police were in town and they'd like to meet me and there was a free meal in it for me. Well, how could I refuse?'

Biggs — probably the most famous Englishman in Brazil — was pleasantly surprised by 'the lads' as he calls them when he showed up at their suite at the Hotel Nationale in the centre of Rio. 'Sting was a good guy. We played some table tennis, supped a few beers and got a little sloshed. It was all most civilised.'

However, one thing has always stayed in Biggs' mind about Sting. 'He was bloody determined not to let me win a game of table tennis. That guy's a fierce competitor and I can fully see why he's become such an incredible success story.'

Interestingly, not once did Sting ask Biggs a question about his part in Britain's most infamous robbery. 'I don't think he was all that interested.'

As usual, Sting's mind was on one thing only — continuing his own fame.

FIFTEEN

FEMME FATALE

*'I want to be a famous actress ... and I
will be. There is no failure in my terms.'*
- TRUDIE STYLER

WITHIN A FEW WEEKS OF THE HIGH COURT BATTLE with Virgin, the
British tabloids had gone Sting-crazy. His affair with Trudie Styler
was out in the open and his marriage was clearly over.

Many were astonished by the way that Trudie had captivated Sting
with her whipcord-thin, angular body, oversized mouth and the long
deep scars — legacy of a childhood accident — which slashed
unapologetically across her left cheek.

With the media baying for his blood, Sting made an extra-
ordinarily insensitive move by flying off, with twenty-seven-year-old
Trudie, to a party in the south of France hosted by arms dealer
Adnan Khashoggi.

Only three weeks earlier Sting had issued a statement insisting that
although they had separated, his marriage to Frances was not over.
His public relations advisors had been hoping they could water the
story down by implying that no one else was involved. However, that

statement simply further fuelled the rumours flying around London at the time.

At the elegant Hermitage Hotel in Monte Carlo, where Khashoggi was celebrating his forty-eighth birthday, Sting and Trudie kissed and cuddled at a dinner table also occupied by Ryan O'Neal and Farrah Fawcett.

Sting's new companion — wearing an expensive white mini-dress — giggled delightedly when a tribute to The Police was played. They were even served a soup named 'Material World' after one of the band's songs.

The couple slipped off early to their luxurious suite before returning to London the following day in a private Lear jet owned by Khashoggi. Upon spotting hoards of waiting pressmen at Heathrow Airport, Sting instantly separated from Trudie and rather clumsily insisted he had been with Frances at the party. 'My wife has been with me all the time,' he told reporters. 'Now leave me alone. I'm extremely tired.' Then, a scuffle flared up between Sting and the paparazzi and one cameraman was thrown down a flight of stairs by a bodyguard.

At London's Stringfellow's nightclub a few nights later, Sting openly held hands with Trudie and boldly introduced her to eager pressmen as 'my mistress'. He told reporters, 'We're here so we can get over the pressure and then be left alone.'

Reporter Garth Pearce was at Stringfellows that night and Sting introduced Trudie to him. Pearce was struck by how unhappy the singer appeared to be. 'He wore the hunted look of a man who suspects everything and everybody,' said the writer. 'He was always so relaxed, so clear-eyed and clear-headed about his intentions, enjoying the success that his music brought.'

Years later, Sting admitted that calling Trudie his mistress was a dreadful mistake. 'That wasn't clever of me,' he recalls. 'Irony — because that's what the remark was — doesn't translate into newspaper print. I learned that lesson the hard way in print and got my fingers burnt. But I won't have anyone prying into private life.'

The strain of the Virgin court battle and his disintegrating marriage had brought Sting to within a hair's breadth of a nervous breakdown. He even began using Police concerts to make sweeping verbal attacks on those who offended him. He was in danger of completely losing touch with the world he had grown up in.

During sessions with a Jungian analyst, which followed the end of his marriage, Sting was supposed to encounter his dark side but, in fact, he made up most of the dreams he told his analyst. It was shameful but he did not want to let go of his true thoughts at the time.

*   *   *

Meanwhile there was Trudie. Having first set eyes on Sting when she was his neighbour four years earlier, she had now become his full-time mistress. It was all a long, long way from the tiny council house on the outskirts of Birmingham where she had been born. Trudie's father — a hulking former farm labourer — worked in a factory as a lampshade packer.

The Styler family were very poor and their existence became even more meagre after Trudie's father was made redundant. There were two other sisters, Sabrina and Heather. It was a million miles from the home life of the acting family that Frances Tomelty belonged to.

At the age of just two and a half, Trudie was mown down by a runaway baker's van. The vehicle's exhaust pipe ripped open her head and left her with scars across her cheek and an enormous strawberry-coloured stain. When she went to school, the kids would shout 'Scar Face, Scar Face' at her in the playground.

She completed her A-Levels and then announced she wanted to be an actress. It was hardly a happy family to grow up in. Aged just seventeen, Trudie ran away from home and headed for Stratford-Upon-Avon. 'It was a summer's night. I hitched a lift and knocked on the first door I came across and asked the lady for a bed. I stayed with her for a week and then found a job as an au pair with a family described in the advertisement as "theatrical".'

It was this family who adopted Trudie and taught her the most basic social graces. 'They also taught me not to hit children, not to swear and how to cut grapefruit. I'd never seen one before.'

They even taught her to drop her strong Midlands accent, in exactly the same way that Sting lost his Geordie brogue.

Thus, Trudie Styler the actress was born ...

*   *   *

Back on the professional front, things became worse for Sting when he appeared at a concert in Newcastle to find that only twelve thousand people had turned up as opposed to the expected thirty thousand. It was hardly the kind of homecoming he might have expected and he started to wonder if the poor attendance was a direct backlash of public opinion following his marriage difficulties.

Critics who attended the gig complained that the show was ill-directed and offered absolutely no surprises. By the end of his performance, Sting was relieved to have got off-stage without breaking down in front of the audience which included his mother, father, brother and two sisters.

Sting was starting to wonder if leaving Frances was going to prove the biggest mistake of his life. He was paranoid about the response from his fans and there was a sense of complete isolation about his situation at that time.

It was Trudie who kept him in one piece. She was genuinely in love with Sting and determined not to let their affair end up as yet another rock 'n' roll relationship that faded into oblivion. Sting was at his most vulnerable and he actually felt that Trudie was the only person in the world at that moment whom he truly trusted. Their problems eventually bonded them together but there were severe difficulties at the outset.

As The Police began to crumble, Sting's behaviour was fairly abysmal. He later described himself as behaving 'like a complete cunt'. It became very scary for those around him, especially Trudie.

In the early days of their relationship, she seriously considered leaving Sting. He had no idea what was going through her mind at the time and she only revealed her true feelings on the subject many years later. At that time, Sting saw himself as a perfect person. No one and nothing were going to get in his way.

It didn't help that there was little time for a real courtship. By the second week of August, The Police were off on the next leg of their North American tour. The month-long trip climaxed with an appearance at the first Californian US Festival which was held at a giant outdoor park near San Bernardino.

That same month *Brimstone and Treacle* was released in cinemas across Britain. Sting's role as disturbed young man Martin Taylor prompted some disturbing reviews by the critics but it seemed from his performance that he did not have to delve very deep to play the character.

'He's definitely an exaggerated version of me,' Sting told one writer. He was very proud of the role. 'It's quirky and weird and unusual. I'm not sure if it's going to be a box office smash, but then it isn't meant to compete with *Star Wars*.'

The *Brimstone and Treacle* soundtrack featured half a dozen solo tracks from Sting, which were especially significant because The Police were still supposed to be together at that time. Yet again Sting had done something on his own.

One of the songs, 'Spread A Little Happiness', was issued as Sting's first solo single and had the effect of further fuelling rumours about his future with The Police.

Interestingly, it was Andy Summers who eventually admitted to one writer at the time, 'We're all doing our own things now and there's room for it — it's part of what comes with being successful with something like The Police. It creates a platform to go off and do other things.'

At the end of 1982, The Police set off for Montserrat once again, where they were to start work on their fifth album. December also saw the emergence of two more of Sting's solo efforts — his versions of classics 'Tutti Frutti' and 'Need Your Love So Bad' — on the Dave Edmunds-produced soundtrack for the movie *Party Party*.

Sting secretly took Trudie to the Caribbean with him but it turned out to be a disastrous decision when Trudie stormed back to London within days of travelling across the Atlantic and told friends that there had been a dreadful row.

The bust-up between Sting and Trudie happened just after they had celebrated Christmas at a mansion he had hired on Montserrat. Sting — eaten up with guilt about not being with his family at such an important time — became sullen and moody and the inevitable occurred.

At first, Trudie was sympathetic about Sting's emotional state but when he began throwing a temper tantrum she took the biggest risk of her life and walked out to make sure that he realised she would not allow him to treat her so badly. The plan worked because it sent a loud and clear message to Sting that if he wanted to keep Trudie he would have to treat her as an equal — it has been the key to their relationship ever since.

Proof of this came in no uncertain terms six months later when Sting successfully forced a number of British tabloids to retract stories that claimed he was about to go back to Frances after dumping Trudie. The articles were complete nonsense as everyone close to Sting knew full well. Frances had long since been relegated to the position of ex-wife.

It wasn't until March of 1983 that Sting's live-in relationship with Trudie became official, thanks to a heartbreaking statement by Frances that finally acknowledged the end of her marriage to Sting. She told newsmen, 'I am still very bruised by what has happened. But there's no question of us being reconciled. Instead, there will be a divorce. I want to bring to a close a part of my life which is finished forever. Ever since being a little girl, I have been brought up to believe that marriage was what came at the end of the rainbow. All I ever wanted was simply to live out the fairy tale ... but perhaps I put too much emphasis on it.'

Frances had been provided with a spacious house in Hampstead in which to bring up their two children but she was undoubtedly sad at the break-up. She said, 'I told myself I had to face it. I wasn't the only single parent in the country and I didn't have copyright on pain.'

The extraordinary thing about The Police at this time was that, despite the huge sums of money being spoken about in relation to the band, they were still receiving regular monthly salaries with the occasional bonus from record sales or concert tour income.

The trio even paid PAYE and had their National Insurance deducted at source. The group's accountant, Keith Moore, had devised a scheme — with Miles Copeland's approval — which meant that the group were treated more like employees of a company than rock 'n' roll stars.

The band members trusted Keith Moore. But, with hindsight, it seems clear that Moore was allowed too much control of The Police finances. Eventually Moore began abusing that power. The strangest aspect of this is that Miles Copeland and the band knew that there had been criticism of Moore's track record. However, unbeknownst to the band, he was declared a bankrupt in 1975 and had even been banished from the Institute of Chartered Accountants. Somehow he convinced Sting and the others that he could still be trusted. For the moment, however, Moore seemed unable to put a foot wrong.

*   *   *

The *Synchronicity* album released by The Police in June 1983, was profoundly affected by Sting's reaction to the break-up of his marriage to Frances and his subsequent relationship with Trudie. He even admitted a few months later, 'I'm grateful I went through the crisis. I worked hard to survive it. I grew. My best creative work so far is a result of trying to work out these problems.'

Yet, typically, a few days after that outburst, he insisted, 'In a sense I'm very suspicious of myself. I wonder if I manufacture pain in order to create.'

The first single that emerged from the *Synchronicity* album was 'Every Breath You Take', which was immediately misinterpreted by many as a simple love song. As Sting later explained, 'It is a fairly nasty song that deals with surveillance, ownership and jealousy.'

The song was composed by Sting when he left Montserrat to stay briefly at James Bond novelist Ian Fleming's house, Goldeneye, in

Jamaica. Sting couldn't sleep in the tropical temperature with mosquitoes buzzing overhead, so he got up in the middle of the night, went straight to the piano in the drawing room and created the basic format in about ten minutes.

The *Synchronicity* album title was yet another play on words from Sting. This time it was his fascination with C G Jung's concept of synchronicity. Sting was convinced that the psychologist's idea of collective consciousness tied in well with the working relationship among the three members of The Police.

Whenever Sting was asked for an explanation of the album's title, he used it as an excuse to talk about how good the friction among the trio was. 'As long as it's a friction that comes from ego. It should come from a passion about music. If I have an idea I believe it, I'll kill for it and I would hope that the others feel the same ... that's where the tension and anger come in, and it's not a bad thing.'

By this stage, there was absolutely no doubt that Sting was running The Police in terms of what songs were used on albums. Andy Summers tactfully told one journalist at the time, 'I don't always agree with the choice of material that goes down, but mostly Sting's songwriting tends to be so good that it's hard to argue. And I enjoy playing his material.'

Yet another movie role followed when Sting was hired to play one of the villains in *Dune*.

The incredibly long shoot in Mexico was gruelling but at least the traditional self-confidence that had gained Sting a reputation as something of an arrogant bastard was completely knocked out of him by those difficult experiences on *Dune*.

Actress Sean Young was cast as Chani in *Dune* which commenced principal photography on 30 March 1983. She seemed to develop a tremendous crush on Sting and appeared to be trying to manoeuvre herself into a situation where he would seduce her. Sting was terrified by Young's in-your-face attitude and did not find her that attractive.

It was an intriguing response from Sting because he was proving to himself, above everything else, that he could be faithful to Trudie. According to one crew member on *Dune*, Sean Young became increasingly angry as her efforts to seduce Sting failed.

However, even before he set eyes on Sean Young, things started to go badly for Sting. A load of expensive digital music tapes 'disappeared' in Customs at Mexico City airport. Then there were constant bouts of illness, brought on, Sting believes, by the smog, altitude and poor food.

Mexico's altitude — 7,200 feet — means thinner air. There were careful instructions to drink only purified water, peel all fresh fruit and vegetables, avoid salads and eat only in certain recommended restaurants.

Sting's character in the little-seen movie was called Feyd and he tortured and killed numerous people. He also had to carry around a shaved cat in a cage and frolicked in a steaming shower wearing nothing but a green leather codpiece. At one stage, Sting astonished the movie's producer by suggesting that he should strip naked for the role 'because I thought it would be the right way to play the scene'. His offer was politely declined.

There were also scenes in which he had to work with more than a thousand extras and things certainly got very out of control. 'I was never really discouraged. It takes an elephant gun to stop me from doing anything and they couldn't get one of those through customs.'

Reflecting on his role, he added, 'Feyd is evil ... with a large jockstrap. I think Feyd is the product of inbreeding within the ranks of the Harkonnen upper classes for a few hundred years. He's intense, rotten and quite deadly but he has a good side.' Sting then smiled diabolically, 'But you don't see that in the movie. I think he likes ... animals.'

By the end of his five-month stint he was exhausted and dreaded having to adjust mentally to cope with rejoining The Police for their next major tour of the United States.

Legendary Hollywood producer Dino De Laurentiis was so impressed by Sting's professionalism on the set of *Dune* that he offered the singer the lead role of Fletcher Christian in a new version of *Mutiny on the Bounty*, due to be filmed later that same year. Sting was caught between two professions. He knew that he needed to devote some time and effort to The Police and he was also fed up with being on a movie set, which he found incredibly tedious. In the end, he turned down the offer and De Laurentiis cast a relatively unknown actor called Mel Gibson in the role instead.

On 23 July 1983, Sting was back in The Police driving seat as they began yet another marathon world tour at Chicago's Comiskey Park. Subsequent North American concerts, which ran through to the end of August, saw the trio playing numerous giant outdoor stadiums, including a show at New York's legendary Shea Stadium on 18 August.

Playing in front of an estimated seventy thousand fans, Sting quipped, 'We'd like to thank The Beatles for lending us their stadium!' Sting was ecstatic at the opportunity to play his classic 'So Lonely' in front of such a huge crowd. He described the group's peak performance at Shea Stadium as, 'This was Britain conquering the US just like The Beatles had done before us.'

The concert itself was the crowning glory that summed up their newfound domination of the music scene on both sides of the Atlantic. Wearing a flowing white T-shirt and red trousers, Sting bellowed out his favourite numbers as three twenty-foot video monitors conveyed pictures to anyone stuck at the back of the vast crowd.

Even the moon came out, right on cue, as the band hit 'Walking On The Moon'. 'I knew then that we could never repeat this,' says Sting. He decided there and then that the group should disband while still at the top. 'It was time to stop. It was the best thing we could have done. We were at the top. We could not get any higher.'

However, Miles Copeland saw it differently and he insisted that The Police would stay together for the time being, even though the magic had long since gone.

After the concert, at a celebration party which ran until 4 a.m., Sting needed absolutely no reassurance about the band's success. 'I have a best friend, who I've known since schooldays in Newcastle, who has always said I've been waiting for this moment. The Beatles have been the blueprint of my life. They're the reason

I started singing and the reason I'm a musician.'

Behind all the euphoria at Shea was one simple and lavish piece of preparation which ensured that the band would not tire easily on their thirty-date tour of America. At a rent of fifteen thousand dollars a week the group had moved to a carefully guarded mansion in the Hamptons, seventy miles east of New York, three weeks before the Shea Stadium extravaganza.

There, amid a mock Adam fireplace, marble pillars and cut-glass chandeliers, Sting, Stewart and Andy lived in splendid isolation, travelling every night by private plane to various concerts and returning in the early hours.

The property even included three professional chefs on twenty-four-hour standby to prepare anything the group required, a fully equipped gym, a jacuzzi and a swimming pool, plus all the latest movies on video.

Miles Copeland had devised the entire scenario, insisting that the tour would be less tiring if they had one base to go back to each night. 'Every top group gets exhausted and run down by all the travelling, change of hotels and airports. At least this way they feel happy and comfortable. It makes good sense.'

Back in Britain, a rumour was spreading through the music business like a ripple across a pond — Sting had had a heart attack. Phones rang late into the night as the industry's insiders did mental calculations of the cost of the losses in millions of dollars.

The story was sparked off when Sting spent the night in the intensive care unit of a hospital in St Paul, Minnesota, and it was certainly true that specialists had, at first, suspected a coronary.

However, the real story, when it emerged, was much less dramatic. Sting had broken a rib three days earlier in a fight with Stewart Copeland after the Shea concert and it had sparked pains similar to those of a coronary.

The incident did not surprise anyone inside the group's hierarchy but when the story got into the newspapers it was held up as yet further evidence of the enormous pressures building up for the band and the bad relationships among its principal members.

Observers said that the fight was a direct result of the incredible tension The Police had been under. Life inside the group had become as unlike the stereotypical image of a rock band as Miles Copeland's style of management was alien to the rest of the industry.

Miles Copeland considered the flare-up between his brother and Sting to be just one of many symptoms of the tension that inevitably existed during such a complex and gruelling tour. He was more concerned with other things, like how to market the group. He told one writer, 'The secret is to remember that while marketing a band is all about reminding people of their existence, overexposure can produce boredom among the consumers. A band can retain its exclusive image and its mystique in the same way as a perfume can.

'The secret of longevity lies not in reacting to the market but in determining it. Reacting to it means you have little faith in what you are doing and that is the beginning of the end. As far as we are concerned, the myth of the short lifespan of the rock group is over. The Police are here to stay.'

The group were in great danger of being overexposed and the rows among the band members were one of the worst kept secrets in the music industry.

Above: First stardom. Stewart Copeland, Andy Summers and Sting, aka The Police.

Right: Sting never hesitates to strip off his shirt and flex his fabulous muscles during live performances

Right:
August 22, 1992:
After nine years
and three children,
Sting and Trudie
finally tie the knot
at St. Andrew's
Church, Great
Dunford, near
their Wiltshire
country mansion.

Left:
Departing
for their
honeymoon
in 1992.

Left: Wedding guests Miles Copeland and glamorous partner arriving at Sting and Trudie's wedding.

Below: They seemed a picture of perfect happiness. Shortly after this picture was taken, Sting split with his first wife actress Frances Tomelty.

Right: Sting celebrates yet another award with Trudie.

Below: Sting, Amazonian Indian Chief Raoni and adventurer Jean-Pierre Dutilleux signing copies of the controversial rainforest book that caused a rift between Sting and JP, after it was revealed that the Belgian had accepted a cash advance for the charity project.

"Lurch" and "Noddy" were just two of the delightful nicknames endured by Sting at his grammar school, St. Cuthbert's in Newcastle.

Right: Sting and Trudie co-star in their own movie *The Grotesque*, released in 1996.

Below: Paula Yates, shown here in provocative pose, got the hots for Sting during a steamy interview on '80's TV rock show The Tube. However, the star's close friendship with Paula's estranged husband, Bob Geldof (*opposite*), has continued to this day.

Right: Sting and his brother, two sisters and parents lived in this cramped flat on Gerald Street, Wallsend, above what is now a take-away Chinese restaurant. It was then the dairy where his father worked.

Below: They later moved to a brand-new house on the Marden Farm Estate in nearby Tynemouth. Sting hated the modern property and longed to be back on the mean streets of Wallsend.

Left: Not long after making his first million with The Police, Sting purchased this classic Georgian house in Highgate, North London.

Below: In 1991, he moved Trudie and the children out to their picturesque Wiltshire mansion, Lake House.

Top: Spot the superstar: The Newcastle Big Band provided Sting with a perfect launch pad into his musical career in the early 1970s. He then progressed to Last Exit (above) who soon built up a strong following in the North East of England.

Above: Sting with Brazilian friend Gilda Matoso. Her loyalty to the star was rewarded when he offered her a plum job promoting the rainforest world tour.

Left: Sting received a rough ride in the Brazilian press. This was one of many caricatures of his friendship with Amazonian Indian Chief Raoni.

Right: Sting ended up winning a boozy game of pool when he and Ronnie Biggs met up in Rio. The Great Train Robber reckons the star "hates to lose at anything."

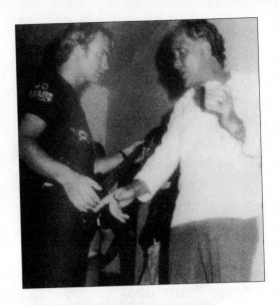

Below: The over-sensitive Brazilian government sent this "spy" to follow Sting and his entourage during the rainforest world tour. The official reported back all sorts of outrageous allegations about the singer's behavior.

SIXTEEN

THE BEAT GOES ON

*'I think people get a thrill when I strip off
on stage. They seem to. Once you've made the
decision to strip off then you're talking
about sexuality, eroticism if you like.'*

— STING

IN THE MIDDLE OF THE US TOUR, Sting continued to talk openly about his use of drugs, although he was now only using cannabis. The endless offers of a puff on a joint made his job as a rock star easier to handle. Sting actually stopped taking cocaine after the break-up of his marriage to Frances.

Trudie was sorting him out in every sense of the word. Sting cut down on his drinking and gave up cigarettes altogether. He fully acknowledged that perhaps he was a 'little immature', explaining, 'I sometimes wonder if I wouldn't be more mature had I not been a success. When you're a rock star you're allowed to be a petulant child.'

However, Sting still had not discovered complete and utter happiness. He went on, 'I seem to be two people — on the one hand a morose, doom-laden character and on the other a happy-go-lucky maniac.'

In late 1983 Sting first encountered a woman who was to become one of his and Trudie's best friends, although bubbly, down-to-earth American Deborah Cohen's first encounter with Sting was not exactly a happy one.

As head of marketing at A&M records in Paris, she was ordered to meet Sting at Charles de Gaulle Airport to make sure he switched planes for a trip to Los Angeles. As she later recalled, 'I just had to make sure he got from one terminal to another even though he had a two-hour layover.'

Sting was equally astonished when Deborah turned up to 'nurse maid' him through. 'I can't believe they sent someone to do this,' were Sting's first words on meeting Deborah Cohen.

'But we got talking,' she explains, 'and he asked me where I was from. I told him Salt Lake City and he said, "Oh". It was the same sort of reaction everyone gives to the news. They all seem to expect you to come from New York or LA.'

A few minutes later, Sting was checked through into the correct terminal by Deborah Cohen and they were about to go their separate ways when she turned to him. 'Would you do me a very special favour?' asked Deborah.

'Sure,' said Sting reluctantly.

'Whenever planes fly over Salt Lake City, for some strange reason the captain always announces the fact over the address system. Would you go to the bathroom and flush the toilet at that moment?'

Sting laughed and agreed to do it.

Four months later, Deborah met Sting when he returned to Paris and the first thing he said to her was, 'I did it.'

As Deborah later recalled, 'He became my friend for life then.'

The final few weeks of 1983 consisted of yet more gigs in Britain which then overlapped into the new year before a return visit to the US combined with a trip to Australia.

Sting was amazed when *Synchronicity* became the group's best-selling album as he considered it their most esoteric work to date.

Not surprisingly, the pressures on the trio had been mounting throughout this period. The nonstop touring got harder and harder each time they embarked on yet another gig. Tempers were shorter and patience was a word from a bygone era. Rumours about a break-up of The Police started to gain real momentum. Miles Copeland was forced to issue a statement denying a split but it had become obvious to everyone involved that the band wanted to spend more and more time apart.

During the North American gigs, Sting admitted that his solo efforts had become almost therapeutic. 'The band is just one part of our lives. It's not the entire be-all and end-all of our lives. If it was that'd be awful. I couldn't stand it. I need a private life and I need private modes of expression.'

At Atlanta, Georgia in November 1983 the end of the group became clear for everyone to see. Miles Copeland explains, 'It had become more competitive and other things began to rear their ugly heads.'

Sting elaborated, 'I wanted only my songs on the record. I thought that was the best thing the band could do. I had to fight every step of the way. It was ruthless and difficult.'

Andy Summers was the only member of the band who thought that to fold the band might have 'been a little premature. We have continued to sell a lot of records and still do'.

In addition to all this, Sting felt he had devoted too much of his time to music and not enough to acting. He had decided actively to seek certain roles and soon landed starring parts in *The Bride* and *Plenty*. It was the perfect escape route from the warring Police and it took him off the music scene for much of 1984.

Sting was haunted by the dreadful track record that rock stars-turned film stars had. It was an incredibly difficult transition, especially as it had long become clear that dropping a big-name rock celeb into a movie in no way guaranteed box office success.

Sting admitted at the time, 'Most actors have a lot of time to train, to find out the skills of acting in relative privacy, whereas musicians spend all their formative years learning to play an instrument. Suddenly, you're offered a chance to be in a movie and you have to learn almost overnight how to act and also you have to do that in the glaring spotlight, on screen in my case. It actually has its bonuses because the pressure is good for me. You have to learn — it's sink or swim basically.'

The Bride was directed by Frank Roddam who had first encountered Sting when he helmed *Quadrophenia*. Originally Roddam — another native of the North East — had planned to offer Sting a cameo role, but after testing him backstage at a Police concert in Chicago he realised how much his acting abilities had improved and offered him the leading role of Dr Frankenstein.

Sting was very excited about *The Bride* project and regularly spouted to journalists about the movie, 'It's actually a sequel to *The Bride of Frankenstein* — it's not a remake. It's what happens after and it's done in the style more of Mary Shelley's original novel than the Hollywood invention of the thirties. It's not a horror film; it's a kind of fairy story really and I become a monster. I make monsters for a living and I end up as a monster. It's also a Pygmalion story in that I've invented this girl, who I teach how to behave in society. And it's a love story.'

Sting's love interest in the film was leading lady Jennifer Beals. The entire crew and cast noticed how well Sting and Jennifer connected. They even exercised together every morning at whatever location they happened to be in. Beals told one associate that she thought Sting was 'fun, sweet, supportive, and he didn't isolate himself in any way. Plus — he'd kill me if he heard me say this — he's in amazing shape for an old man'.

Any suggestion of a romance was dismissed by both Sting and Jennifer. He even insisted, 'We didn't really say much to each other that wasn't scripted, though Jennifer's read enough to be able to talk about books. She's stimulating.'

The truth was that both stars were completely paranoid about any suggestion they might be having a fling. Sting was worried about Trudie and Jennifer was about to marry. When Sting was asked by an inquisitive journalist if he was having an affair with Jennifer, he replied curtly, 'Of course not, you fool,' but the rumours persisted. There was talk of long periods inside each other's trailers and crew spotted the couple hugging affectionately. In the end, however, Sting caught up with Trudie and Jennifer returned to New York and her boyfriend Bob Simmonds.

Sting went directly from shooting *The Bride* to the set of *Plenty*, co-starring Academy Award winner Meryl Streep and the distinguished Sir John Gielgud. Sting was bowled over to be working in such esteemed company and saw it as further evidence that his acting career was being taken seriously. He was at ease in the company of actors and genuinely believed that his career as a thespian would outlast his day job as a rock icon.

As Sting worked busily on the set of *Plenty*, his earlier efforts in *Dune* hit the big screen to appalling reviews and reports of an escalating budget that eventually settled at the sixty million dollar mark. Director David Lynch was singled out by the critics and the film took virtually nothing at the box office.

The irony of the situation was that Sting's 'starring' role in *Dune* consisted of only about five minutes of actual screen time. However, he was ordered to go on the promotional trail on behalf of the movie by the producers who actually hoped that a lot of people would go and see the film on the strength of Sting's involvement.

'The film is very strange,' admitted Sting during an interview on the *Today* show in America. 'It's not like *Star Wars*. I think it's actually more original in its look and appearance. I think it looks great, I really do.'

The critics rounded on *Dune*. The *New York Post* critic Rex Reed declared, 'You only think you've seen rotten ... Wait until you see *Dune*. This pretentious exercise in pointless insanity is so bad it's in a class by itself. It's diabolically bad. After fifteen minutes of gibberish, I gave up trying to figure out what the hell was going on and started snoring. There isn't a drug strong enough to get me through another experience like *Dune*. Not in this lifetime.'

That December, Sting switched media and acted in two radio adaptations based on Mervyn Peake's novels about Gormenghast. Sting had earlier acquired the screen rights to the novels and had written his own screenplay but he eventually decided to put them out on radio instead.

When the first play was broadcast the esteemed *Daily Telegraph* proclaimed, 'Sting, who is immediately more famous for being a pop star, is also a good actor. He possesses the power to make the malevolent heart of the dark drama glow with eerie precision.'

The Mervyn Peake projects certainly helped Sting to gain some long-overdue respect as an actor. It also convinced him that he should look out for a meaty stage role to get his teeth into because that might actually prove a more fruitful route to the top of the acting profession.

*   *   *

There is a term in aviation called 'V1 rotate speed'. This refers to the point at which an aircraft careering down a runway reaches a velocity beyond which it must take off. By 'V1' there is insufficient tarmac left to slam on the brakes. Towards the end of 1983, Sting and his comrades in The Police hit V1 for the last time. The problem was that there was barely enough fuel left to get them safely to their next destination.

Music business observers believed that Sting was planning a jazz-orientated project to launch his full-time solo career. Then he went on BBC Radio One and told presenter Annie Nightingale, 'What I am preparing for at the moment is the ability to walk away from all this. I'd like one day to say I've had enough and quit.'

Sting actually formed his new band by sending out an open notice to the jazz community, by word of mouth, that he was looking for a new backing group. 'The people who came through the door were staggering — people whose records I own,' he later explained.

Sting ended up with an all-black outfit, all aged under twenty-five, including Omar Hakim, Branford Marsalis and Darryl Jones who had played bass with jazz maestro Miles Davis.

Initially, the band were not even told they were making a record but that they had to prepare a live show, playing Sting's new songs at New York's Ritz, with just one week's rehearsal. 'It was a way of making us into a group. I'm more interested in spontaneity and excitement than I am in sound. The sound can look after itself if you're playing with energy,' Sting explained enthusiastically at the time.

It later emerged that a vivid dream about giant blue turtles invading his immaculate walled garden in Hampstead, destroying the well-ordered lawns and flowerbeds, had finally convinced Sting he should break away from The Police and start a new solo career — hence the title of that first solo album *The Dream Of The Blue Turtles*.

The key figure in helping Sting to turn those dreams into millions of dollars in record sales was a middle-European countess in her eighties who also happened to be his analyst and had originally been a disciple of Jung back in the twenties.

Sting knew that many people simply presumed that because he was seeking the help of an analyst, he must be going mad. In reality, he approached his sessions with the countess as an academic exercise to see what he could discover about himself and his dreams. In other words, he had a genuine curiosity. He also had a unique ability to turn such crises into highly profitable compositions. 'Dreams can be sometimes frightening, sometimes wonderful, sometimes bizarre. But they let you use parts of your brain you don't use when you're awake,' he explains.

The lyrics on the album were a drastic departure from the traditional Police style. Many of the issues that Sting felt strongly about came burning through. 'I feel I can't beat about the bush any more. I'm more outspoken than I've ever been because the issues have never been quite as serious,' he commented after forming the new band.

Throughout all of this, there were continuous denials of the break-up of The Police. After a series of stunning rehearsals with his new group, Sting travelled back to London on Concorde and was reunited with The Police for the annual British Music Industry Awards.

At a ceremony held at London's Grosvenor House Hotel, the trio received a special presentation for their outstanding contribution to British music over the previous seven years. After accepting the award, Sting told the audience, 'We've been very lucky. We're a good team. We have a lot of talent and inspired management. To solve the problem of dividing the awards trophy in three, we're giving it to Miles Copeland.'

Following the awards ceremony there was speculation that The Police would make a live double album but the plan came to nothing and Sting admitted to one journalist, 'I don't know about our future plans. I think it's very important not to just go out because the accountant says, "Oh, you better go and make a million bucks." Because that way is stagnation as far as I'm concerned. I think The Police have to get back when we have a new idea or new way of presenting ourselves. I don't want to just present the old formula, even though we know it works. That's not interesting.'

Within a few days of the awards ceremony, Sting was back in New York working on his solo album with his new group. Three low-key solo concerts at the Ritz in New York followed and then he and the other new band members headed for Barbados to start recording.

It was clear that The Police were gradually being wound down. As Sting commented at the time, 'I get very claustrophobic, very frustrated in one sense. My head can cope with more than one thing and needs to, so I'm keen to get away from the stereotypes and people's conceptions of what I am. I like people to be puzzled by what I'm doing next.'

However, The Police were to hang on for a while longer. Many observers inside the music industry reckoned they were planning to make a bucketload of cash and then call it a day but Sting was not capable of manipulating the system in that way. He continued to insist, 'Just because I'm doing a solo album doesn't mean it's the end of the road for The Police. We're not joined at the hip. I just thought it might be interesting to work with different musicians.'

*   *   *

Keeping up his political stance, Sting overdubbed new vocals to 'Every Breath's' backing track for the satirical *Spitting Image* TV programme. Playing out under pictures of Reagan and Chernenko, 'Every Bomb You Make' echoed concerns expressed in response to the recurring question of reconciling wealth with a social conscience. 'In a sense, because I'm not worried about the gas bills, I'm horrified at Thatcher's missile bases — someone who's desperately trying to pay the rent or get a job maybe isn't.'

Among the parodies of Police records which appeared in the early eighties were US disc jockey Weird Al Yankovic's rather obvious 'King of Suede' and the P.C.'s 'Too Depressed To Commit Suicide'. However, perhaps the most bizarre Police-related project ever produced was the 1983 orchestral version of Police hits entitled *Arrested*, which featured strings, horns and special guest rock musicians, among them Ian Paice (ex-Deep Purple), Gary Moore (ex-Thin Lizzy) and Chris Thompson (Manfred Mann's Earth Band) — all players of Andy Summers' generation, who represented the antithesis of the New Wave and whose remarks, when faced with the mid-seventies punk revolution, were probably highly uncomplimentary.

*   *   *

In Britain, Sting was trying to find some time to relax. One answer was to indulge himself in a brand-new hobby — buying racehorses. It was the perfect sideline for someone who had never lost the urge to gamble after starting at the age of twelve.

Over a short period of time he spent more than a hundred thousand pounds on four horses, encouraged by a trainer he hired to turn the animals into winners. Within eighteen months Sting had had ten winners.

However, there was another reason why he had purchased the horses, apart from his long-held love of gambling at the track. In some ways, Sting found it much easier to deal with racehorses than to cope with the constant bickering with Stewart and Andy that was now marring The Police.

When asked if this was the case by rock journalist Annie

Nightingale, Sting tried to put on a brave face. 'People are always trying to plant dissension between us. But we've worked together for so long we know each other very well. I think we thrive on arguments. Every day there's a fresh one. The day we have nothing to argue about is when we break up.' That day was fast approaching!

In late 1983 news leaked out that Sting's live-in lover Trudie Styler was expecting his third child in January 1984. To many observers this was further proof that Trudie was as good as married to Sting.

Public exposure of the couple had remained low key following those cringe-making days when he introduced her to the world's media as his 'mistress'. Sting was determined not to hurt Frances, Joe and little Katherine. In fact, Sting and Trudie were already virtually inseparable. She was determined to make sure she played a role in every aspect of his life. She even put her career as an actress on ice to make sure that she could accompany Sting wherever he went.

Trudie's determination to keep close to Sting soon became legendary among the back-up team that travelled with The Police to every concert. One said, 'Trudie was glued to Sting the whole time and he didn't seem to mind one bit.' But then Trudie had seen what happens when a rock star leaves his wife at home.

To the numerous females who tried their hardest to get icons like Sting into bed at the drop of a hat, Trudie was the ultimate barrier to overcome. 'What's she got that I haven't,' bitched one groupie when she spotted Sting and Trudie kissing and cuddling backstage during an American gig.

Trudie happily admitted she had given up everything to be with her man. 'Everything will have to wait until the baby is born. Right now the baby comes first. I think the press are very surprised about the suddenness of it all, but really it's not that sudden.' Then, as if to reassure everyone that their relationship was very serious, she added, 'Sting and I have been going out for two years now.'

The arrival of another child was just as important to Sting as the previous two births. He was regularly spotted stroking Trudie's stomach and cracking jokes about the baby just before she gave birth. Sting admitted to one writer, 'We're doing so much travelling that the baby will probably be born on a plane. I love kids. I spend as much time as I can with my kids. But unfortunately one of the drawbacks of a job like mine is that you're away from home so much.'

The birth of Sting's third child did not exactly underline his reputation as a caring, sharing parent. He actually missed the moment of birth because he had popped out of the hospital to get something to eat.

The child turned out to be a healthy, bouncing baby daughter weighing seven and a half pounds. They named her Brigitte Michael but she has been called Mickey ever since her birth.

The birth, at a National Health-run West London Hospital in Hammersmith Broadway, was just the same for Trudie as for all the other expectant mothers at that hospital — except for one big difference. Sting had reluctantly splashed out on a bodyguard for mother and daughter because of fears for their safety following yet another threatening letter.

From the moment Trudie entered the hospital the guard was on duty round the clock and only left when Sting turned up to collect mother and daughter in a chauffeur-driven limo. However, the guard's presence upset a number of the other mothers at the hospital. One commented, 'It was very unsettling having the guard there. It all seemed rather silly.'

A few weeks after the birth, Sting took Trudie to see her friend Pam Gems's new play in London and was greeted by a barrage of photographers as he left the theatre afterwards. The old Sting would have glared furiously. The new Sting politely asked the paparazzi if they knew the way to fashionable Joe Allen's restaurant where they were heading for dinner.

Now that the baby was born, Trudie didn't stay at home for long. She took the lead role in the provincial tour of a play called *Key To The World*. Her role, as a strutting, loud-mouthed music writer who smokes cannabis and has one-night stands with rock stars, seemed a little daring. She could hardly be described as living in luxury as she was earning a paltry hundred and fifteen pounds a week and living in a seventy-five-pound-a-week cottage in Leicestershire with her daughter and a nanny while Sting toured the world.

By March 1984, Sting's divorce from Frances was finalised after he agreed to a reasonable seven-figure settlement for his former wife. The 'quickie' *decree nisi* was granted on the grounds that the couple had lived apart for more than two years. There was no mention of Sting's relationship with Trudie and friends were predicting that Sting would marry Trudie 'sooner rather than later'. In actual fact, Sting had no such intention. He had decided that marriage was nothing more than a piece of paper. Certainly he loved Trudie, but to marry her seemed a futile exercise.

Interestingly, Sting's dad Ernie was one of the few family members back in Newcastle to give any response to Sting's ever-changing romantic life. As if to illustrate the difficult relationship that undoubtedly existed betwen father and son, Ernie said pointedly, 'I have met Trudie. She's quite a nice girl. Nothing wrong with her. But, personally, I'd rather see him back with his wife. Still, he's a big boy now.'

Ernie's comments underlined the very characteristics that Sting had inherited from his father: stubbornness, a refusal to be tactful and a devil-may-care response. These were all qualities that had helped Sting to get to the top but that didn't make it any easier to hear his father's words.

Shortly after Mickey's birth, Sting was voted 'the man with Britain's sexiest bum'. The poll — in *Woman's World* — put him just ahead of Rod Stewart and Mick Jagger. Other favourites with readers of the magazine included Cliff Richard, snooker players Tony Knowles and Alex Higgins and athlete Daley Thompson.

Around this time Sting made a significant admission to one music journalist which seemed to sum up the cynicism of the eighties that was running rampant at the time. He insisted that he hated rock music. 'I enjoy writing and performing rock, but not listening to it. They talk about the "new music" but they're still using the same chords, the same old backbeat that Fats Domino had. I'm just not interested.'

Meanwhile, Frances — who had maintained a dignified silence about her break-up with Sting — felt it was time to start living a new life away from the glare of the vast spotlight that constantly shone on her former husband. 'I enjoy living on my own,' she insisted from the large north London house that Sting had bought for her as part of their divorce settlement. 'There is more space. When you have to think about career, children and husband, it doesn't leave much room for yourself.'

Typically, Frances was honest enough to admit that there were bad days. 'Sometimes it is lonely. I have just come out of a marriage and it is only in the last couple of months that I have begun to enjoy being on my own and learned how to use the time — how not to give too much time to the children.'

It was not as if Frances had retreated into her own little shell, either. She started dating and even admitted that the men had to 'pass an audition. If they don't like children they're out. A date with me tends to be: "I'm going out for a walk, do you want to come along?" ' Then she added, 'I would worry about money if I was a millionaire. Besides, having financial support from another quarter brings its own guilt — especially if I'm going off to rehearsal when my son has a cold. Having children gives you a sense of perspective.'

Shortly after Frances's first public comments on the end of her marriage, Trudie provided a full-length interview to the *Daily Mail* newspaper, arranged to balance the books after the piece about Frances was published.

In the article, Trudie insisted that she wanted more children by Sting and she made it absolutely plain that there was no question of their relationship being a passing phase.

In the spring of 1984 it was reported that Sting had been secretly rushed to a private London hospital to have an operation on his 'nasal area'. No one would say whether the singer had undergone plastic surgery or an operation to cure a sinus blockage which had troubled him for most of his life. Sting's nose was certainly less prominent when he next appeared in public.

In late 1984 Sting made a secretive approach to the Soviet Embassy in London to try to find out if he could do some solo recording work in a Moscow studio.

The Soviets advised Sting that he would be more than welcome in their country. No doubt they knew of his Marxist leanings in the past. The communists were well aware that such a prominent figure could greatly help to promote the Soviet Union and its political system in the eyes of the world. Naturally, Sting did not look at it like that at all.

Sting's image as a supercool rock star took a bit of a knock when he and Andy Summers attended the glittering seventieth birthday party of so-called grandfather of punk, William S. Burroughs. As had been the case for many years, musicians tended to seek out the eccentric writer because he was considered such a hip character.

Sting and Summers had their photograph taken next to the writer at the party in a luxurious apartment in New York. However, what Sting did not realise was that Burroughs had absolutely no idea who he was and the writer even warned some of his other guests who might have been carrying drugs, 'I don't know whether you're holding, but someone told me that those guys were cops.'

SEVENTEEN

ON CAMERA

'Trying to stay sane has not been easy. I've
seen the chasm open. I've seen enough to
realise that I don't want to fall down that chasm.'
- STING

DESPITE HIS UNDOUBTED LOVE FOR TRUDIE, Sting remained deeply
wounded by the end of his marriage. In February 1985, he conceded,
'I worked hard to survive the crisis. And I believe I grew as a result. I
think my best creative work so far has come as a result of trying to
work out my problems.'

Typically, he was still using his own pain and anguish to inspire
songs that were going to earn him tens of millions of pounds.

Sting made a heartfelt confession to *The Sunday Times* when
he wrote a first-person piece about himself which appeared
simply under his name with no comment on the contents. It makes
interesting reading.

I probably have lost a lot of friends, or burnt a lot of friends, in
some cases very badly. I've always justified it by the level of my
success. There is a certain amount of guilt in success, obviously.

But then, if you look at my background, it wouldn't suggest to anyone that I would have ended up a 30-year-old millionaire living in a Georgian mansion in Hampstead, owning racehorses and with a record-buying public in millions.

And therefore there is a certain amount of 'You don't actually deserve this', the feeling that you must have done it by some kind of Byzantine trickery. You can end up really hating yourself for that sort of trickery. It's another ingredient of self-destruction. This is particularly true in rock 'n' roll, which is such a transient thing.

A certain amount of inspiration, and the enjoyment of what you do. That's the prime mover. But then again there is what you might call strategy, where you look at the market and see what sells, and you see what image is required. To a certain extent you taper your creativity to that particular mode. That is not to say that you have to compromise what you do. In a sense, we were very lucky, in that what we actually felt like doing coincided, historically, with what the market felt like buying.

In a sense, you see, the upheaval that punk rock had caused within the industry brought total confusion; the executives in the industry didn't have a clue what was happening, and they were terrified for their jobs. They were too old for it; they didn't understand what was going on; they felt isolated by the phenomenon. And they were really trying anything. We came in on the back end of the tidal wave of revolution — opportunists that we were — which is why I talk about strategy. We flew a flag of convenience which was: 'We are marketable, yet we are part of this new revolution; take us on. We will succeed accordingly.' Which is exactly what happened. We became the biggest selling act in the world inside three years.

I wouldn't say that we ever kowtowed. We were just there at the right time. But now we have almost total freedom, artistically. We can do what we like. Look at the irony of my singing a 1930s song, 'Spread A Little Happiness', which goes completely against the grain; it became Number One; it's fun to be able to do that. But if I'd done that at first I wouldn't have stood a chance. Obviously, I have spent five years polishing and honing an image. First of all, looking the right way was terribly important. Then saying the right things, giving coherent answers to intelligent questions. It did strike me as odd that one of the first serious interviews I did involved my opinion on nuclear fission. Luckily, I knew about it and gave a fairly coherent answer. But I thought — how funny; all I did was sing a song, and here I am answering questions like this. The other week, for example, I was being asked what I thought about Lebanon. But I suppose that if I have a forum, for whatever reason, then I have a responsibility to say something and to think about it carefully.

That piece, in the 29 March 1985 edition of *The Sunday Times,* was particularly interesting because it provided real insight into the way Sting was handling fame and it gave away certain clues as to his future involvement with issues and campaigns completely unconnected with rock'n'roll music.

In June 1985 a ten-month world tour with his new backing band was announced to help to promote *The Dream Of The Blue Turtles.* Sting and Trudie even allowed a TV documentary camera crew to follow them around on and off duty as they prepared to launch Sting's new solo career with a concert in Paris to open the world tour.

At a press conference before his appearance in the French capital, Sting managed to make his visit to the city sound more like a religious pilgrimage than a rock concert. 'Paris has a certain ambience, a certain neutrality.' Describing the documentary, he explained, 'The film is about the formation of this group and the different areas forming a common language.'

Then Sting became extremely politically correct by adding, 'Black musicians are not given enough opportunity. This is a racially mixed band which is an open challenge to the system.' What Sting did not mention was that he was firmly the boss and everyone else — of whatever colour — was answerable to him.

The newly formed group's first live gig was to be at the Mogador

Theatre in Paris, an antique establishment with an interior like an inside-out wedding cake. Backstage, Trudie was nine months pregnant with their second child and experiencing mild contractions as her lover performed on stage. She even had a midwife and doctor on standby.

Sting, who had managed to miss all three of his previous children's births, was determined to be there this time, which was why he insisted on Trudie travelling with the group to Paris, despite her heavily pregnant state. As no airline would carry her, the couple travelled by rail on the *Orient Express*.

Sting's new band ran a sweepstake worth two hundred and fifty pounds on the date of the birth — ironically eventually won by Sting himself, although he did ask Trudie, 'If you go into labour during my performance do you mind having it on your own?'

Meanwhile, the show went on as Sting introduced new songs in charmingly broken French. Hugely appreciative, the fans did not even seem to mind that the TV documentary team had lit the entire interior like a football pitch.

At the champagne reception afterwards, Trudie was still standing and many of the group felt her tummy for twinges after she proclaimed the contractions too weak to mean that the birth was impending.

Hours later, Sting, Trudie and a three-man film crew were crammed into the delivery room at a nearby hospital. Trudie was injected with a drug to hold up the birth as no midwife was available at the time. Six hours later she was released from the hospital still heavily pregnant.

The entire exercise was repeated the following night, with Trudie absolutely exhausted from her extended labour. Asked whether she wanted a boy or a girl, she muttered, 'I think I'll have a Blue Turtle.' It was another twelve hours before baby Jake was born.

The documentary cameras caught it all. The baby's head appeared first before he was pulled out and virtually slung on to Trudie's chest. Sting — wearing a green hospital vest — turned to the camera and said, 'This will make me appreciate my other children as well. What a miracle they were. It is so easy to come in later when they are cleaned up.' He then cut the umbilical cord. 'This is so profound.' Trudie looked on exhausted as Sting held the baby, who had a mass of dark hair, in his arms.

The cameras even zoomed in to catch the moment when proud father Sting was handed his newborn son whom he referred to as his 'little pirate' and then panned to Trudie cuddling the baby.

The ninety-minute documentary was helmed by Oscar-winning Hollywood director Michael Apted and entitled *Bring On The Night*.

Sting later explained why he allowed the film crew to shoot such a personal event. 'Because it is a wonderful moment. When we saw the film, Trudie and I wept through that scene and so did everybody else in the room. I wanted an honest rock'n'roll film. Jake's birth happened to coincide and Michael Apted talked us into including it because not to include an event like that would have been a dishonest account of those nine days of my life. I don't think it is a piece of gratuitous home movie making. I think it's a moving and honest moment, and I'm willing to take the rap.'

Sting's two backing singers are made to sound incredibly exotic when described in the film. One had been a teacher before becoming a singer and the other had been a receptionist in a brothel, earning five dollars for every man she persuaded to enter the house of ill repute. On a good day she earned a hundred dollars. Her duties also involved explaining in graphic detail what the girls would do for their male clients.

The documentary is particularly interesting at the point where sax player Branford Marsalis is clearly taking the mickey out of Sting about his name. There are laughs all round but Sting looks clearly unamused and nearly completely lost his cool when Marsalis insisted on calling him 'Gordy'.

'It was unusual because he normally joins in with everyone but he was very detached and uncommunicative throughout and he pissed a lot of people off,' said one member of the crew.

Other elements of the documentary were sickly sweet, like the occasion when everyone is sitting around a large table having supper together and they burst into a line of song.

Then one member of the group says, 'Sting is a throwback because he cares about the music not the money ...'

Even the ever-cautious Miles agreed to be interviewed before the cameras and came out with a classic response when it seemed that Sting might pull out because of the birth of the baby. 'I have to be brutal with the group. It is Sting's money. These guys are brilliant but their market value is nil. If Sting cancels we have a problem.'

Miles's comments particularly irritated Branford Marsalis who felt that he and the other group members should be better treated. He considered himself to be much more than just a member of Sting's backing group and was particularly aggrieved because Miles had nailed them all down to what he considered a less than brilliant deal on money. Just before the first concert in Paris, another side of Miles was revealed by the documentary film cameras as he rubbished the wardrobe and set designer for making the group wear dull-coloured outfits for the gig. Miles shouted and screamed and the wardrobe lady shouted and screamed back. In the end, the outfits were changed.

The question of marrying Trudie came up again at this time. Sting now had a slightly different reply for the newsmen, 'We have not got time.' He conceded, 'I'm not against the idea in principle. I just don't feel the need — although I'm sure the vicar would tell me differently.'

However, the old, pessimistic Sting was still not far away, even after such a momentous occasion as the birth of a child. He continued to cast doubts on the idea of sticking to one relationship. 'We grow and change,' he explained. 'It's only realistic to accept that and to be prepared for the possibility that a relationship may break up because of it. That's a much better idea than saying, "I love you — this is for ever and ever." That's living in cloud cuckoo land.'

Trudie, as usual, seemed able to cope with such stinging comments. 'Him settle down?' she said. 'Don't be ridiculous. He's a gypsy — a wild boy.' But she didn't mean it. As far as Trudie was concerned, this was for keeps.

*   *   *

Among Sting's new band members, Branford Marsalis — part of a veritable jazz dynasty — became the spokesman and he later admitted that working with Sting was a frustrating experience at times. Marsalis's biggest complaint about Sting was that he never showed any signs of emotion in front of the band. Marsalis spent much of his time trying to make Sting react, to break his concentration and prove he was human after all. 'He will not look into the audience when he plays. He has this sense of decorum, because if he does look down, he's afraid he will laugh. We threw dead chickens across the stage, all kinds of shit, trying to get him. Nothing.'

One time Marsalis got the group's road manager, Billy Francis, to dress up in one of his suits, blacked up his face, gave him a sax and made him stand on stage while Marsalis continued playing just off stage. 'I knew exactly when, during "Roxanne", Sting would look at me. So when he looked up and saw Billy, his eyes jumped out of his head. But he didn't lose it. He said, "On saxophone — Branford Marsalis!" '

Marsalis finally got to Sting when the group appeared in Australia. He explains, 'Every night he'd yell to his roadie, *"Dah-nee, my jahhkut"*. And this night Danny walked on stage, held the jacket out to Sting and then tossed it into the audience. The audience ripped the jacket to shreds. "I don't fucking believe you!" Sting screamed. He went nuts. Because, you see, he'd lost his favourite *jahh-kut.'*

Marsalis added, 'Guys like him you never get to know.'

*   *   *

Probably the most significant aspect of Sting's successful transition to solo artist was that only the previous year Freddie Mercury and Mick Jagger, two comparable vocalists with similar aspirations, had attempted solo efforts that looked rather pallid in comparison.

However, the transition to solo artist was backed by the one man few thought would stick with Sting — Miles Copeland. He steadfastly remained Sting's manager despite the as yet unannounced split with The Police. He publicly praised Sting's efforts on behalf of issues like the miners' strike, even though Sting himself describes Miles as 'the most right-wing person I know'.

For some strange reason there was — and still is — a definite chemistry between Sting and Miles. Some say it is mutual respect. Sting openly insists, 'Miles is a force to be reckoned with. He's the kind of person you need on your side when the going gets tough. People are frightened of him, which keeps them off balance.'

For Sting, Miles was the perfect protector, advisor and, sometimes, even a father figure. He was also rather impressed by Miles who had an MA in economics, taken at Beirut University where his specialist subject was the development of Third World countries.

Miles would often joke, 'My studies concerned the problem of how to take an underdeveloped country and organise it in such a way as to bring it into the twentieth century. My conclusion was that this was pretty near impossible, so I flew to England to develop underdeveloped pop groups!'

The only time a real rift appeared between Sting and Miles came when Miles produced a British TV programme called *Miles Copeland's Britain* which was shown in February 1986. Sting was so furious at being included in the programme that he made Copeland remove three minutes of himself in action on stage because he did not want to be seen to be sanctioning Miles's right-wing views on Britain.

A similar problem had occurred the previous month when Thames's *TV Eye* included an interview with Copeland about the left-wing Red Wedge concert tour which had created a lot of controversy at the time. Sting insisted footage of him be removed from that as well. Sting's attitude was that Miles Copeland was a superb manager but his politics sucked and he would have no part in sanctioning such beliefs under any circumstances. Miles accepted Sting's opinion on the basis that there was no way it should get in the way of a good business deal.

It was around this time that Sting started to find himself appealing to a much wider spectrum of people. His music was becoming phenomenally popular with safe, secure middle-class people who were on the up and up in Britain in the mid-1980s. The one-time rebel was rapidly becoming the housewives' choice.

Sting took his new solo career very, very seriously by spending three months playing around the States (including an appearance at the most famous black music theatre in Harlem) before arriving back in Britain the following January.

In the early eighties, Sting had told one journalist that he would not continue as a rock star after the age of thirty-five because it was 'undignified', but with only eighteen months to go in the summer of 1985, he changed his mind, saying, 'I would hope that my performance will change so as to be natural to a man of my age and dignity.'

As part of that new bid for 'dignity', Sting even started confessing his sins in interviews with popular newspapers and magazines in Britain. He confirmed his involvement with drugs to — of all unlikely candidates — *Woman* magazine and then went on to admit he slept with 'every woman who came in the room' and 'all that stuff'. Sting went on to insist that, 'coming to terms with my dark side was useful'.

'I went from being a school teacher in a mining town to becoming one of the most famous people in the world. The ups and downs have been intense.'

Perhaps, for that reason, it wasn't so surprising that another highly spiritual problem was haunting him at this time. The six-hundred-thousand-pound house — a magnificent, listed seventeenth-century Blake-designed terrace at The Grove in Highgate — which he had purchased for himself and Trudie, was said to be haunted by the ghosts of a mother and child. Typically, Sting secretly employed a spiritualist to confirm whether the spirits did actually exist.

Sting had first encountered the ghost of the woman and her child when he woke up in the middle of the night and saw the figures clearly standing in the corner of the bedroom. By the time he woke Trudie the spirits had gone, but they returned at least three more times before Sting called in a local spiritualist. Sting explained, 'Ever since I moved there other people have said things happen. Like, they're lying in bed and people start to talk to them or things go missing.'

When the ghost returned a second time it really freaked Sting out.

'I was very sceptical until that night after my daughter Mickey was born. She was disturbed and I went to see her. Her room is full of mobiles and they were going berserk. I thought there must be a window open, it's windy, right? But the windows were dead shut. And this baby was lying there wide awake with her eyes open.

'About two days later I woke up and looked into the corner of my bedroom and, clear as day, there was a woman and child standing in the corner again. I heard Trudie say: "Sting, what's that in the corner?" I just went totally cold, icy cold.'

Sting then called in the spiritualist who offered to send his eerie squatters back into the ether but Sting decided he found their aura positive and he wanted them to stay.

There was also a later incident when, he claims, a poltergeist sent a razor-sharp carving knife flying across the kitchen where it embedded itself in a wall.

A few nights later, Sting woke from a deep sleep and, across his bedroom, he saw a misty figure, dressed in Victorian clothes, staring straight at him. At first, Sting assumed it was Trudie and said, 'What are you doing over there?'

Then Trudie sat up in bed next to him and asked, 'Who are you talking to?'

Sting pointed to the lady across the room and Trudie saw her as well. Neither of them panicked. They just stared at her in silence and held each other tight. The room suddenly went icy cold and the Victorian lady began to fade away. They never saw her again.

*　　　*　　　*

Up until this stage in his career, Sting had seemed to be the sort of rock star who avoided hanging out with other celebrities. His opinions on other stars were pretty decided. He said of former Beatle Paul McCartney, 'He's a genius but he should push himself to do work that's more serious.'

Sting described Michael Jackson as a tragic figure. 'One of the rewards of success is freedom. To lose your freedom instead — which is what seems to have happened to Michael — is tragic.'

Sting even laid into Prince (as he was then known). 'Prince is a great musician but I worry about him losing his sense of humour.'

On a lighter front, Sting was the star attraction at the world's largest fête, held in London's Battersea Park. Excited fans kept him so busy he barely had time to get on with his job — auctioning signed photographs and records. However, it was all for a worthy cause and the event helped to raise more than a hundred thousand pounds for Oxfam.

To Sting, these sorts of events were a vital part of his job as a celebrity. He genuinely felt so strongly about various world problems that it seemed to make sense to play some sort of active role in fund raising.

Another worthy cause, which provoked more than just a ripple of comment, was Sting's involvement in declaring war on Britain's ever-increasing drug problem. Having exorcised his own involvement with narcotics, he felt it was time to lay his feelings on the line. He even managed to get the message across in a song that was released in 1985, entitled 'Children's Crusades'. The campaign was particularly aimed at heroin. 'The people who run the heroin industry — all those fat business men — are the most evil men on earth. I wish them in hell,' he told one reporter.

In the summer of 1985, Sting took a highly publicised role in the Bob Geldof-inspired Live Aid concert campaign and cemented a lifelong friendship with Geldof.

Sting was deeply perturbed by the images of the starving children in Africa. 'I want a world where there is no starvation and no threat of nuclear war. As a father, I see it as part of my lot to make this world a better place for my children — and for children everywhere.'

Sting believed that Live Aid was not only good for those millions of starving children but it also helped some of the richest rock stars on earth to be a little more normal. He explained at the time, 'Rock is a very competitive business and that fuels a lot of ill-feeling between bands. But in Live Aid everyone pulled together.'

Sting also enjoyed it because he met so many other famous names for the first time and was delighted to discover that stars like Boy George and Simon Le Bon were 'nice guys.'

He also contributed to a unique Christmas record which was expected to raise one and a half million pounds for the Ethiopian famine fund. The song 'Do They Know It's Christmas?' was specially written by Bob Geldof and Midge Ure from Ultravox with a huge cast in mind.

In September 1985, Sting narrowly escaped death after a diving expedition went disastrously wrong while he was staying at musician Eddy Grant's studio/home in the Caribbean. He had been scuba diving off Barbados when he suddenly ran out of air. Only a dramatic rescue by his instructor saved him.

Sting had gone down sixty feet and the gauge on his air tank showed five minutes' supply left. Then, suddenly, he found himself sucking on a mouthpiece with no air.

Unable to shoot to the surface without risking the potentially fatal 'bends', he desperately swam sideways towards his instructor and grabbed her ankles to signal something was wrong. They then shared air from her tank and she slowly brought him to the surface.

Despite occasional flare-ups between Sting and Trudie, the couple now seemed very settled. They still did not marry but, at the same time, Sting made it clear she was the only woman for him, which was all that mattered to Trudie.

In September 1985, however, reports emerged from Canada that a beautiful TV publicity girl had turned down Sting's sexual advances. Shapely Brona Brown claimed that when she asked Sting at a film preview, 'Is there anything else you want me to do for you?', he replied, 'Yes, I want you. Come home with me.'

Sting had been in Toronto for the opening of his new film *Plenty*, starring Meryl Streep, and Brona insisted that the singer definitely did want to have sex with her. 'He seemed serious. I think he meant it,' she told one associate. 'It was very tempting.' However, nothing happened and, in fairness to Sting, it sounded far more likely that he was wise-cracking rather than being serious. As one friend said later, 'Sting is always saying daft things like that but he doesn't mean it.'

In October 1985, Sting was forced to hire a hefty Swedish masseuse to try to alleviate back problems that had been plaguing him for years. Each night the singer subjected himself to a bizarre beating before he stepped on stage for his US tour dates. Every evening the muscular woman would pummel his body for thirty minutes in order to relax him. On the first night of that tour, associates were concerned when they heard cries of pain coming from Sting's dressing room — until they realised what was happening.

At one of the last Police concerts ever given, at Newcastle City Hall in January 1985, an explosion in a nearby electricity substation resulted in the audience being asked to leave. More than two thousand fans, including many members of Sting's family, were warned that the show could not go on. Before the disappointed audience left the theatre, Sting walked on stage to apologise and then sang 'Roxanne' without accompaniment. At least two people in the crowd were brought close to tears: his parents, Ernie and Audrey, could barely stand the emotion.

Later on that same year, Sting seemed about to star in *King Lear*, to be directed by the legendary Jean-Luc Godard. According to certain Hollywood insiders, however, the deal was held up because he wanted Trudie to have a part in the movie as well. In the end, Sting passed on the project when it emerged that financing the film might take at least another year.

The Police officially broke up in March 1985 when Stewart Copeland admitted that he had signed an agreement to wind up the band following the end of their last tour of America. Stewart stormed out of a meeting with Sting after a huge row erupted which nearly ended in a fist-fight. Sting admitted afterwards, 'We have got very little in common these days. The Police will never make another record.'

It was never made clear why Miles Copeland insisted that the split should not be disclosed at the time. Some claimed it was linked to the group's complex finances. When the end came, it was very low key and hardly caused a ripple of interest inside the music business. Not surprisingly, few inside the music business were surprised by the split when it finally came.

As Sting's old friend Bob Geldof explained, 'When Sting thought he was losing his creative hard-on he decided to quit The Police.'

EIGHTEEN

WINE, WOMEN AND SONG

'It's Sting who's the superstar,
who has the fans, not me.'
                    - STING

THERE WERE MANY DRAWBACKS to stardom, but the thing that bothered Sting the most was the lost souls who became so obsessed with him that it got very scary at times. In 1986, Sting had a run-in with such a fan when Shirley-Ann Cowden publicly lashed out at the star as if she was a jilted lover after he slapped a legal warning on her because she wouldn't leave him alone.

Shirley, aged twenty-three, was furious because she insisted that she had done nothing wrong. 'I intend to sue unless I receive a personal apology from Sting. The letter sent to me implied that I had "serious personality" problems and I was mentally unstable — all without medical evidence. I refute the allegations.'

Shirley, from Cathcart in Greenock, Scotland, first became a fan when she saw The Police in action in 1981. She then met Sting four times and was even photographed outside his North London home. She had seen him seventeen times in concert.

Shirley claimed that Sting ran away the last time she saw him, after previously being perfectly friendly. His press spokesman at the time said, 'We are very concerned about Shirley-Ann. Sting is not being unkind. He just feels it would be more distressing for her if he got involved.'

Around this time, Sting splashed out five million dollars on a Malibu beachside mansion once owned by Barbra Streisand. A year later he spent a further one and a half million dollars on converting it into a virtual palace, complete with pool, gym and sauna. He had been meaning to buy somewhere for a long time and the end of The Police freed the available funds.

* * *

In December 1986, Sting was devastated to learn that both of his parents were suffering from cancer. His mother's illness was worse which was especially tragic for Sting because he was so close to her.

Audrey always appeared at concerts Sting gave in Newcastle and was immensely proud of her son's achievements. Sting had heartily approved when Audrey remarried following a hush-hush divorce from Ernie a few years earlier. Explained sister Angela: 'Gordon meant the world to us, and he would be the first to admit his family meant the world to him. We are all so very close.'

Now, his parents' illness was a double blow for Sting. All those years of self-analysis and self-doubt immediately returned. As he once remarked: 'My life isn't without pain. But then I don't think that life is about happiness anyway. I don't think we are here to be happy. We are here to learn.'

That Christmas was not a happy one for Sting or his family. He went up to Newcastle to try to help but it was difficult. His parents were now living in different parts of the city and there was little communication between Audrey, now fifty-four, and Ernie, now fifty-seven, so Sting had to travel between both homes throughout the Christmas period.

Sting's brother Phil summed up the situation at the time. 'Mum is in worse shape than Dad. Dad has been going backwards and forwards to hospital for treatment and he doesn't know himself how bad his condition is. All we can do is keep our fingers crossed and hope they both respond to treatment and get better.'

Sting went back to London after the Christmas break knowing that, for the time being, he had to get on with his life. His parents' future was entirely out of his hands.

*　　　　*　　　　*

In the middle of 1987 Sting released his second solo album entitled *Nothing Like The Sun*. It had taken him just three months to write and most of the songs had been produced in his New York apartment. He kept in close contact with his family in Newcastle and tried to get on with the job at hand but it was extremely difficult to concentrate.

Sting even banished Trudie and the children so that he could get the album completed. Occasionally, he managed to pop out to New York nightclubs like Nell's but much of the time was spent in the apartment. Most mornings he set himself a gruelling schedule which included going to the gym followed immediately by solitary sessions composing new songs. He also managed to fit in some piano lessons and even took a dance class.

That year Sting also starred in the movie *Julia and Julia* with Kathleen Turner. The film was released to a less than enthusiastic welcome the following year. Sting didn't help things by describing his role when gyrating and writhing totally naked with Turner as 'not arousing in the least'. He went on, 'You're acting. It's hard work. You're thinking what is the function of my character? What am I doing here? Then there are a certain number of things you can't do in bed with a woman if you're acting with her. I mean ... she's a married woman!'

In a diplomatic aside, Sting told one associate that Kathleen Turner was 'a film star in the true sense. She's larger than life and she's incredibly vivacious. Everything works around Kathleen'. (Which meant that Sting had been made to feel the lesser performer during the making of *Julia and Julia).*

The critics were not overly impressed by *Julia and Julia.* The New York *Daily News* described it as 'a surreal, hopelessly silly concoction' while the New York *Times* proclaimed it 'third-rate fiction'.

It seemed also that Sting's music was no longer getting a unanimous thumbs up from all the critics either. The recently released *Nothing Like The Sun* led to one reviewer accusing Sting of being a man 'living in the shadow of his own ego'. However, Sting brushed the knocks aside and had his faith in it sanctioned when the album was voted Best British LP at the 1988 British Rock Industry Awards.

During a trip to Australia after completing *Julia and Julia*, three *Penthouse* magazine models claimed the star let them seek refuge in his hotel suite after a gang of drunks attacked them in a bar.

One of them — beautiful model Bobby Wallbank — said Sting was 'the sexiest man I've met', and added, 'He's a real hunk and is everything dreams are made of. He oozes sex appeal.' It was all good tabloid stuff.

The incident was not significant but Sting's growing interest in occasional journeys into unknown territory were becoming more and more frequent. Sting certainly liked hanging out with oddball characters, people on the edge of normal society. Yet, he insisted that his attitude towards partying was, 'I do it in almost laboratory conditions. It's always in a specific place for a specific purpose. But I wouldn't just go out one night and by accident get drunk. I don't do that. I don't like losing control. There's a need to control my life. And to a certain extent I succeed in doing that.'

It all sounded ominously in line with the eighties yuppies who had become his biggest fans until Sting paused for breath and then added, 'What you really want to know is whether I lick pussy an' stuff like that. Course I do.'

A few years earlier he would not have had the confidence to add that last sentence.

Fans were a continual problem and up to two dozen of them had by this time taken to camping outside his North London home. It must have been the teacher in him that made Sting feel partly responsible for these schoolgirls.

One time he left the house to get a train for a TV interview in Birmingham and then found that all the girls were on the same train with him. 'They're very polite and, anyway, I do still know how to handle schoolkids. Running away when they run towards you makes them hysterical. The best way to normalise the hysteria and the whole situation is to stand your ground, say "Hello" and give an autograph.'

Luckily, Sting's passion for motorbikes meant that it was relatively easy to travel round London without being recognised, thanks to a helmet and dark visor.

Around this time, Sting angrily snapped back at a journalist who dared to ask him when he was marrying Trudie, 'Of course I'm not going to marry her.'

However, Trudie was not exactly what one could describe as a stay-at-home type. Not only had she continued to act, she was not averse to throwing a paint pot or two at Sting if he irritated her. No union is perfect but in many ways that made it healthier.

Trudie also insisted that she did not mind that he hadn't married her. 'I'm not so insecure that I need constant confirmation that he wants to be with me.' Then she added, with a naughty twinkle in her eye, 'I suppose he might go off with someone else — but then, I might, too.'

Although Trudie knew that she could not be with Sting throughout all his many tours abroad, she did make an effort to try to see him pretty regularly. She even took the children to see him abroad. 'I think it's important that they should see their dad in working situations so they can understand why he's away so much.'

Trudie also introduced a strict rule that, however busy she and Sting might be, the children would never be left alone with their nanny for more than ten days at a time. Often, Sting would charter a private jet just to pop home from some far-flung place for a few hours in the peace and sanctuary of his own home.

One time, Trudie called him up from the set of a movie she was making and asked Sting if he would take the children for a month because she was so exhausted working. He immediately flew them out to the West Indies where he was recording a new album at the time.

Meanwhile, Trudie was carving out an image for herself as a tough lady. Journalists had still not forgotten how she smiled when the press photographed her with Sting when he was still married. She was also building an acting career by portraying 'bad' girls.

'All those images of me being a bad girl — they're true and I don't care,' she said. 'I can be bad. I have been bad and I hope to be bad again soon. Bitch, cow, mistress — all those words have been used to conjure me up. God, I really don't care what other people think or say — and they've been throwing stones at me for two and a half years already. I'd prefer more interesting descriptions of myself, like the word "defiant". But I don't really expect much from anybody. I've learned better.'

In the summer of 1986 Sting landed a dream role in a film called *Stormy Monday*. Most of the film's action was to take place in Newcastle and he even found himself being directed by another Geordie, film-maker Mike Figgis who had first encountered Sting nearly twenty years earlier when he had been a trumpeter on the same jazz club circuit as Sting.

The six-week shoot featured Sting portraying a nightclub boss with gangster connections. It was the first part he had ever landed that seemed to suit his mentality perfectly. Wherever he went on location he found memories of his childhood flooding back.

'I actually did one scene at a bus stop where I spent several years of my life waiting to go to school,' explained Sting. 'I remember waiting for the bus in the mornings and wondering what I was going to do with my life. If I had thought that twenty years hence I would be back making a movie, I would have fainted.'

Sting was particularly overawed by acting alongside Tommy Lee Jones who had sprung to prominence in a movie about executed killer Gary Gilmore, which had been inspired by one of Sting's favourite books, *The Executioner's Song*, written by Norman Mailer.

Sting's other co-star in *Stormy Monday* was actress Melanie

Griffith, ex-wife of *Miami Vice* star Don Johnson. Griffith behaved a bit like a throwback to the old Hollywood stars of the 1940s and 1950s, who were used to stretch limos and trailers. The two did not become particularly close and Sting complained that Griffith found it virtually impossible to relax when the cameras stopped rolling.

One member of the crew later recalled, 'Sting and Melanie were complete opposites. She had a vast trailer while Sting was more than happy to muck in with everyone else. She had fresh food brought to her trailer and he would sit with the crew and have a friendly chat over lunch.'

When Sting suggested to Melanie that she join him by the catering lorry one day for lunch, the crew member revealed that she turned to Sting and said, 'I don't think so,' and flounced off.

However, Sting was more concerned with visiting old childhood haunts in his hometown. He even went to all the schools he attended as a youngster. 'I drove through the gates of my grammar school and I had the same queasy feeling I used to have when I was late and hadn't done my homework,' Sting later recalled.

He also regularly visited his seriously ill mother. She was now close to death from the cancer that riddled her body but, typically, was fighting it on all fronts. Somehow Sting managed to produce a fine acting performance, despite the emotional turmoil caused by witnessing his mother's gradual decline.

Stormy Monday was a similar type of film to the most acclaimed British gangster movie of all time, *The Long Good Friday*, starring Bob Hoskins and Helen Mirren.

Explained Sting at the time, 'One of the themes of our movie is the attempted rape of the city by planners and speculators which, in fact, has already happened in Newcastle.'

In the movie, Sting spoke in a thick Geordie accent. 'I made up a life story for the man I play so that I felt I knew him. I hope I'm getting better at acting because I am acting with good people. I reckon the part worked but I don't see it as my career now to play Geordies. I definitely don't want to become a professional Geordie.'

During one meeting with a reporter to help to promote *Stormy Monday*, Sting made an intriguing remark when asked how he managed to keep his career as a rock star going as well as being an actor. 'I am tired but I am very fit. I don't think there is any alternative to this lifestyle, except being dead.'

While making *Stormy Monday*, Sting found himself in the familiar surroundings of Julie's nightclub after he had called up old Geordie friend John Harker and arranged to meet him for a drink. Harker was surprised to find the multi-millionaire rock star leaning against the bar unrecognised, having queued for half an hour to get in. It was only afterwards that he realised the entire occasion was most probably essential research for Sting's role in the movie.

Sting was in Montserrat recording a new album when his beloved mother Audrey died. He had actually just finished a game of billiards with a crew member when the call came from his brother Phil. 'It's all right now, it really is. She's not in pain any more,' he tried to console his distraught brother but both of them sobbed down the phone.

Sting put the receiver down and walked to his suite where he sat on the bed for hours just thinking. No one dared disturb him.

After being told she had only a month to live, Audrey had fought the disease for two years. She never lost her great sense of humour and, in Sting's eyes, remained a glamorous woman right up until the end. Sting later tried to explain the influence of his mother by saying, 'I quite literally got music from my mother. It was she who encouraged me to play the guitar; it was she who listened to me.'

Then he added, 'At the same time, it was she who created a lot of tension in me. I was the first child and I think the first male child has bigger psychological burdens to carry than any other children, because it's like a love affair.'

Years later, Sting wrote 'The Lazarus Heart' specially for his mother. The song came to him after yet another weird dream during which he felt that she was cutting him open with a knife.

'She was very powerful in a symbolic way — a very Freudian mother. I'm very aware of her presence. I feel closer to her than ever before. She was stuck in this body that was useless to her for two years and she was such a free spirit that her death was a freeing for her.'

*　　　　*　　　　*

Around this time, Sting became politically more choosy about his film roles when he backed out of a movie because the project — due to be shot on location in Zimbabwe — did not take a hard enough stance against apartheid. The singer had been due to star in *The Lost Weekend* with Stephen Spielberg's wife Amy Irving.

In July 1987, Sting was invited to appear at the annual Umbria Jazz Festival with his musical hero, the revered seventy-six-year-old composer, pianist and arranger Gil Evans.

The invitation undoubtedly caused a few raised eyebrows among the jazz purists in attendance at the festival, who included Miles Davis, Cab Calloway and Wynton Marsalis. Evans had asked Sting to join him after the two met backstage at the legendary Ronnie Scott's club in Soho, London.

Thirty-five thousand people applauded thunderously, joining in with Sting for some of his more familiar numbers and clapping along with the powerful rhythm section. It was a night he would never forget. He put all his sorrow about his mother behind him and played to his heart's content.

Sting and Trudie showed up at the Cannes Film Festival in 1987, even though he did not have any specific movies in competition. Their close friend Deborah Cohen joined them for a few days and all three were invited on to record tycoon Robert Stigwood's yacht for a highly intimate dinner.

The following evening, a precocious young Belgian named Jean-Pierre Dutilleux introduced himself to Sting and Trudie at the bar of the Albion Hotel where the singer was staying. He told them he had just been nominated for an Oscar for a documentary he had made about the plight of the Indians in the Brazilian rain-forest. Sting showed nothing more than a passing interest in what

Dutilleux had to say, even though he said he was a close friend of Stewart Copeland.

Next day, the young Belgian bombarded Sting with phone calls and Sting had to tell reception to stop putting them through. However, Dutilleux — who described himself as an adventurer — was not going to be put off that easily. He saw Sting as the perfect figurehead for a grandiose scheme he had been developing for years to save the Indians' land.

Sting and Trudie stayed in Cannes for three days and Sting flew in his trusted assistant David Fox for a special lunch to celebrate Fox's thirty-ninth birthday. Sting also managed to find time to have a strictly business dinner with A&M boss Jerry Moss.

Throughout the trip, Sting was haunted by the image of his sick father. On his last visit to see him in hospital, he thought he had been sent to the wrong bed because the disease had so eaten away at his father that he could no longer recognise him.

Sting was particularly disturbed by the fact that he found it so difficult to talk to his dying father. Eventually, he took Ernie by the hand and told him that they had the same hands. Ernie agreed and smiled weakly before saying that Sting had put his hands to much better use than he had. It was the first time his father had ever paid him a compliment.

In the late summer of 1988, Sting, with Tracy Chapman, Peter Gabriel and Bruce Springsteen, took part in the Amnesty International Human Rights Now! tour which was to take in London, New York, Philadelphia, LA, Oakland, California, Japan, Zimbabwe, Brazil and Argentina.

Every member of each audience was asked to sign the Declaration of Human Rights Petitions which could be found at the entrance to each venue. Peter Garbriel summed up the thinking behind the tour when he said that it was vital that 'ordinary people can visibly demonstrate they have real power to influence change'. That sentiment was echoed by Springsteen's words to the audience in Philadelphia, 'It's in your hands.'

Critics of the gigs said that, for all its good intentions, the audiences were never that transfixed by the half-hour films shown between sets, which depicted the UN's thirty human rights. Audience members were groaning by the time the programme got to number fifteen. However, Sting believed that human rights awareness was a crucial part of life and he hoped to plant a seed that would grow to fruition in the next generation.

However, there was no doubting the entertainment value provided by Sting on the tour. While his devotion to the cause was unquestionable, it was also clear that the tour was good promotion for him. London rock critic Marcus Berkman wrote in the *Daily Mail*, 'The set of the night was undoubtedly Sting's. Every time I see him live I marvel more at the verve and virtuosity of his band.'

The Amnesty world tour also marked the development of Sting's close friendship with rock icon Bruce Springsteen.

Bruce had first dropped in on a Sting show just before the Amnesty tour started. Then they further cemented their friendship when Bruce joined Sting for 'Every Breath You Take' and Sting returned the favour for 'The River' during their first American gig of the tour.

At one of the regular Amnesty press conferences that were held before each engagement, Sting and Bruce cracked jokes at each other, which broke up the very formal atmosphere and had journalists cringing.

When one wag asked 'the American performers' whether they were giving tips to the others on reaching an American audience, Bruce cut in, with a grin on his face, 'Have you ever tried to tell Sting about anything?' At another point he told the assembled music hacks, 'I play my songs and between sets Sting lectures me on what's wrong with all of them.'

Everyone chuckled, then Sting came back with a straight face, 'I'm going to be a better person for having known you, Bruce.'

New York *Daily News* writer David Hinckley reckoned at the time, 'This particular buddying is too good to be dismissed as mere professional respect. Remember the players. Sting, a man usually considered so aloof and cool we should leave all his shows with frost on our heads. Bruce, the voice of Chevrolets, fries and wild summer nights down the shore. This should not be happening. It's great. What was it someone said about Ginger Rogers and Fred Astaire? She gave him sex and he gave her class? Oh, OK, so it's not really that simple. Sting actually comes equipped with a pretty good sense of humour. Bruce knows a few multi-syllabic words himself.'

Hinckley was absolutely spot on. Sting and Bruce did hit it off as great friends and have kept in touch ever since with visits to Bruce's pad in upstate New York. They even shared a holiday on a luxurious yacht on the Mediterranean in the summer of 1995.

One friend explains, 'Not only do Bruce and Sting get on like a house on fire but Trudie and Patty are great soulmates also and they have a bundle of kids between them.'

*   *   *

Sting eventually found himself in hot water in South America when he upset the governments of both Chile and Argentina by holding a concert that featured the song 'They Dance Alone'.

It is even reckoned that he indirectly helped the Chilean opposition in its efforts to unseat the country's military dictator, President Pinochet.

Sting appeared in a fifteen-minute television broadcast put out by the opposition in the run up to the country's sole-party election for Pinochet who was standing for another eight-year term. The programme featured 'They Dance Alone,' which Sting had earlier written specifically for the relatives of 'disappeared' political prisoners. It featured footage of a solitary woman tracing the steps of a traditional folk dance in an empty hall.

The concert was broadcast on radio in Chile, where the song had already been dedicated to the thousands of tortured prisoners who had disappeared since the brutal regime of General Pinochet had come to power.

In Chile, Sting played in front of thirty thousand kids. Amnesty

International had given him a message to read out in Spanish, which said, 'The next song is for the Disappeared'. Looking at the machine guns being carried by the armed police surrounding the venue, Sting decided not to read it out. 'What we took to Chile was the message of the music, which is, anyway, pretty rebellious. It's like giving out pamphlets, but cleverer,' he later said.

During his much publicised visit to Chile on behalf of the Amnesty Tour, Sting bumped into his old friend Herman Rojas, the Chilean record executive who had first met Sting during his early days with The Police.

Rojas came backstage with a beautiful girl called Carla who was desperate to meet Sting and had even taken to calling him 'El Mino' (the stud) because she was so obsessed with going to bed with him. She never got close enough to him to find out.

Meanwhile, Sting told a world-televised press conference that he was deeply affected by the situation. 'The idea of mothers grieving and being denied justice for their children, husbands or fathers symbolises the search for truth and justice.'

Later, Sting was standing behind those same mothers at a press conference with stars like Sinead O'Connor and Peter Gabriel. Rojas watched Sting go on stage as part of the show, and noted that Miles Copeland was doing exactly what he had been doing almost ten years earlier. 'He was pushing the kids off the edge of the stage if they got too close to Sting. It was hardly the sort of way to behave at a peace concert.'

At one stage, a Chilean was shoved back into the audience by Miles Copeland and he turned and screamed at Sting's manager, 'What are you doing, man? This is our fucking country.'

Rojas adds ominously, 'Some people at the concert that night wanted to kill Miles Copeland. He created a really bad feeling between the public and Sting.'

*   *   *

Just before Christmas 1988, an extraordinary report surfaced in the press claiming that Sting had joined forces with arch Conservative politician-turned-novelist Jeffrey Archer to present Arthur Miller's adaptation of Ibsen's anti-fascist play *An Enemy of the People* at the Playhouse Theatre, owned by Archer. It later emerged that Sting had actually put up twenty thousand of the eighty thousand pounds it cost to put on the play.

NINETEEN

RUMBLE IN THE JUNGLE

'The Land is one great, wild, untidy,
luxuriant hothouse made by nature, for herself.'
- CHARLES DARWIN, 1836

THE RIVER AMAZON IS SECOND IN LENGTH only to the Nile and first in terms of the volume of water carried and the size of the area drained by it. All its tributaries flow through a vast plain that stretches from the plateau of Guyana in the north and the Andes in the west to the Brazilian plateau in the south. However, it was the Amazon basin with its hot, humid climate and dense covering of tropical rainforest — one of the principal sources of oxygen for our entire planet — that was to become Sting's obsession.

In the mid-1960s, rich mineral resources were discovered in the subsoil of the region and subsequently developed by the Brazilian government who flattened and destroyed thousands of square miles of rainforest. These projects have included a motorway of over three thousand miles in length. There have also been the slash-and-burn clearing of the forest, logging, mining and ranching which have destroyed more than half of the forest.

By the mid-1980s, experts were predicting that the entire forest would be destroyed within a hundred years, with catastrophic consequences for the planet.

In December 1987 Sting was in Rio de Janeiro for a concert when he agreed to be whisked off to the middle of the Brazilian jungle, thanks to the efforts of one man, Belgian photographer and self-styled adventurer Jean-Pierre Dutilleux. The events that followed were to change Sting's life in a way that nothing before or since has ever done.

Dutilleux was on his way to the airport in Rio when he passed the coach which had just picked Sting up before his concert in the city. Dutilleux turned his car around, tracked Sting down to his hotel and confronted him in the bar.

At first Sting did not want to know.

While Dutilleux was talking to him he kept saying over and over again, 'Dolphins, penguins, who gives a fuck, JP?' Sting even turned and moaned, 'I'm on tour. I'm tired, I want to be on the beach. Why the hell would I want to go to the jungle?'

'Look,' said JP. 'You will thank me for the rest of your life about this trip.'

'OK,' replied Sting. 'How do we do it?'

'Well, we have to hire a little plane, we have to buy some fishing hooks, some machetes ...'

'What for?'

'You have to take the Indians gifts, to strike up a relationship.'

'How much will it cost?'

'A couple of thousand dollars.'

Then Trudie stepped in and said, 'We should go with him.' The funny thing was that up until a few moments earlier Sting had not given a thought to the Indians.

Dutilleux was so overcome with delight at getting Sting to agree to go to the jungle that he hugged him there and then in the bar of the hotel.

However, within hours of Sting's decision to go, various executives in his record company started insisting that they wanted to come on board the project as well. As Dutilleux explains, 'They all thought it would help their career and put them in good standing with Sting — precisely the wrong reasons for doing such a project.'

Interestingly, Dutilleux believes to this day that Sting would never have got involved in the rainforest campaign if Miles Copeland had not been out in the lobby discussing some deal or other on the phone throughout Dutilleux's initial meeting with Sting in Rio. 'Miles was unhappy when he heard about the planned trip and banned me from taking any photographs,' explains Dutilleux. 'But halfway through the stay in the jungle, Sting just turned to me and said, "JP, you must take some pictures." Miles was even more upset when he heard about that.'

Sting was feeling particularly vulnerable at the time because his father had died of cancer as he was travelling across the Atlantic. One of the first people to meet him on his arrival in Rio was an attractive brunette, Polygram Records publicity officer Gilda Matoso. She later became a close friend who has kept in contact with Sting to this day.

She recalls, 'We already knew when his plane touched down that his father had died but he insisted on going ahead with a press conference planned for that afternoon.'

At the press conference Sting kept his sunglasses on the entire time to hide his tear-stained eyes.

Journalists were briefed not to ask Sting about his father but they still threw some emotive questions at him. Fortunately, he had Trudie and his team of Miles Copeland, co-manager Kim Turner and right-hand man Billy Francis on hand.

Band member Branford Marsalis recalls, 'When his father died you couldn't see any sign that he was under stress. He wasn't trying to pretend he wasn't dealing with it — he wasn't fucking dealing with it. Denial to the tenth degree.'

However, the deaths of his mother and father made Sting want to do something in their memory and perhaps going to the jungle was one answer.

By this time, Sting was probably the biggest star in Brazil. His photos were on posters plastered everywhere. Anyone who looked vaguely like him was instantly mobbed. One dustman with blond hair was almost raped by a mob of Sting-hungry women on Ipanema Beach.

Sting's old friend Deborah Cohen recalled, 'I took a two-block walk with him to the cinema one afternoon and it was frightening. Within a few hundred yards we had a huge crowd following us.'

Deborah noticed that Sting puts up a special protective guard whenever he does not want to be approached by fans. 'He has the ability to put them off. He just gives out an icy-cool vibe and no one goes near him. It is quite remarkable.'

During that same visit to Rio, Sting discovered a favourite restaurant called Satyrico in Ipanema, which specialised in seafood and pasta. However, his first visit there almost turned out to be his last when Miles Copeland grappled with a fan who was pestering Sting for his autograph, without realising he was physically disabled.

'Miles told the guy to "Fuck off, we're trying to eat dinner here." Then he swung around and the guy fell to the ground. It was only then we realised he was a cripple,' said one guest.

A vast two-hundred-thousand-strong crowd greeted Sting two days later at the Maracana stadium. 'I felt it was like a wake for my father. I was out there in front of two hundred thousand people and it was a celebration of my parents and a way of me saying thank you to them. I felt very strongly that they were there,' he later recalled.

The following day, Gilda Matoso organised a visit to a picturesque fishing village up the coast from Rio. Sting, Trudie and African–American keyboard player Delmar Brown made the trip but it was marred when the local police stopped their convoy and ordered Delmar Brown out of the car he was travelling in because, as Gilda recalls, 'The cops are very colour prejudiced outside the cities.'

When Sting emerged from another vehicle, the police suddenly became very apologetic and waved the party on.

In the quiet little town where they lunched, Sting actually seemed relaxed for the first time since arriving in Brazil. 'It was the first time I actually saw Sting smile throughout that trip because he was so cut up about his father,' explains bubbly Gilda.

At a concert in Brasilia, held a few days later, Trudie turned to Gilda Matoso during Sting's performance on stage and said, 'Do you know where we are going tomorrow?'

'I'm going back to Rio,' came the reply from Gilda.

'We're going to the jungle. Why don't you come?' asked Trudie.

'No thank you,' came Gilda's no-nonsense reply.

It was then that Trudie revealed that Jean-Pierre Dutilleux had persuaded them to go and visit the rainforest and Chief Raoni who had become spokesman for the Indians.

Accompanied by Trudie, Sting had agreed to stay in the rainforest with the Kayapos Indians of the Xingu region. The Indians had first been discovered by the outside world only fifteen years earlier. Jean-Pierre Dutilleux had already made an Oscar-nominated documentary about them before he persuaded Sting to make this trip.

However, even before Sting got to the rainforest he found a mountain of bureaucracy had to be overcome just to get permission to fly to the jungle. With sixty acres being destroyed every minute of every day, the logging companies were not anxious for a high-profile personality to attract attention to the situation. Eventually, permission was granted after Dutilleux pulled some strings to ensure the visit went ahead.

So, armed with a weird and wonderful collection of presents for the Indians — including fish hooks, torches, fishing lines, machetes, knives and aluminium pots — they loaded up their six-seater plane for the journey. That was when Sting first laid eyes on one of the most bizarre characters he had ever met.

Captain Kelly stood over six and a half feet tall in sandals, shorts and sleeveless flak jacket; his arms, legs and chest were covered in exotic tattoos that vanished teasingly inside his clothing. Around his neck and wrist were Indian necklaces and bangles; a jungle knife was strapped to a snake-skin belt. He wore a pair of bright red spectacles that looked like they belonged to Elton John and a haircut that made him resemble a fugitive from *The Monkees* — all nicely topped off with a broad Mancunian accent. Captain Kelly was to be their guide.

It emerged that Kelly had once owned a string of rhythm and blues clubs in the north of England and used to hire groups like Zoot Money's Big Roll Band, which featured a certain guitarist called Andy Summers. Later, he sold the clubs, moved to Brazil, opened a pub in São Paulo and then started helping the Indians.

After a hair-raising flight through thunderstorms, Sting and Trudie landed in Indian territory. There were once six million Indians in the Amazon basin. By the time Sting arrived, there were just two hundred thousand. Many had been massacred by gunfire, others by blankets impregnated with the flu virus being dropped on villages; others had been destroyed by alcohol and the demoralisation of their culture.

The Xingu Indians lived in a protected area roughly the size of Belgium. They were considered a showpiece tribe who also happened to be peaceful, although they were protected by the hostile tribes of the Lower Xingu, some of whom killed motorists who had broken down on the Trans-Amazonian highway which ran through their forest.

Sting's first impression on arriving at the village is worth noting:

Nothing can prepare you for your first glimpse of an Indian village. The symmetry of enormous thatched long-houses arranged in a perfect circle and surrounded by the chaos of the jungle. Someone flashes a mirror at us. It's a signal from another world, but as we get closer to the centre of the circle we can make out the markings of a soccer pitch and goal posts. It was the first indication that this journey was to shatter a number of fantasies we had about the Indians as well as confirm others.

Tiny figures emerge from their houses to watch our descent to a nearby airfield. Another bumpy landing. As the door opens the jungle heat is almost solid and the silence of the late afternoon, after the twin engines have come to a stop, is wonderful and frightening. The jungle wall is as silent as a tomb.

Our hosts suddenly appear at the other end of the field. Some are on bicycles, others are wearing football strips, some are naked except for a piece of cloth around their waists.

Sting was particularly struck by the look of the Indians.

All the men had a kind of Henry V haircut matted with red dye.

Their faces looked Tibetan, which reminds me just how far their ancestors must have travelled from the centre of Asia, north across the Bering Strait to Alaska and south, through what became Canada and the United States, to Central America and finally to a southern tributary of the Amazon basin; moving about one hundred miles per generation according to studies by anthropologists.

Sting and Trudie put on a brave face when they were told they would have to wash in the river and that their beds would consist of a couple of hammocks. Within minutes of arriving, Sting, Trudie, Captain Kelly and Jean-Pierre had stripped naked and headed for the river bank.

As they swam naked, Sting noticed a tall man with shoulder-length hair, ceremonial beads and Levis urinating in the river. Between his chin and his bottom lip was a large wooden plate. This was Chief Raoni.

During that trip, Sting discovered that the best drugs were made from natural vegetation. He took part in a 'Dead Man's Root' swallowing ceremony, ritualistically gobbling the mystical rainforest root and disappearing into a seven-hour trance during which he experienced death, met God and woke up having seen himself in a deeply unflattering light.

Sting also took the 'tea' — made from ayahuasca — for the first time. It was an emotive, elating, yet horrifying experience — he felt a bottomless fear that he was dissolving, losing control, and nothing could save him. Here he was, Sting, the ultimate control freak and he was losing it, floating through the forest in a swirl of paint that the Indians had dabbed on his face, a face he'd contorted into a mask that helped to make him a millionaire twenty times over. Here in the jungle, with the tea-induced high rushing through his body, he was maskless, flowing into the trees, no longer impermeable, part of the greenness sliding around him.

The fear he felt after taking the 'tea' for the first time was certainly unequalled by anything he had encountered during the sessions of Jungian analysis which he had begun after the break-up of his marriage to Frances.

When the 'tea' took its full effect, following those initial fear-ridden minutes, Sting began to pull through into a new set of emotions. What came next was two hours of the most intense weeping, followed by pure joy, his body swirling out beyond the thatched huts, the fires, the hammock where he slept.

Sting found that he was outside himself — in that perfect state of detachment he'd always sought as a sleepless young man with drugs or women in the best hotels, or while singing 'Roxanne'. Now he could hide from nothing, the mask could not save him from melting into the million trees, the billion leaves that surrounded them in the jungle.

Throughout, the Indians' hands were near him, guiding and reassuring him on his drug-induced journey. To have been alone at that time would have been madness. At one stage, Sting imagined he was dead. Then Raoni drummed his fingers on Sting's chest and said, 'Lot of pain here.' Quite unexpectedly, tears sprang from Sting's eyes.

The world had thought that Sting was in the jungle to save it, but first of all he was looking for something he couldn't name, and then he found it — a father he could love when his own had just been snatched from him.

Night-time in the village consisted of Sting and Trudie being guarded by some of Raoni's warriors who stood by their hammocks and farted and laughed through most of the evening, much to Trudie's disgust.

However, Trudie's biggest problem in the jungle was her complete and utter fear of snakes. Back home in Britain she had been known to run screaming from a room if a snake even wriggled across a television screen. Out in the jungle they were everywhere and, to make matters worse, it turned out that the snake was the Indians' most powerful symbol of strength.

Over the following few days, Sting and Trudie were treated like gods and met witch doctors and wild beasts such as panthers. They even cycled to another village to meet other Indian tribespeople.

In some ways, Sting considered the trip to the jungle to be another wake in memory of his father. He was overwhelmed by the rainforest's haunted vision, its mysterious beauty, and he was determined to do something to ensure its preservation. Sting became convinced that he had to stop the destruction and began mulling over a plan to convince as many people as possible that there was something everyone could do.

Meanwhile, the ever-sensitive Indians realised that Sting was still heartbroken about his father's death. They did everything in their power to console him. They even had a nickname for him — 'Potima' — which meant 'The liver of a little armadillo'. They gave Sting a full covering of warpaint to cheer him up — the dye was also a useful repellent against the mosquitoes that bombarded him and Trudie every night. There was also the occasional tarantula!

By the end of the trip, Sting found himself completely swept up by the Indians and vowed that he would do everything within his power to help their cause. He told Chief Raoni:

I am honoured to be your guest and you have treated me kindly. I believe that the forest is yours, but the white man has no real home. He is lost in a world that he doesn't understand. He has ceased to communicate with the spirits of the earth and the forest, the river and air, so he is alone. Unhappy, he searches for happiness and when he sees happiness in others he becomes angry and wants to destroy it because inside he is empty. I am not a politician, I am only a singer but many people listen to me. I promise you that whenever I can speak on your behalf I will do so. I shall tell your story to whomever I can because you are the only protectors of the forest and if the forest dies then so does the earth. Even a white man can understand this.

On the plane trip back to civilisation, Sting promised Jean-Pierre Dutilleux that he would speak to Amnesty International. 'I also want to write something. It's not the noble savages I have a sense of, but the nobility of the species. My faith in man has been restored despite all the bullshit. In some ways Western man is in reverse evolution; we've forgotten our real potential. The Xingu can remind us of what we really are. They must survive.'

Friends like Gilda Matoso noticed a huge change in both Sting and Trudie's personalities when they returned from the jungle to continue the tour. 'They could talk of nothing but the jungle. There was no other subject worth discussing,' explains Gilda.

Another friend, Deborah Cohen, says, 'Sting was completely and utterly entranced by the plight of the Indians. He was a changed man.'

At the end of that exhausting tour of Brazil, Deborah Cohen accompanied Sting to a luxurious private spa in the mountains overlooking São Paulo. Sting, Trudie, Miles and Deborah, plus the rest of the entourage, spent two days there gradually unwinding but Sting still couldn't stop talking about the Indians. 'As everyone enjoyed massages and rub downs, he just went on and on and on,' says Deborah Cohen.

Sting returned to the jungle on two more occasions. Accompanying him both times was Carlos Paiva, a Brazilian production co-ordinator working on behalf of a French TV documentary crew who were making a programme about Sting's journey into the rainforest. Paiva became very close to the singer.

On the second trip they visited not only Raoni's village but many other settlements and even had the luxury of two twin-engine planes. (Sting and Trudie travelled in separate aircraft for much the same reason that Prince Charles never flies in the same plane as his heirs.)

The routine was much the same as on the previous trip except that Carlos Paiva had the unenviable task of cooking meals like spaghetti because Sting felt he could not risk illness by tasting any of the local delicacies such as roasted snake and grilled lizard.

On the flight back out of the jungle, Trudie and rainforest official Brian Marcos almost died when their twin-engined craft got lost. Carlos Paiva, who was also on board, recalls, 'We were using the forest as a guide because there is no radar in the jungle. We had just heard about a Boeing 737 that had crashed into the jungle that day and there was an appeal going out to look out for survivors.

Ahead of us was Sting in his plane. Suddenly we hit some low cloud and completely lost track of Sting's plane. We knew we had to look out for this vast river because it was a flight path point but we could not find it anywhere.'

For the first fifteen minutes Carlos and the pilot did not tell Trudie of their fears in the hope that they would soon work out the correct route. 'But after thirty minutes I knew we were in big trouble. We had even lost radio contact with Sting's plane. We had less than an hour of gas left. Trudie realised what was happening and we tried to make light of it but she started to look very scared. All of us were frantically looking out of the window of the plane to see if we could see any airstrips to land at.

'Then we spotted a strip in the middle of the jungle. We did not know whether to land in case it was a drug dealer's and then we would all be killed. Then a guy came out of his hut by the airfield and radioed to us so that we could relocate ourselves on the map. We had just fifteen minutes of fuel left at that stage and by the time we found the next safe landing strip there was virtually nothing left in the tank.'

When Trudie was reunited with Sting that day they found themselves surrounded by journalists who had travelled to the middle of the jungle because they were reporting on the missing airliner. Later, Sting and Trudie discovered that the aeroplane had crashed for exactly the same reasons after the pilot got lost in the jungle and was forced to make an emergency landing.

A few months later, Sting attended the Alta Mira Indian conference in a one-street town in the middle of the jungle. By this stage the Indians were very bitter about their treatment and there was much suspicion that Raoni had befriended Sting to get some money from him. Carlos Paiva explains, 'There was also a lot of politics involved. It was a very intimidating atmosphere and there was absolutely no protection for Sting.'

When Sting and the rest of the party arrived in Alta Mira there were no hotel rooms left so they managed to rent a rundown shack on the edge of town which was soon overrun by reporters.

Word soon filtered through from the centre of town that Sting was not wanted and would be 'chopped into little pieces' if he stayed on any longer. The local police were fairly indifferent to the threats as they themselves were the daily recipients of similar warnings. Sting bravely decided to ignore the dangerous situation and remained in the town to attend the conference.

Then rumours that Sting had fallen out with his Indian hosts started to be published in newspapers around the world. The stories claimed that the singer had been chased out of the town by the Indians and was under a twenty-four-hour guard by the Brazilian army. The truth was that a number of landowners were so incensed by Sting's involvement that they had decided that he should be killed so that world attention on the rainforests would fade.

When Sting got wind of the threats, he was extremely scared. He knew that out there in the jungle anything could happen. There was little real protection for him. The police were in the pocket of the landowners. There were negative stories in the local press. Sting was greeted by a wave of hysteria. People were being whipped up to mistrust his motives.

Various groups were blamed for spreading the malicious story, including a right-wing political party and the hydro-electric company planning to destroy much of the forest to make way for a dam, and it was even suspected that a group of Indians jealous of Raoni might have started the rumours.

Meanwhile, back in London, Miles Copeland was going quietly crazy. He had been against the entire rainforest campaign because he felt it was too dangerous for Sting personally and it might actually backfire on his image as a world-ranked rock star. Now he was hearing rumours about death threats but he couldn't even reach Sting on the phone.

The singer was stuck in a dead and alive hole in the middle of the Amazon jungle. He felt he was doing something for the good of other people and there was no turning back.

In the end the conference turned into a mini-victory for Sting because he gained real respect for his efforts on behalf of the Indians. However, on the way back from that third trip, the party had to pass through a bizarre rundown settlement called San Jose Bungy Bungy where the only aircraft fuel for a thousand miles was stored. Sting,

Carlos and their entourage had to sleep in a shed/hotel that consisted of dormitories next to a lively brothel used by the local woodcutters and a cabaret bar filled with miners having non-stop fights.

There were no phones in Bungy Bungy and Sting and his friends were transported to and from the airport on the rusty flat-bed of a rundown pick-up truck. Then Sting was offered roast monkey for dinner!

'It was like the Wild West at its worst,' explains Carlos Paiva, who accompanied Sting on that trip. 'But what made it so awful was that the cabaret bar only had one record and they kept playing it over and over again.'

Sting and his compatriots tried to sleep through the racket but in the end all three got up and trooped down to the bar where they were greeted by the sight of partly clad women draped over various men swigging from whisky bottles.

More scantily dressed women lined the bar and were offering men sex for the price of a drink or a few dollars. It turned out that at least a dozen of the women had travelled to the town specifically to try to pick up some business after hearing that Sting and his entourage were in the area.

On the same trip, one of the planes crashlanded on an airstrip when the pilot forgot to put down the landing gear. Life in the jungle was certainly no picnic.

TWENTY

An Englishman Abroad

'The Indians have been fucked up
the arse since they were discovered.'
- Sting

By early 1988 Sting and Trudie had become completely obsessed with the rainforest and the plight of the Indians. Close friend Deborah Cohen visited them in their Highgate home in north London around that time. 'I'll never forget the day I walked in. Sting was sitting in a chair by the fireplace, Trudie was on the floor at his feet and they were talking about the Indians like a couple of excited teenagers.'

Within minutes of Deborah's arrival, Sting turned to her and said, 'We have to do something about the Indians. We are thinking of setting up a foundation for them.'

Deborah tried to sound enthusiastic but in the back of her mind she was worried that maybe Sting was getting into this whole thing too deeply.

Shortly after that, Deborah moved to London to work at MTV and rented Trudie's apartment just a short distance from the couple's

Highgate house. As a result, she saw a lot of the political infighting that went on during the setting up of the Foundation. 'Some of it was outrageous. Certain people tried to muscle in on it because they saw it as a way of ingratiating themselves with Sting,' explains Deborah.

In February 1989 Sting returned to Brazil, accompanied by Jean-Pierre Dutilleux, with the specific aim of trying to persuade Brazil's President Sarney to agree to their plans for a Rainforest Foundation. The idea was for Chief Raoni to join Sting on a world tour to publicise the scandalous situation in the rainforest but they needed to get him a passport first.

Their assignment in the Brazilian capital of Brasilia was not easy and Raoni only got his passport after much haggling. However, the more important question of whether the president would allow the Indian areas in the jungle to be proclaimed a National Park was far more complex. President Sarney agreed in principle but Sting knew full well that they still had a long way to go.

The chief himself rounded on journalists when he attended a Rainforest Foundation meeting shortly after a number of negative stories appeared in the Brazilian press. 'Why do you journalists tell lies? Which of you is against our Foundation? Come on, tell me! If any more journalists tell lies about us, I will chase after you with my war club.'

Sting couldn't help smiling at the last remark as it perfectly summed up his feelings towards certain reptiles in the press.

His rainforest fund was the first foreign campaign to save part of the area and he intended to promote the plan by taking Raoni with him on a world tour to heighten awareness of the situation. Critics of the proposal said that much of the scheme had been formulated without the involvement of other Indian tribes in the area.

Father Julio Geige, head of the local missionary organisation which supported the Indians' fight against the construction of a dam which would flood sixty-five thousand square miles of forest, said Sting's plan was 'full of good intentions. But it will face the problem of buying land for Indians which the Indians consider already theirs. If Sting had been more patient, and listened to more Indians, he could have become part of the solution'.

Meanwhile, Trudie was steadfastly supportive of her lover. 'We knew we had to do something to publicise their plight before it was too late. Unfortunately, it has taken a year to finalise the plans. And now we've got to move fast if we're going to preserve that land for generations of Indians to come.'

Sting's association with the Brazilian rainforest was already so well known throughout the world that he was invited to perform an opera written by a secondary school teacher on behalf of the rainforest campaign. Sting happily sang alongside eleven to fifteen year olds at St Augustine's School in Billington, Lancashire. He was so impressed that he pledged to help the school to raise fifty thousand pounds to pay for a trip to Brazil.

At the beginning of 1989 Sting turned up in Brazil once more and asked his old friend Polygram publicity officer Gilda Matoso to help organise some press coverage so that he could publicise his plans to save the rainforest. Gilda was surprised when she got a person-to-person call from the Sting himself. 'Well, Gilda, I'm here and I have made up my mind to create a big foundation for the Indians to raise funds for them. I want to do a big magazine interview because I want to touch the president about this.'

Gilda went ahead and organised an interview with Brazil's biggest circulation magazine *Vega* (*Look*). Only hours later, she was fired from her job with Polygram.

That evening she was due to meet Sting to oversee the interview she had arranged with *Vega*. He immediately noticed that she was very pale and withdrawn.

'What's wrong, Gilda?' asked Sting.

'I got fired today. I'm not with Polygram any more.'

'What are you going to do?' said Sting, trying his best to console her.

'I don't know,' she said before bursting into tears.

Sting held Gilda in his arms and tried everything to calm her down. 'Don't worry. You can run the press for the rainforest campaign.'

Gilda was touched and so began an extraordinary six-month relationship.

'That's the sort of guy Sting is. He remembers his friends,' explains Gilda today. Weeks later, she discovered she was pregnant so the job became of special significance.

For the first half of 1989, Sting bravely toured the world with Chief Raoni. The Rainforest Foundation managed to raise one million dollars towards the protection of a hundred and fifty thousand square miles of Brazilian forest.

In April 1989 Sting turned up in Britain with Chief Raoni in tow and launched his campaign to save the forest by introducing the bemused Indian to Britain's press at a specially organised meeting at his North London home.

Raoni was staying at Sting's house at the time with his cousin Paiakan. Also at the house was American-Indian Red Crow who was part of the touring party and who had previously visited Raoni in the jungle.

Sting's old friend Deborah Cohen was still working with MTV in London at the time and renting Trudie's flat around the corner from the mansion. As a favour to Sting, she was asked to put up a very unusual member of the party.

She explains, 'Basically, this guy was a spy working for the Brazilian Government, who was sent on the tour specially to report back on what everyone was up to. Trudie asked me to put him up so that they at least had him at some distance from the main party.'

Sting and Jean-Pierre Dutilleux had allowed the 'spy' on the trip because they knew the Brazilian Government would never have permitted Raoni a passport if they had refused. 'He was described as an ecological student but we all knew he was really a spy,' explains Deborah Cohen. 'I had to keep an eye on him keeping an eye on Sting and Raoni,' adds Deborah who has a refreshingly open take on why Sting was roped into the rainforest campaign: 'Raoni needed a beautiful blue-eyed gringo to go out and tell the world what was happening in the jungle.'

Sting and Trudie's Brazilian friend Carlos Paiva helped to organise the world tour and he confirmed the existence of the Brazilian Government spy.

At one stage, Paiva even stole some of the notes written by the spy, photocopied them and then translated them for Sting and Trudie who were intrigued to find out what the spy was reporting back to his masters in Brasilia.

'The notes said things like he suspected Sting was smoking marijuana and that he was a secret agent, possibly working for the CIA,' explains Carlos Paiva. In fact, many of the farmers and woodcutters whom Sting encountered in the jungle had thought the same thing.

The spy on the world tour even noted down the numbers of the accounts where donations for the Foundation were to be deposited because he wanted to try to smear the campaign by suggesting Sting was keeping the money.

In one note, the spy stated that Trudie was a 'bad woman, who was using the situation to her own advantage.'

At one stage, Sting was so infuriated by the existence of the spy that he asked Carlos Paiva to contact the Brazilian embassy in London and insist they send out a more professional snoop. 'Sting was insulted that they should send such an amateur after us. His thinking was that at least they could come up with someone more worthy,' explains Carlos.

When the tour ended, the Brazilian Government were so incensed that their spy had been uncovered by Sting and his party that the man was stripped of his job and had a nervous breakdown. A couple of years later Carlos Paiva bumped into him in Rio and he openly admitted lying, cheating and deceiving everyone on the world tour. 'He felt terrible about what had happened and said he had quit in disgust at what he had been asked to do.'

One night, while the world tour was in London, Deborah Cohen — who had lived in Brazil previously despite being American by birth — received a panic-ridden call from Trudie to go over to the house in Highgate. 'They wanted me to make some rice and potatoes for Raoni because he was getting difficult about his food,' recalls Deborah.

The scene that greeted her was bizarre. The back garden of

Sting's mansion, which overlooks Hampstead Heath, had been converted into what looked like part of a village in the middle of the Amazon. Raoni had laid out branches and blankets in a circular pattern and Red Crow was smoking a peace pipe as Sting's young children played around them.

The first thing Deborah Cohen noticed was that Raoni's trademark CD-in-the-lip was not there. Instead, his entire lip hung down grotesquely and there was a giant hole where the piece of wood normally fitted.

Then her eyes panned further around the once-manicured garden of Sting's million-pound mansion. Raoni and Red Crow had built a fire and made a makeshift 'sweat lodge'. At that moment, Deborah was hustled out of the garden along with the kids as Raoni, Red Crow and Sting stripped naked and sat around the 'sweat lodge' in which herbs and spices were thrown on to the fire to form a do-it-yourself sauna.

The three men then gradually worked themselves into a trance-like state. Raoni began chanting Indian songs as the other two looked on and the peace pipe continued to be passed around.

Deborah Cohen recalls, 'It was a very funny scene. Here we were in the back garden of a respectable London house amid the most bizarre scene I have ever seen in my life.'

Meanwhile, the spy who was staying at Deborah Cohen's flat turned up at the front door. 'I was dispatched to get rid of him. The last thing we wanted was him reporting all this back to the Brazilian Government.'

An appearance on the Terry Wogan BBC TV show gained the visit even more promotion in Britain but many music business insiders were unimpressed. They saw Sting's role as little more than a spokesperson for Raoni.

Jean-Pierre Dutilleux insists to this day that he was the only white man who truly understood Raoni. He says, 'Raoni was on a mission on behalf of his people. He would not leave the jungle until the spirits and his people had given their blessing. This was the right time for the Indians to speak out for themselves. Raoni had to confront this alien world.'

Dutilleux describes Raoni as 'the Gandhi of the jungle'. He insists, 'Raoni has never personally profited from the situation. He still lives in the same hut with no money, no electricity, no water. He does not want to know how to count.'

In Paris, Raoni crossed the River Seine and asked if they were on their way to visit a new tribe. When JP and Sting had all but given up trying to get a meeting with President Mitterand, it was Raoni who insisted it would happen and kept their spirits up and was proved absolutely correct when they were granted an interview.

In Rome, Raoni, Sting and Dutilleux had an appointment with the Pope. Dutilleux remembers, 'We went through countless tunnels in the Vatican and crossed the Sistine Chapel and suddenly a bunch of priests burst out in a round of applause. Then we arrived at this little office where the Pope was to meet us.'

However, the Indian chief was far from impressed, because, as Dutilleux recalls, 'I told him he was the chief of the missionaries. Unfortunately, Raoni does not like missionaries and he would never allow any of them on his land.'

Sting, Raoni and Dutilleux stood about and waited for the Pope to turn up. After twenty minutes, Raoni got very angry and told the others he did not want to stay any longer. He was about to leave when the Pope finally appeared.

The Pope stepped back when he first saw his three visitors who looked absolutely exhausted and unshaven after their gruelling tour. Then he began talking in English. Raoni soon cut him off. 'You have a god and I have a god too and he is right here with me. And my god is saying to your god that your missionaries should get off Indian land. We respect your religion now please respect ours.'

The Pope looked completely stunned, gave each of the men a plastic rosary and disappeared. Raoni was so incensed that Sting and Dutilleux had to hold him back because he looked as though he was about to hit the Pope.

'It was a disaster,' recalls Dutilleux.

In Japan, however, the reaction to this bizarre trio was far more receptive. On arrival in the land of the rising sun, Raoni was convinced that the Japanese were related to his Amazonian Indians because they looked very similar. At one engagement, Raoni had his Japanese audience in hysterics when he told them, 'You are all Indians. You just forgot how to use a bow and arrow.'

However, there was another reason for Raoni being so happy in Japan. Dutilleux explains, 'Raoni loved Japanese girls and there were two particular girls whom we christened his groupies. They reminded him of his wives and he kept disappearing with them.'

Tour organiser Carlos Paiva confirms, 'Those girls were Raoni's groupies. They adored him and looked after him. He was happiest in Japan. It was really love at first sight and Raoni was like a soppy teenager. Some mornings we couldn't get him to leave his room because he wanted to stay with them all day.'

Raoni even photographed the girls in a number of saucy poses and took the snapshots back to show all the other Indians in his village at the end of the tour.

On the way to Switzerland by bus from Italy, Raoni was so bowled over by the sight of Mont Blanc that he persuaded the party to stop and walk into the woodlands at the base of the mountain.

There, in the middle of the countryside, Sting showed his lighter side by taking a leak and allowing Carlos to take a photograph of him doing it.

In Amsterdam, according to Jean-Pierre Dutilleux, Sting got involved in a verbal clash of egos over Latin crooner Julio Inglesias.

He explains, 'Inglesias was in town and I suggested that maybe he should join in the rainforest efforts and appear with Sting and Raoni. Sting told me, "You've got me, you don't need him." Inglesias was huge in South America at the time and it would have been great to get him on board.'

Dutilleux's relationship with Sting was also in trouble because of a clash of egos. The Belgian still saw the rainforest and Raoni as his project, while Sting considered he was now the figurehead. However, many people have said Dutilleux was a difficult man to work with.

There was also another, more familiar, problem on the world tour that has never before come to light. One of the women members of the entourage developed an incredible crush on Sting and flung herself at him at any opportunity.

On one embarrassing occasion when Sting was alone in his hotel room in Rome, the woman — an attractive brunette — showed up at his door dressed in nothing but a coat which she dropped to the floor the moment he opened the door. 'Sting slammed the door shut and rang one of his assistants and the entire incident was hushed up,' recalled one member of the world tour party.

Carlos Paiva explains, 'Trudie handled the whole thing brilliantly. She knew this woman was trying to get into bed with Sting but she turned the situation around and treated it like a joke. In the end the woman gave up.'

Stormy Monday was premiered in Britain in January 1989 and got reasonably good reviews. However, Sting used the publicity surrounding the movie to launch a scathing attack on Hollywood. 'The problem with a lot of my films is that I've often been the most experienced actor on the set,' he told one writer. Sting then went on openly to dismiss some of his previous big-screen efforts for the first time. *The Bride* was: 'dreadful — I was the best thing in it'.

He described *Dune* director David Lynch as 'a monster, a geek from the Mid-West'. Some observers were wondering why it had taken Sting so long to work out the deficiencies in many of his previous movie projects.

Unfortunately, *Stormy Monday* did not perform well at the box office. It was perceived as a well-intentioned film that had too many holes in the plot actually to thrill an audience for almost two hours.

TWENTY ONE

CITIZENS OF THE WORLD

'Death isn't much of a party subject,
but it's been valuable to me to think about.
Maybe it'll be valuable to other people too.'
- STING

STING AND HIS PARTY OF RAINFOREST SAVIOURS collected enough 'air miles' during their world tour to go back and forth to the jungle as they pleased but that didn't make it any less exhausting.

In Australia, a knackered Sting found himself so swept up by Chief Raoni's superstitious beliefs that he allowed the Indian to bless a helicopter before any of them would agree to fly in it. 'Even the pilot became convinced it was going to crash unless Raoni blessed it,' explained tour organiser Carlos Paiva.

During the world tour, Raoni got into the habit of splashing mouthwash on himself as if it was perfume. Carlos explains, 'The mint smelled like wood to him and that reminded him of the forest. He first found it in one of those airline kits you get on long-distance flights.'

Once, on a long-haul flight, Paiva took a photo of Raoni and the flash woke up the Indian chief. He got his own back by pickpocketing the camera from Carlos and secretly doing the same thing back. It was only when Carlos got the film developed that he realised what had happened.

On the same flight, Sting and Raoni cavorted like a couple of kids, taking photos of each other. A close bond had been formed between the two men. It was almost as if wise old Raoni had become Sting's missing father figure.

Today Jean-Pierre Dutilleux concedes, 'Raoni still likes Sting for what he did and recognises his contribution. But what matters at the end of the day is that we achieve what we set out to do. Nothing else matters.'

Dutilleux chooses his words carefully, but he now believes he 'got burned by the whole rainforest thing'. He claims that behind-the-scenes problems marred things even during that first trip to visit Raoni. In particular, there was a lot of tension between the eccentric Captain Kelly and Sting. 'Sting felt Captain Kelly's alleged chequered history potentially damaging to the Foundation.'

Dutilleux says the rainforest campaign took a terrible toll on him personally, especially when some newspapers and magazines began questioning the wisdom of the project. 'I was nearly destroyed by the whole rainforest business, especially the press and TV coverage afterwards.'

Dutilleux was very reluctant to be publicly drawn on his true opinion of Sting but he did say, 'I know more about Sting than anyone on this earth and one day I might reveal all. I have so much to tell that would shatter some illusions. I played puppet to Sting for long enough and I ended up being so heavily criticised for it. There is so much to tell.

'I should have known better. Sting has a big ego. When we were together in the jungle I tried to talk to him about church and religion and regular subjects and he refused to talk. He's an anti-social asshole.'

Dutilleux even claims that, one day in the jungle, Sting turned to him during an argument over egos and said, 'JP, I am famous because I'm talented.'

However, it was the Brazilians, according to Dutilleux, who ended up resenting Sting for what he was trying to do in the rainforest. 'They did not like him interfering. They thought it was none of his business. That's why the Brazilian branch of the Foundation started off as a disaster. People would say, "Why is his wife one of the chiefs of the Foundation? What does she know about it?" '

Then, in a blistering attack, Dutilleux said, 'I just wish I'd found someone else to save the Indians.' He referred to the Foundation's current efforts to raise money as 'pathetic'. Says Dutilleux, 'Sting gives these pathetic dinner parties once a year to raise money, but it isn't the real thing.' It is not known whether "these pathetic dinner parties once a year" to which Dutilleux refers are the annual New York Carnegie Hall concerts Sting and Trudie organise which regularly generate donations of US$1.3m a year, net of expenses.

Explaining why he had got involved, Sting told the world, 'Raoni was so direct, so warm and so honest that I just had to say yes. He asked me if he could come to Europe and I thought it would be so good to let people listen to him.'

Then Sting admitted, 'Don't underestimate Raoni. He understands only too well the value of publicity. In a sense he has manipulated me rather than the other way round. When I first met him, I said, "Look, I'm only a singer. What can I do?" But when he wants something he has only to look into your eyes and you cannot say no. He has great charisma.' Sting seemed to accept his role as 'giving people a face with which they could identify the problem. After all, now he is the most recognisable Indian on earth'.

By this stage, however, many were starting to wonder if Sting had actually allowed himself to be taken for a ride. The singer steadfastly refused to accept that this was the case. 'Raoni took it all in his stride. He is an amazing man, utterly incorruptible. The Kayapo have a word, *kendu*, which means another world. The worlds may touch but they never merge. He viewed us with simple detachment. He could not understand why we would wish to live with traffic jams, but his innate sense of grace would forbid him from criticising us.'

The tour worked well from Raoni's point of view because it gave his cause a lot of exposure.

Just a month after returning to his village in the rainforest, many of Raoni's people were under threat from malaria which threatened their existence even more imminently than the destruction of the forest. 'It is appalling news and threatens everything we are trying to do,' a distraught Sting told one news reporter. 'The reports we are getting now are really tragic. It appears the whole village is infected and there have been many deaths.'

It had not gone unnoticed that the Brazilian Government had failed to keep to their promise to help Sting to set up the nature reserve in the forest. Sting denied that he had been exploited by the Brazilian Government. 'I don't think I'm being used at all; if anything, I'm an embarrassment.'

Until the end of 1990, Sting continued to visit Chief Raoni in the jungle and to attend meetings with Brazilian Government officials. 'There are forces in Brazil that don't want the president to help us — obviously, the military being one of them — because they see the jungle as their last vestige of power.' Yet the Rainforest Foundation eventually earned 2.5 million dollars in a single year, and an area the size of Italy was finally protected.

Perhaps surprisingly, Sting still continued to believe that his way was best and he pledged to fight on. 'I'm still, in a sense, a believer in transcendent cures for various problems,' he explains. 'Contemplating your navel will perhaps move the mountain one day. I think people can change one by one. If you work on yourself, you change the world in a microcosmic way — but it's getting a bit late, unfortunately. I feel that with certain issues, like the environment, for example, you have to be active. You can't just sit there with your legs crossed and hope that the air is going to be fit to breathe tomorrow. I think we don't have very long left, frankly.'

In the middle of all this — as if to remind himself and the world that he was still a very active rock 'n' roll star — Sting splashed out two million dollars to buy a New York apartment from fellow singer Billy Joel.

Sting had actually fallen in love with the property after being invited to a party there a few months earlier. Joel — who had been planning to sell the apartment for some time — was delighted when Sting put in the offer. The two-storey flat overlooked Central Park and even had a music room. Joel insisted he was looking for somewhere smaller to live.

However, problems were lurking for Sting. The years of touring and the newfound involvement in the rainforests had sapped him of creative energy. He was so exhausted by the endless travelling and campaigning that he literally dried up.

In retrospect, he blamed himself for what had happened, even confessing that one of the main reasons why he threw himself into so many projects was because he was trying to escape the depression brought on by his parents' deaths.

The friendship Sting had established with Chief Raoni and other members of the Kayapo Indian tribe should have helped him to be even more creative, but heartbreak over his parents' deaths actually sent him spiralling into a long period of mourning.

Sting explained at the time, 'Having lived and spent a lot of time with these so-called primitive people, I realised that death is something that is obviously important to them because they mourn. I figured that I'd have to go through some sort of process where I would get this stuff out. Once I'd worked that out, I realised that I was going to have to write a record about death. I didn't really want to.'

By late 1990 Sting had woken up to the fact that some people in the jungle saw him purely as a meal ticket — an easy way to have some of the luxuries in life that had passed them by. He fully understood that giving lavish presents to the Indians would only make matters worse. 'It's no good making the Indians permanent beneficiaries of endless handouts. That would just destroy their culture and their sense of worth,' was how Sting reacted to one claim that Raoni was trying to take advantage.

The turning point came for Sting when one old man in Raoni's village asked him to buy the Indians a helicopter. Sting turned to Raoni and said: 'You have got to explain why I can't.'

Not long afterwards, it emerged that Raoni himself had even asked

Sting to buy him a plane. The singer was philosophical about it all. 'He's always doing that,' he told writer Hunter Davies. 'One of the other chiefs has one to fly him to São Paulo for Coca-Cola supplies. Indians are the same as whites. I don't see them as noble savages, but they still deserve a chance to protect themselves against so-called progress.'

Sting's close friend Gilda Matoso in Rio said that everyone was 'very amused' by Raoni's attempts to get Sting to buy him an aeroplane. Another friend recalled Sting introducing Raoni to three American businessmen after telling the Indian, 'They'll buy you a plane if you convince them you really need one.'

Said Sting, 'If one had the gift of hindsight, you know, I wonder whether I would have been involved at all in this. We were young, we really didn't know all the ins and outs of it, but we have learned, I think. If we have made mistakes, we have rectified them.'

Sting even forced Jean-Pierre Dutilleux out of the organisation in a row over proceeds from their co-authored book, *Jungle Stories,* which was supposed to help raise funds for the Foundation. JP now admits that he kept his share of the advance for the book, but insisted, 'I am a professional writer. I have to survive. I had to take the advance. We are not all multi-millionaire pop stars like Sting, you know.'

Sting's friend and colleague Carlos Paiva believes that the main reason why the Brazilian branch of the Rainforest Foundation was such a disaster in its early stages was because it was 'set up in such a rush. We announced it before it was ready and that was a huge mistake. People criticised us because other organisations like Greenpeace were so much better organised.'

Carlos says he warned Sting and others that things were not going well. 'I was very concerned. The Foundation was not concentrating enough on raising funds in Brazil. In the end the office here was costing a fortune to run.'

Carlos Paiva says he was 'very hurt' by the attitude of the Brazilian branch of the Foundation, whom he accuses of doing little to justify their salaries to help the rainforest. 'People were starting to be very rude about Sting. It was very hurtful.'

However, Sting steadfastly refused to close down the Foundation and his faith in the crusade did eventually bring about a very worthwhile conclusion.

*   *   *

Sting's close friend Gilda Matoso gave birth to her child on 18 January 1990, just days after yet another flying visit to Rio by Sting and Trudie.

On that occasion, Sting went to the infamous Rio Samba School where he was invited to join in a procession with a tambourine. 'He pulled off his shirt and really let himself go,' recalls Gilda. Three hours later, she had literally to drag Sting out of the school because he wanted to dance all night.

The following afternoon, Trudie and Sting accompanied Gilda to a friend's fifteenth birthday party. Neither the parents nor the child could believe their eyes when Gilda walked in with her celebrity friend. 'They nearly fainted. It's not often an international rock star turns up at a teenager's party.'

However, it was also around this time that the Brazilian press seemed to turn against Sting over his efforts to save the rainforests.

Gilda Matoso says he was very hurt by the criticism. 'He just couldn't understand it. He felt betrayed to a certain extent.'

Meanwhile, Chief Raoni continues to campaign on behalf of his tribe. Jean-Pierre Dutilleux saw him recently in Brasilia where he was lobbying various government officials. 'He was staying in a filthy rundown hotel,' says Dutilleux. 'He could have stayed in a plush hotel, but he would rather sleep on the floor and eat rice and potatoes.'

For Sting, the rainforest campaign was a catharsis, a release from the pain and anguish suffered after the premature death of his parents. If it didn't exactly turn out the way he hoped, then so be it, but overall he believes the campaign achieved a lot.

TWENTY TWO

WRITER'S BLOCK

'The nightmare of success and pressure catches
up with you. It's a nightmare you can't avoid
if you go through what I have been through.'
                                                    - STING

THE GIANT JUMBO JET SUDDENLY PLUNGED out of the sky in a steep
dive, pulled out of it at treetop level and then skimmed across the
countryside, swooping under power lines and bridges. It zoomed
along crowded streets at just above head height, its wingtips mere
inches from buildings on either side of the road. Up front in First
Class, rock superstar Sting braced himself for the inevitable crash.
Then, as usual, he woke up in a cold sweat.

This was yet another version of the anxiety-filled dream that kept
recurring during the mid to late 1980s. The meaning of the dream was
clear to Sting. The plane was the symbol of his rather extraordinary
life plus a subconscious fear that it was out of his control. He just
wished the old, familiar dreams about drugs, sex and rock 'n' roll
would return.

Sting was very worried during this period. He did not write a song
for almost three years between 1987 and 1990. He knew that the

death of his parents had affected him deeply but he still could not come to terms with the fact that he seemed to be suffering from writer's block.

For the first eighteen months after the deaths of Audrey and Ernie he had the excuse of touring with his band. After that, he really started to grow anxious. Here he was, a person who made his money from writing music, and not a single idea had crossed his head in three years.

He started to find it increasingly difficult to sleep and would wake in the middle of the night to find himself obsessed with discovering the cause of his problems. Why wasn't he writing? Was it because he didn't have anything to say? Or maybe he had something to say but was too afraid to say it?

Eventually, Sting sought medical advice and, through analysis, started to reassess his life. He had undergone Jungian dream analysis long before his parents' death and those teachings made him realise the key to his inner turmoil lay in his upbringing and the fact that he could not come to terms with what had happened to his parents. 'When your father dies too early, as mine did, before I really got to know him, it leaves a particularly big gap,' he later admitted.

That gap was only filled when Sting managed to write and produce *The Soul Cages* album. The record became an outlet for his grief. 'I suppose it's a way of mourning. I don't think we really have that in our society any more, and it's a shame,' Sting recalls. 'We tend to look upon death as something we just have to get over as quickly as possible.'

At the time of his parents' death, Sting actually found that the easiest way to cope with losing both of them within one year was to deny it had happened. First of all he did that huge tour and worked himself to a standstill. It was a long time before he woke up one day and realised that he had to deal with it.

Throughout this difficult period in his life, Sting found himself thinking back to the huge ships that used to be constructed at the end of his street when he was a child growing up in Wallsend. 'Growing up in the shadow of a ship gives you a sense that you're destined to be a traveller,' reflected Sting.

He certainly wasn't one of those people who had to look at their astrological chart every morning before deciding what to wear. He had become very cynical and jaundiced about such things since finding fame. However, he did believe there was something in his dreams that was significant and he was convinced that examining his fantasies made his real life seem a little richer.

Sting had grown accustomed to the freedom to travel when and where he liked. In some ways he was a nomadic person. He found it impossible to stay in one place for longer than six weeks and he actually looked forward to those gruelling world tours because they kept him on the move.

Sting's take on the three cities in which he owned property is fascinating.

Los Angeles: 'I find it interesting because I think in many ways it is a city of the future. Certainly in terms of what you might call exaggerated alienation. You're always in cars in LA. You're never on the street. It's very futuristic.'

New York: 'An interesting place artistically because you're thrown together with all different kinds of artists. It's like a big university, where everyone is on top of each other.'

London: 'Everything in London is ghettoised. A painter will never ever meet a poet, a poet will never ever meet a composer. And being working class, I don't have as much social mobility as you might think. Of course, it's my fault, too. I send up the whole thing because I know where I'm from. Every time I go somewhere like the Royal Academy dinner, I keep expecting that any minute someone will grab me by the scruff of the neck and throw me out.'

Sting's next acting role was the on-Broadway part of Macheath in *The Threepenny Opera*. Before it hit New York, the play was performed for an exclusive audience in Washington DC. That first night was attended by US President George Bush and at least forty Secret Service protectors complete with earphones.

'It was a very strange night,' explained Sting afterwards. 'The Secret Service wanted to check my sword-stick, presumably in case I was going to assassinate the President.'

Unfortunately, notorious Broadway theatre critic Frank Rich panned the singer for his performance once the play hit New York. He said of Sting, 'He seems to hope that a large cane and smug, insistent pout will somehow convey the menace of a murderer, rapist, thief and arsonist.'

Rich described Sting as 'a plausible actor in films like *Plenty* and *Stormy Monday* but stiff on stage.' Then he went on, 'How could these scathing songs, forged in the crucible of the century's apocalypse, sound as numbing as they do from the stage?'

Sting was hurt by the criticism but philosophical enough to take it in his stride. He told the London *Daily Mail* theatre critic Jack Tinker, 'I had come here to learn this craft, the craft of acting as opposed to appearing on stage in big rock concerts. But I had to do it in full view of everybody. I've not been allowed to go into rep and I never went to drama school. So I had no alternative. I was famous before I decided to do it.'

He then explained the thinking behind his determination to continue pursuing a serious acting career. 'I structure my life so that if I have two choices where one is sane and the right thing to do, I will invariably do the other. Call me a chancer if you like. One day I'm bound to come a cropper.'

He was also heavily influenced by Trudie when it came to picking new roles. 'She was very instrumental in it. She said: "Before you're forty you should play Mac the Knife." I normally take her word. She's very intuitive and in tune with what I need. You only live once and if you're given an opportunity like this you take it and see if you can pull it off.'

Sting's theatrical career took a serious dive when the classic Brecht-Weill musical of London low-life shut down because of dwindling audiences just two months after opening on Broadway. However, Sting transformed the final performance of the show into his own personal joke. He had grown a sinister-looking moustache for his role as Macheath. When it came time for his jailhouse scene, however, he appeared on stage sporting a face covered in lather. Then, while singing and performing acrobatics from various pipes that served as cell bars, Sting shaved as the actors and audience roared. Afterwards, he ordered a bus to the stage door, piled the cast and crew inside and had them driven to his apartment near Central Park where a huge New Year's Eve party was held and everyone got very merry and forgot all about the disastrous run of the play.

Shortly after that it was announced that Trudie was expecting the couple's third child that summer.

Despite the bravado shown by Sting after *The Threepenny Opera* flop, the singer was actually very depressed by his apparent failure on Broadway, particularly because he was singlehandedly being blamed for the failure of the play. Critics were saying he should stick to singing and give up any of his long-held aspirations to make it big as an actor.

Yet again Sting was trying to stretch himself in another field while, in fact, ninety-five per cent of his ten million-dollars-a-year income came from his musical career. When doctors warned Sting that his punishing schedule was threatening seriously to damage his vocal cords, Miles Copeland stepped in and insisted he take a break from all other activities. Copeland was savvy enough to know the full value of protecting his best investment. He also told Sting in no uncertain terms that there was no way he was going to let him sacrifice his musical career for acting – not yet anyway.

It was yet another example of the continuing influence of Miles Copeland over Sting. After more than ten years together they had actually grown even closer, despite the enormous differences between them in political and social terms. Sting continued to recognise just how valuable Miles' management was to his career. Copeland mapped out every move with military precision and he considered Sting to be at least twenty years off retirement.

For more than a month during his voice problems, Sting was literally banned from talking except when it was entirely necessary. He communicated with most people by passing notes to them and constantly inhaled soothing steam from a vapouriser.

Sting dedicated *The Soul Cages* album to his father — along with two colleagues from *The Threepenny Opera,* director John Dexter and actor Ethyl Eichelberger, both of whom died in 1990, and the album became dominated by imagery drawn from the singer's childhood in Newcastle. 'My relationship with my father was complex and it wasn't resolved. I feel as if something has balanced out now by having done this record. It's the only way I can do it.'

Sting's image as a wild man of rock continued to be watered down on a virtually daily basis. Not only were the fans who attended his concerts looking more and more like self-satisfied yuppies but he seemed to be doing his bit to make himself seem so ... nice.

When he attended a press conference for one record launch, he turned up with his five-year-old cocker spaniel William, dressed like an ad out of *Country Life.*

To fuel the respectable side of rock further, Sting and his band seemed intent on gaining a reputation that was almost defiant in its perverse lack of excess. 'You need vitamins and exercise every day,' insisted Sting. It was like music to the ears of the thirtysomethings lining up to see his concerts.

On tour, the new drug-free, girl-free Sting insisted that his band watch videos of *Fatal Attraction* on the coach going to all concerts 'as a lesson not to get involved with strange women', explains one current member of the Sting crew. 'I think it was also partly Miles Copeland's idea. They made it clear that they did not approve of any of us pulling chicks at gigs.'

Sting even occasionally gently reminded his fellow musicians of their 'obligations as family men'.

The crew member adds, 'In other words, they were warned they'd get fired if they were caught with stray women after any gig. When *Fatal Attraction* was first shown on the tour bus we all laughed but Sting kept a straight face throughout. We realised then that he really did expect us to keep away from any stray females.'

That moral line has been kept up to this day and, as recently as the spring of 1995, *Fatal Attraction* was still being played on Sting's touring buses.

Backstage, Sting's only real vice appeared to be his favourite plaidon-suede pink Gaultier jacket which cost him an impressive eight hundred pounds. 'I prefer to spend my money hiring four of the best musicians in the world,' explained the newly crowned King of the Clean Cut and Sober, 'rather than stick it up my nose and in my arm.'

It was all music to the ears of his newfound yuppie, family-orientated fans.

TWENTY THREE

Family Man

*'The majority of people I come across
in pop are pretty thick. There is no
reality in glamour.'*
                    - TRUDIE STYLER

IN STING'S PICTURESQUE HOUSE IN HIGHGATE, north London, there was a framed *New Yorker* cartoon in the downstairs bathroom which depicts two businessmen calmly chatting at a bar. One says to the other, 'Oh, I'm pretty happy — I just wish my life was more like Sting's.'

The cartoon seemed to encapsulate Sting's vast number of achievements quite neatly, of which his continuing relationship with Trudie was probably the most remarkable feat of all.

'Trudie has changed me. She is a true friend, we are buddies, we hang out together and do things together. She can criticise me without it being fatal to the relationship and I can do the same to her. The first thing that hits people about her is her sense of humour. She is very funny. When I get serious or pretentious she really demolishes me with quips, which is good for me. She is a very funny woman, she is passionate, intelligent and she is a bitch when she has to be.'

Sting had even managed to rebuild a friendship with first wife,

Frances. It was all so *civilised*. 'I worried how the kids would cope with the break-up of our marriage. It used to be something exceptional, but it is now normal that marriages break up,' explains the singer. 'The problems I, my ex-wife, kids and current girlfriend face are not exceptional, but they are problems you have to face up to.

'I am lucky. I have a very good relationship with all my kids and my ex-wife. I think we have done rather well, we are still good friends and we have something very important in common.'

Yet, despite these reassuring words, Sting — typically — could not resist contemplating the unthinkable, just as he had done years before he parted from Frances. He was haunted by what would happen if he and Trudie split up. He even admitted, ominously, 'I don't believe in the idea that if you are in love then it will last forever. I think that is nonsense. I think that romantic love, by definition, cannot last forever. I think there is another kind of love that is more down to earth — a kitchen-sink relationship that comes from sharing responsibilities.

'Saying it won't last forever means having to look at it afresh every day and ask: "What is happening? Do I want it to happen and if I do what do I do to keep it?" I don't think you can rest on your laurels and say we are in love and that is it. I think that if you do that you are heading for a surprise.'

Throughout all this — and despite owning houses on both sides of the Atlantic — Sting was determined to bring up his children in a safe, friendly environment, which meant avoiding America as a full-time base. He confessed his pro-British beliefs when he said, 'I want them to go to English schools and have English accents. I like being English myself.'

Sting's single 'An Englishman In New York' proved his point. The main inspiration for the song had been the eccentric so called 'Queen' of England, Quentin Crisp, whom Sting had first met when they appeared together in *The Bride* four years previously.

Crisp takes up the story in his own inimitable tones:

> *Mr Sting's secretary called me up and asked me if I would go to a certain restaurant on West Broadway and have a meal with Mr*

Sting. It was a nice place and the manager was so impressed to have a star in the place that he gave us the wine on the house.

Then Mr Sting told me he was going to write a song about an exile in New York and it was going to be about me. He then asked me if I would appear in a video that would accompany the song and I agreed, naturally.

It was a bitterly cold day when we filmed it in the middle of New York and Mr Sting kindly let me retreat to his apartment when we were finished. It was a weird place, completely bare except for one cot for their baby. Mr Sting gave me something to eat and I went away contented.

Whether his song was much good musically I would not know. But after I appeared in the video I kept getting letters and parcels from people who wanted me to forward them to Mr Sting but I had no idea where to find him.

I was impressed by Mr Sting because he always looks directly at you and he seems to understand about the world. Mr Sting is a highly aware person who doesn't seem to be basking in his own greatness. There is no film between him and the world.

On the set, he did not interfere with the director and he always ran to work which was most impressive. But he never wanted to pry into my life.

Sting himself was incredibly impressed by Crisp and later described him thus: 'He embodies a feminine ethic that I find very attractive. It's not sexual — but he's very gentle, polite, well-mannered and giving. So although the song is about a man, it is really about feminine power.'

*   *   *

Sting's attitude towards conservation was already renowned throughout the world. However, there were a number of unlikely spin-offs.

He was begged by anti-blood-sports groups in Barcelona, Spain to

243

change his mind about appearing in a Spanish bull ring. He was scheduled to perform at the Plaza Monumental but animal lovers pleaded with him to move the concert to a nearby soccer stadium. One animal rights campaigner commented, 'The mere fact of accepting to perform there seems to be condoning the butchery that is usually carried out on the premises. Somewhere that is usually used for slaughter, torture and slow death of innocent beasts does not seem the most appropriate place for artistic occasions.'

Sting was outraged by the suggestion that he was supporting bull fighting and steadfastly refused to change the venue. 'Just because someone plays a concert in a bull ring, it doesn't mean they are into blood sports,' insisted a spokesman for him.

It was an interesting response because it clearly indicated that Sting's attitude towards the business of touring and making an income was still a high priority.

*   *   *

Sting has another obsession which few people know about and which would certainly surprise his ecologically correct audiences. He has a particular penchant for striptease clubs and topless bars. Whether this is related to Sting's legendary sex drive is not known.

This interest started to come to public attention in the late eighties but the truth was that ever since penning the brilliant 'Roxanne', Sting had retained a fascination for the seedier side of life. There was absolutely no question of him seeking out the sexual services of prostitutes, but he was certainly very interested in studying women of the night just as an artist studies a landscape.

Once, Sting cavorted with a belly dancer in an Athens nightclub along with his great friend Bruce Springsteen when Sting threw a four-hour party at a taverna to celebrate his thirty-seventh birthday. Other guests included singer Peter Gabriel. Miles Copeland, who does not usually attend such functions, looked on with an amused expression as Sting stripped down to a pair of shorts before joining in a smoochy dance with the belly dancer.

Trudie was nowhere to be seen and New York photographer Arnold Grahame commented, 'It was the wildest party I've been to. Sting was dancing like a teenager. Everybody got pretty tipsy.'

As one friend later explained, 'Trudie would have heartily approved. She knows that Sting has a healthy interest in such places. But she trusts him implicitly.'

In fact, Sting *and* Trudie have often visited transvestite and straight clubs in some of the most notorious red-light districts in the world, including those in Paris, London and Rio. 'Sting has never hidden his fascination with that side of life and he has actually encouraged her to go to such places,' says another friend. Sting genuinely believes that prostitutes and strippers are essentially 'good people'. Women fascinate him and he saw no reason to stop being intrigued.

TWENTY FOUR

CONTINUING DRAMAS

'At last I've found my niche in society.
And that is to be a rock star.'
                                    - STING

STING CONTINUED TO EXPERIENCE PROBLEMS with his voice and he began using a humidifier with increasing regularity, even when performing live. One New York *Times* writer was so astonished that he wrote, 'In the olden days, if any sort of haze floated round a singer's head it was incense or marijuana. But mystic enlightenment and old-fashioned mind-altering substances have given way, in our health-conscious decade, to the humidifier.'

Around the same time, following more mind-altering sessions with a psychiatrist in London, Sting admitted to one friend that he was seriously contemplating training to be a Jungian analyst.

When *Rolling Stone* magazine asked him for his reaction to being frequently accused of pretentiousness, he replied, 'What is pretention?'

Then he was asked, 'After all these years, aren't you tired of the name Sting?'

Sting replied in all seriousness, 'It's no sillier than Beethoven or Mozart.'

On a different level, Sting continued to make generous and very personal donations to good causes. He even gave his own treasured saxophone to Mother Theresa's fund for the homeless. He had played it on many of his previous albums but modestly insisted, 'It is just a small gesture which I thought might help keep the ball rolling for a very deserving cause.'

About then, Sting became the target of yet another obsessed girl fan who bombarded him with phone calls. Junkie Elizabeth Griffin, aged twenty-two, even changed her name to Roxanne and adopted the singer's surname of Sumner. It was all very bizarre.

Police finally tracked her down after tracing her phone number and officers raided her flat in Exeter, Devon and seized a diary which contained the star's personal telephone number.

Roxanne insisted, 'All I can think of is him. I can't even sleep because of him. He has taken over my life. I've got four of his phone numbers, but he's never there when I call — and I phone him all the time. He's a rotten pig for not speaking to me. Now I don't want to see him face to face — I'd want to kill him for making me like this. I've even had trouble from my family because of him, and I blame him for everything. People think I'm crazy, but I'm not. This is like a nightmare and I just wish I could get him out of my mind.'

The Roxanne situation perfectly illustrated the sort of problems Sting faced as a celebrity. He had always been reluctant to use bodyguards but on occasion they had become an inevitable part of his life. Threats from love-crazed female fans were one thing, but when threats against Sting's children were received it had the knock-on effect of forcing the singer to hire bodyguards to escort his children to and from school.

In 1990, a number of notes arrived at Miles Copeland's IRS Records office in London, warning that there were plans to kidnap one of Sting's children. That was when Sting and Trudie first considered moving out of London because Trudie felt it would get the family further away from the problems of the city and those types of threats.

The notes talked about plans to 'slice the kids up one by one' and at one stage Sting was so worried about his family that he moved them into a hotel. The singer became convinced that their Highgate house was being watched and he feared that the children could be snatched at any time.

In the end nothing happened but both Sting and Trudie were badly shaken by the threats and Trudie decided that she would continue pressing Sting to consider living in the country.

On a more traditional rock star level, Sting then got himself embroiled in a rather juvenile row with fellow singer Rod Stewart.

It all started when Sting boarded a plane in America, which had been hired by Stewart the day before. He sat down and found a message carved on a table. It read: 'Where's your sense of humour you miserable git Sting [sic].'

One of the stewardesses aboard the private jet even admitted to Sting that Stewart had carved the message. Sting was astonished that Stewart would bother to be so childish and decided that he had to do something to get his revenge.

When he returned to Los Angeles later that same week, Sting drove over to Stewart's Beverly Hills mansion and chained up the electronic gates at his house so that they wouldn't open. Security guards waving pistols then ordered him to leave the premises.

Stewart called up Sting's agent the next day to complain. In an attempt to diffuse the situation, Sting eventually sent Rod and his girlfriend a bunch of flowers.

Sting spent a lot of time in California at this point. At one stage the British tabloids even claimed that he had split up from Trudie because he wanted more freedom. One report insisted that Trudie had given Sting an ultimatum to: 'Stay at home or we are finished.' It went on to claim that the couple were living apart but there has never been any evidence that the report was accurate and Sting was soon seen in Trudie's company again.

Back in London, Sting's former wife Frances spoke openly for the first time about the problems that were associated with being married to Sting. It had been many years since their marriage fell apart, but only now was Frances prepared even to refer to Sting openly. She was convinced that she lost some major acting roles because she preferred to stay at home and look after the couple's children, Joseph and Kate. 'It has broken my heart rejecting major parts. But it is my choice to be with them. I have to spend some time away, but I limit it as much as possible and only accept roles that fit in with my plans,' she said.

Although Sting and Frances had long since buried the hatchet, she still refused to mention Sting by his name. 'I have a good relationship with him and the children see quite a lot of him and they also spend holidays together,' she said.

*   *   *

As the 1980s came to a close and Thatcherism faded, attitudes towards the mega-rich heroes of yuppydom began to change and Sting became a popular target for social commentators who saw him as a classic 1980s' icon.

Julie Burchill, writing in the *Mail on Sunday*, launched into the singer on the basis that he was too clean living and accused him of making rock music 'too safe and bland'.

She wrote,

> *It is basically just junior league entertainment, after all, and for all its sound and fury can only ever have a pacifying effect, diverting young energy from more important issues.*
>
> *Sting doesn't seem able to grasp this fact of life, however; that pop is a playpen for the self-indulgent children of the West to make a racket in.*
>
> *Dangerous? When was a pop star dangerous, pray? When that fat joker Elvis was waggling his meaty hips in one's face? When The Beatles wanted to hold your hand?*
>
> *When The Police were releasing such rabble-rousing gems as 'De Do Do Do, De Da Da Da?'*
>
> *Phooey.*
>
> *As the decade ends with young people dying in the name*

of real revolutions, perhaps — just as a mark of respect —
we can bury, once and for all, the spoilt, selfish and
unimpeachably safe fantasy of Western pop rebellion.

Interestingly, Sting's response to such criticism was to admit to friends that he was growing a little bored with all the campaigning on behalf of the seemingly endless litany of rock-star causes — and he insisted he would not be writing any songs about the plight of his friends in the Brazilian jungle.

'I've never considered whether I want to sing about this issue. I'm a little bored with the idea of singing for causes,' he said. 'I don't want to be involved in politics. But I sometimes like the chess aspect of it. But I'm a dreamer, a Utopian, I would be no good at full-time politics. And it's exhausting, exhausting.'

The other disturbing problem Sting faced as the decade came to a close was a distinct feeling that he was being heavily overexposed thanks to his multi-talented efforts in singing, acting and good causes.

When America's cable TV network *Home Box Office* presented 'Sting in Tokyo' there was something of a backlash, with low ratings for the programme. One critic even wrote, 'The British blond with the pointed face, the social conscience and the serious, somewhat aristocratic approach to rock 'n' roll has been a familiar figure these last couple of years — on the concert trail, on TV awards shows, on video specials, on the Amnesty tour. Good as some of his music is, there's probably a saturation level out there somewhere. If you like Sting, and you can't get enough, this is a good straight ahead portrait of the artist in 1989. If you want a rest, this is a good time to take it.'

Meanwhile, Sting was using the vast New York apartment he had bought from Billy Joel more and more. Trudie was even spotted in the Big Apple's equivalent to Harrods, Bloomingdale's, on a shopping spree. She picked up twelve sets of sterling silver cutlery at three hundred and fifty dollars each set and then bought twelve goose down pillows at two hundred and fifty dollars a pop.

Another interesting friendship that developed for Sting in the late 1980s was with Italian fashion designer Gianni Versace. Not only did the heavyweight clothes guru fly in to see Sting's first night in *The Threepenny Opera,* he also threw a tea party especially for Sting at the elegant New York East Side townhouse of noted interior designer Suzie Frankfurt.

The families of Sting and Versace got along well. He visited Versace's vast country home in northern Italy and was so impressed that he began taking regular holidays in the same region.

By the middle of April 1990, rumours were rife that a large part of the hundreds of thousands of pounds raised by Sting's Foundation to help save the rainforests had been spent on administrative costs. British investigative TV programme *World In Action* set about an exposé of what they thought was wrong with Sting's Rainforest Foundation.

Welfare experts criticised Sting for 'naïvely' barging into a complex situation. 'On balance, it has not been helpful to the cause of the Indians at all,' commented Stephen Corry of rainforest campaigners Survival International in April 1990.

Sting and his fellow Rainforest Foundation Trustees were incensed at what they regarded as the blatant inaccuracies of the *World In Action* programme. The TV programme suggested that Chief Raoni was living in a run-down hostel virtually penniless and that the Rainforest Foundation had abandoned Raoni and his villagers to the ravages of malaria. In fact, when visiting Brasilia to lobby the Brazilian Government, Raoni chose to stay with his fellow Indians at the hostel provided for the Indians by the Brazilian Government — not at the hotels offered by the Brazilian Rainforest Foundation. Rather than having abandoned Raoni and his tribe to their malaria-infested village, the Rainforest Foundation was in the process of organising and paying for the move of Raoni's village to a malaria-free area. That move had been delayed because of the rainy season and the need to deter malaria-infected villagers from moving to the new village and perpetuating the malaria problem.

World In Action's picture of Raoni lying in a hospital bed, apparently suffering from malaria, made Sting choke. Raoni was in hospital having an operation on an arthritic knee — in a private room paid for by Sting.

Sting and his co-Trustees sought legal advice from an eminent libel QC. He advised them that the *World In Action* programme was defamatory. The time and cost involved in fighting a libel action was enormous. Could the Foundation afford this during these embryonic days? Sting's view prevailed — if the Rainforest Foundation did not achieve the rainforest demarcation they had set out to achieve, maybe the *World In Action* criticism (if not the detail) was right. Conversely, if the demarcation was to be achieved, this would put paid to the constant sniping of the disbelievers and prove *World In Action* wrong. Sting's advice was followed. All efforts were concentrated on achieving the demarcation which was achieved, but after many years of effort and problems.

In August 1990 Sting's fifth child, daughter Eliot Paulina, was born while the couple were staying at a vast villa near Pisa, in Italy. They were paying twenty-five thousand pounds a month to rent the property which was once Duke Forese Salviati's palace. The villa is often used by the Queen Mother and Prince Charles.

The new baby was named after an old black woman whom Sting had met in Barbados. To the family, however, she became known as Coco from the moment she was born.

The couple were in fine spirits when they arrived at Pisa register office to record the baby's name. When asked what she would be called, Sting replied, 'What about Schillaci?' after the star of that year's Italian World Cup.

Sting's humour was only slightly dampened when his request for dual citizenship for the child was turned down by the clerk because neither parent was Italian.

Still the question of marriage to Trudie seemed to be ignored. Sting told one journalist who dared to ask, 'I don't see any reason to get married. I don't need to be ratified by the church and the government.'

In November 1990 it was claimed that he had asked for one million pounds to record one song for a new coffee advertisement to appear on British television. The star's agent told executives at advertising agency Duckworth Finn Grubb Waters that Sting wanted payment in advance. 'We were staggered. I can only assume that he didn't really want to do it and suggested a ridiculous figure to put us off,' explained agency account director Susie Galbraith.

The constant knocking got to Sting so badly around this time that he called in a Chinese mystic to help him. Michael Tse stayed for two nights at Sting's New York apartment and the two men practised the ancient art of Qigong to help him to relax more.

During the three-hour sessions, Tse would stand behind Sting and transmit relaxing energies to him. Then they would go through an exercise routine called The Wild Goose, when Sting would move like an animal.

Tse had been flown over specially from Manchester to help Sting to shake off his bleak moods. 'He was a good pupil who tried to learn hard,' commented Tse who was introduced to Sting by Trudie who had also attended sessions with him in the past.

Shortly after this, Sting proved that he had put his earlier fears about stalkers behind him when he astonished holidaymakers by travelling back from a holiday in Italy in a crowded package holiday flight.

Without even a pair of sunglasses to shield them from the *hoi polloi*, the couple, plus daughter Mickey, aged seven, Jake, aged five, and baby daughter Coco, at seven months, braved a British Rail ride back to Victoria Station in London before hopping in a black taxi to go to their home in north London.

Back on the rainforest campaign trail, Sting remained determined not to fail, despite all the setbacks.

Brazilian President Fernando Collor de Mello finally agreed to give protected status to an area two-thirds the size of Italy, the homeland of the two thousand Kayapo Indians whose cause Sting had championed for so long.

Sting heard the news just as he was about to start a series of concerts at London's Wembley arena. He said it was a victory 'for everyone who cares about human rights and the environment'. He hailed it as a historic act. 'Brazil is setting an example for the world. Now we have to do all we can to help to ensure the decisions become reality.' The new park would cover seventy thousand square miles around the River Xingu. By any account, that achievement of the Rainforest Foundation was considerable, although it was never widely publicised.

Meanwhile, Trudie's career was reviving at quite a pace. To the amazement of Sting, she agreed to star in a small budget Italian film called *Mamba*, a creepy crawlie suspense drama which centred on a deadly game of hide and seek with Trudie's most dreaded enemy — a snake.

Then she managed to fit in appearances in *Miss Marple* and a Kelly Monteith comedy series as well as in a West End stage play. There was also a Channel Four series called *Head Girl*. 'I was really just ticking over. Now I feel as if I have turned the corner,' she said.

On the charitable front, Sting delighted the Music Therapy Foundation by giving them his favourite car to auction — a recently restored MGB GT.

Sting was determined to do good in the world. No one would make him back down from his pilgrimages.

TWENTY FIVE

BAND WITH NO NAME

*'Rock is old now. You can't get the thirty-five year-olds
who come to our shows into a state of hysteria.
We are entertaining people who are not going
to become hysterical.'*

- STING

STING'S TWO SPRINGER SPANIELS, William and his brother Hector, careered down the road ahead of their master, barking wildly, delighted to be liberated from the house. Everyone said Willie was like his master, a free spirit who had to have his way the whole time. When the family vet said that the dog should be doctored, Sting refused on the principle that he wouldn't want the same thing done to himself.

On that blustery day, Sting was just as pleased as his two dogs to be outdoors. Wearing his favourite brown suede jacket, brown suede shoes and black jeans, the stubbled outline of a beard along his cheeks, he walked at a brisk pace, relishing the cold afternoon air and the physical movement.

Back at the house Trudie, their three children and one of his two children from his marriage to Frances were preparing tea. The house sat only slightly back from a very busy street, with houses right next to it on either side, including one that had belonged to Samuel Taylor Coleridge, the poet and critic who had blazed the trail for the British Romantic movement two centuries earlier.

Outside Sting's front door on that cold blustery day lay the familiar urban world of traffic, honking horns, construction sites, pedestrians and pets. Around the corner and a few blocks down a hilly street, however, lay Hampstead Heath, a rolling, verdant landscape ribboned with walking paths. The balance of country and city suited Sting perfectly.

As Sting walked on to the common that day he had every reason to feel happy. At last the demons that had haunted him for most of his life seemed to have been exorcised. He actually felt content with his lot for the first time ever. He had become the pop idol adults could admire yet he still had an uncanny ability to acknowledge the perception of his life and even mock himself to a degree.

An hour later, Sting came back to the house, started a huge log fire in his den and sat down on the ragged sofa in front of the fireplace. It was only mid-afternoon, but the grey sky outside was already beginning to darken, deepening the shadows that took shape along the room's dark, wood-panelled walls. Sting, drinking his favourite concoction of tea and honey, which helped to sooth his vocal cords, had life in the palm of his hand.

In just another eight weeks he was scheduled to embark on yet another globe-trotting adventure. This time, he was going to head up a tough, streamlined, four-piece band featuring Kenny Kirkland on keyboards, Dominic Millar on lead guitar and Vinny Colaitua on drums. First of all they intended to whip themselves into shape by performing in small clubs in San Francisco, Los Angeles, Chicago and New York before hitting the big arenas.

Unlike many rock stars of his age, Sting harboured no fears about his ability to carry his music with some measure of decorum into the future. Sting firmly believed there was a way of getting older and still being a performer without embarrassing yourself. 'It's the gang thing,' he says. 'You don't have to be in a gang when you are an adult. You can be on your own. And that's why I'm not in a band.'

Sting's immense inner confidence had allowed him to try all sorts of different things. But now, as he coasted into the 1990s, he knew that he had to start to pace himself more carefully. 'I've tried very consciously to break the mould, to do things that rock stars don't normally do or aspire to. Of course, you end up being called pretentious. I'm not pretentious. I'm just willing to take a lot of risks, to the extent where I don't mind being ridiculed and I don't mind failing, because I think the process of trying to burst out of the stereotype is worth doing. I don't really think that people know what to expect from me ...'

Sting concerts were becoming low-key, respectable reviews rather than good old rock'n'roll coverage. On stage, he had widened his scope considerably, even including such material as Jimi Hendrix's 'Purple Haze', much to the surprise of his mainly middle-brow, middle-class audience. However, he still continued to provide every audience with its fare share of Police classics and some critics reckoned that was the riskiest part of his act.

As Adam Sweeting wrote in *The Guardian*, 'The chief problem of revisiting The Police material is that it's much better than his later stuff, basically, featuring unforgettable hooks and crafty manipulation ...'

Sting's knack of attracting respectable followers was quite remarkable. When Sir Michael Tippet, one of Britain's leading composers, was a guest on the radio programme *Desert Island Discs,* he included Sting's 'So Lonely'. Sting later commented sheepishly, 'God knows why. Harmonically it's very simple.'

Around this time, Sting made a highly emotional trip back to Newcastle to appear in a special jamming session at the Buddle Arts Centre. It was a clandestine operation, carried out in the utmost secrecy. Last Exit drummer Ronnie Pearson takes up the story: 'Someone rang me late one night and said that Sting wanted me to play that Friday night with Last Exit. I was gobsmacked and delighted.'

Sting turned up at the small arts centre with his three regular band members and they did about an hour before the original members of

Last Exit came on and did two tunes. 'It brought the house down,' explains Ronnie Pearson.

The group came back for an encore that got an even more rapturous round of applause. 'No one was the slightest bit fazed by it,' explains Ronnie. 'I hardly noticed all the missing years. We all seemed to gel so well. It was marvellous.'

Afterwards, Sting and his entourage accompanied the Last Exit members back to his suite at the Gosforth Park Hotel in Newcastle and they sat down, supped beers and discussed old times. 'No other pop star would do that,' says Ronnie. 'It was like old times and I'll never forget it as long as I live.'

It was only afterwards, back at the hotel, that anyone had the courage to ask their one-time musical partner why the concert had been organised in the first place.

Sting's explanation was painfully simple. 'I had this daft idea and I came up with it and all of a sudden someone had arranged it for me.'

Such is the way when you are a multi-millionaire rock'n'roll star.

The singer was guesting for Little Mo's Blues Band, fronted by Sting's old mate Gerry Richardson. Earlier that afternoon, Sting had got back to his hotel suite in Newcastle to find Gerry's van pulling up outside. He immediately said hello and started helping him to haul his gear into the ballroom, where they talked a bit, just like old times.

Now it just so happened that that same day the annual dinner dance of the local architects' association was about to settle into the hotel ballroom when someone spotted him. 'Ooooh! It's Sting!' bellowed one woman. 'It really is!'

Strapping on a borrowed bass, smiling with perhaps just a hint of embarrassment, Sting let out a brisk, 'One, two' and plunged into a fervently chaotic rendering of 'Every Breath You Take'. There was no stage, not even a platform. Men and women fell into line, gawped at the superstar in front of their very eyes and urged anyone with a camera to snap away.

Sting howled a final chorus in the general direction of the tune, then ducked away from outstretched hands bearing pens for autographs and dived through a side door.

Back in the hotel dining room with family and friends, his absence had barely been noticed.

Sting was back in Newcastle. If the return to his birthplace made for ambivalent feelings for the singer, it certainly made for good TV. Two crews from Britain and France followed him everywhere the next day.

Trudie joined Sting to provide some sort of emotional support system against the pressures of the media and the personal anguish that might be sparked by 'coming home' to all those mixed memories and emotions.

However, there were some lighter moments as Sting showed the camera crews around his old haunts. At one point, they tiptoed through a grimy tunnel under a railway line and Trudie delicately inquired, 'Is this where you shagged girls?'

'I wish,' came the reply before Sting started necking with Trudie as if to prove that he had no need to shag anyone other than her.

Then Sting plunged into his very mixed emotions about Newcastle. 'I still have a love–hate relationship with Newcastle. It wasn't a great place to grow up in. What did we have? There certainly wasn't any work. I wanted to get the fuck out and I was given the means to escape: by education, by having some sort of talent. And, also, by having the desire to leave.'

The following day, Sting rolled up to his brother Phil's beachside bar in Tynemouth for the sake of the TV cameras.

The tensions between the brothers had disappeared many years earlier. In front of the cameras, Phil produced an old acoustic guitar — Sting's first, apparently. He pointed out the screws their father had used to repair the instrument after their mother had smashed it over Sting's head to stop him from pummelling Phil during an argument.

That trip to Newcastle left Sting once again pondering about things. In particular, it made him examine his own behaviour as a father. 'It's only when you have children and you look in the mirror and you start to see your parents in your own physical features that you think, "Yeah, I can understand that person, I can love them despite all the mistakes we both made." I was just coming round to that when my father died. And then it was too late. But, in some way, my father has now been mourned. And I feel he appreciates it, appreciates the effort.'

One person who did not see Sting during his prodigal's return to Newcastle was Last Exit guitarist Terry Ellis. He was extremely hurt that he was not included in the Buddle Arts Centre concert. He explains, 'The first I knew about it was when I read about it in the paper. It was very hurtful. For some reason I was overlooked.'

*   *   *

'Life is like a two-week holiday. And when you reach forty you're in the second week.' That grim joke was a favourite of Andy Summers and almost ten years after the demise of The Police, he joined Sting on stage at the Hollywood Bowl in Los Angeles to celebrate Sting's fortieth birthday in front of more than ten thousand fans. A vast firework display, in the centre of which the number forty sparkled and exploded, heralded the end of the show on 2 October 1991.

Behind the smiles, however, Andy Summers was surprised because Miles had him sign a contract before allowing him to go on stage with Sting. Typically, Miles had had a document specially drawn up which prevented Summers from having any rights over his own performance. But he signed and the show went on.

A&M record owners Herb Alpert and Jerry Moss gave Sting a 1971 vintage Riva speedboat built in Italy. They estimated he had sold more than two hundred million units (records, tapes and CDs) in his thirteen years on the label.

A birthday party held at the A&M studios following that sell-out concert was attended by Jackson Browne, Don Henley, Rosanna Arquette, Bob Dylan and Herbie Hancock.

The party was meant as a surprise for Sting. Planned for weeks by Trudie and senior staff at A&M Records, it was, by Los Angeles standards, modest. Invitations were dispatched in bottles, though not all those who received these messages understood the reference to the Police song.

Held on a sound-stage behind the record company's Sunset

Boulevard offices, the party was dominated by obscure speeches in praise of Sting, including the presentation by Jerry Moss of a photograph of the speedboat the company had bought him.

Then two very odd things happened. A video tape of Pavarotti was aired in which he wished Sting the best for his birthday and turned his congratulations into a serenade that went on and on. Then, as people finished shuffling their feet, Little Nell, the New York nightclub queen, appeared beside the video screen to deliver an only slightly more effective rap burlesque summation of Sting's career.

Pavarotti's involvement was no great surprise. Earlier that year, Sting had collaborated with Italian conductor Claudio Abbado and the Chamber Orchestra of Europe on a new recording of Prokofiev's *Peter and the Wolf* for Deutsche Grammophon, a major classical label.

Sting was particularly proud of his fortieth birthday, even though many people in his position would probably not have wanted the public fanfare. 'As I happened to be doing a show that night, why should I pretend that it's not a celebration of some kind?'

The party also included a video of the singer's five children doing a Hawaiian rock-a-hula birthday tribute.

The day after the party, Sting found himself looking through the pages of the latest issue of *Country Life* magazine when he spotted a vast mansion for sale in Wiltshire, called Lake House. He was captivated by the look of the place.

A few hours later, his trusted accountant Keith Moore and his girlfriend Santos Banger turned up at the house to discuss certain financial matters including the renegotiation of Sting's contract with A&M Records, which had successfully — and lucratively — been completed by Miles Copeland to the tune of sixteen million pounds for four albums, a remarkable deal. It was at this time that Keith Moore re-directed, for his own tax liabilities and without Sting's knowledge, a £691,000 banker's draft payable to "Inland Revenue re G M Sumner", which Sting had intended for payment of his own tax liabilities. This theft was at a time when Sting was already paying Moore the not inconsiderable sum of eight hundred thousand pounds a year in fees to be his accountant.

Moore had previously been investigated by his own professional disciplinary body and found guilty of professional misconduct over the financial affairs of both Queen and Big Country, albeit for relatively minor breaches of professional standards.

In 1977, Queen dismissed Moore, alleging Moore had invested some of the band's money in bars and restaurants without their knowledge. Seven years later, Big Country discovered that their earnings were almost inaccessible in the complex web of accounts created by Moore.

Warning signs were there even earlier when Moore was declared bankrupt in 1975, owing millions of pounds to clients, although this did not become public knowledge until after the Keith Moore fraud against Sting had been investigated. Moore specialised in setting up accounts which, according to Big Country singer Stuart Adamson, 'made it very difficult to access our money'. He explained, 'Eventually, the accounts became a maze that only he had the keys for. He had onshore and offshore companies, publishing ones, companies you buy socks from. It was almost impossible to know where our money was.'

Big Country nipped Moore in the bud by firing him in 1986 but they were forced to take him to the High Court to make him return all their financial statements, even though Moore claimed outstanding fees were owed.

Both groups lodged complaints with the Institute of Chartered Accountants and Moore was removed from the register of members for a brief time.

The simple fact was that Sting trusted Keith Moore. Moore appeared efficient at his tasks and was sensitive to Sting's need to concentrate on his career, avoiding the financial complexities which had mushroomed around his enormous worldwide success. Moore had acted for Sting since the late 1970s. As far as Sting and Miles Copeland were concerned, neither Keith Moore nor Miles touched Sting's money. It was all paid into bank accounts controlled solely by Sting and Trudie. At least, that was the theory. They had not reckoned on Keith Moore proving to be not only clever at his legitimate work for Sting but even more clever in deceiving Sting and his various bankers out of over seven million pounds over a five-year period. Moore took the money from various bank accounts a couple of hundred thousand pounds at a time, with Moore making a careful point of misleading Sting into believing only Sting and Trudie controlled the monies.

Back in California in 1991, following Sting's birthday party, Moore found himself being taken for a walk on the beach by Sting, still holding that copy of *Country Life*.

Out on the edge of the Pacific Ocean, Sting was pointing to the ad for Lake House, 'That is the house I want,' he told his trusted accountant.

Moore hesitated for a moment, fully aware that he had had similar conversations with Sting in the past. At one time an estate in Scotland had almost been purchased, with Sting pulling out at the last moment because it had too much land around it to maintain.

This time Sting was serious. After uncovering the kidnap plot against their children, Trudie had made him promise that if he could find the right place he would move his family to the countryside. A few days later, Moore started negotiations to buy the property, even though Sting had never even been to see it.

Before he flew back to Britain, however, Moore got a snappy phone call from Trudie at his suite at the Beverly Hills Hotel. She was furious because the accountant had dared to inform Sting during their earlier meeting that he felt the one hundred and fifty thousand pounds a year that Trudie spent on clothes was 'rather excessive'.

'You don't understand,' fumed Trudie. 'I have to buy him all his clothes as well because he won't get anything himself.'

Moore listened and said little in response. One time Trudie had forgotten to forward her credit card bills to the accountant for him to organise payment and, as a result, had had her card rejected whilst shopping at Harrods. On that occasion, Moore was obliged to fax Harrods a letter assuring them that the items would be paid for.

In 1992 Sting received an honorary doctorate of music from the

University of Northumbria in his home town of Newcastle. Proudly watched by Trudie, he was handed his certificate by the Vice-Chancellor, Lord Glenamara, in recognition of his contribution to the arts and his campaigning on ecological issues.

Sting was understandably delighted and told one reporter after the ceremony, 'Businessmen and captains of industry get them but people like me generate just as much money as other industries.'

On the same day, the university also awarded an honorary fellowship to Sunderland Football Club for its role in the community.

In January 1992 Sting, the man of property, finalised the purchase of Lake House for more than two million pounds. His country retreat consisted of fourteen bedrooms, eight bathrooms and magnificent grounds on the banks of the River Avon in Wiltshire. The deal was carried out in such secrecy that the house was purchased under the name of Gradecode Limited, one of Sting's many holding companies.

Lake House also had an oak-panelled drawing room with an elegant marble fireplace, two dining rooms — one with panels dating back to 1633 — a library, kitchens and vast cellars. On the top floor was a self-contained, four-bedroomed flat and staff quarters. In the grounds there were two cottages, two apartments, garages, a boathouse, water garden, swimming pool, tennis court, paddocks and woodland.

The Wiltshire mansion was built by George Duke and occupied by his descendents for more than three hundred and twenty years. Then, in 1912, a huge fire destroyed much of the property. At the time it was the home of Percy Illingworth MP and Liberal whip, his wife, children and ten servants.

The house, near Amesbury, was purchased just two months before Sting completed his world tour. Perhaps surprisingly, some of the longest-standing locals welcomed the arrival of the singer with open arms.

Retired war hero Brigadier Michael Blackman OBE, aged seventy-six, lost his home, as the sale was with vacant possession, having been a tenant for twenty-four years. However, after meeting Sting and Trudie, even he commented, 'I thought he was a very pleasant, rather quiet young man. I do not think he will upset things. He was looking for a family place to get some peace and quiet.' Sting had decided also to keep on his London house so that the family could still stay there whenever they were in town.

Shortly after purchasing the house, Trudie travelled back to Brazil to work on a TV documentary about Rio transvestites, entitled *Boys From Brazil.*

The programme told the story of two transvestites, Luciana and Samira. They were born men but dress as women and regard themselves as a third sex.

Producer Trudie openly admitted that she found them hell to work with — sordid, feckless and suffering from perpetual premenstrual moodiness due to the female hormones they took to give them breasts and smooth skin.

Trudie's programme received some unwanted publicity from the London tabloid *The Sun,* which exposed the shocking truth about how she and her production team provided a one hundred pound facility fee to a black magic cult so that an innocent goat could be sacrificed in front of the cameras as part of their documentary.

'STING'S WIFE FUNDS GOAT SACRIFICE WITH BBC CASH' ran the headline. Trudie admitted, 'They're used to that. Chickens, goats — anything to get the programme made.' Not surprisingly, the 'scandal' proved to be a complete storm in a teacup.

During the shooting of *Boys From Brazil*, Trudie 'adopted' a little street orphan who followed her and the film crew everywhere they went. 'At the end of the shoot, the little girl gave Trudie a ring and she burst into tears. It was heartbreaking.'

*　　　*　　　*

A short time after starting at his new local school in Wiltshire, Sting's son Jake was diagnosed as having dyslexia.

Then Jake's schoolmates convinced him that he was adopted because his parents weren't married. The moment Sting heard about it, he decided it was time to grow up and settle down. He explained, 'The idea of having to get married was really quite alien. But the kids would come home from school and say, "Are you two married? We'd feel better if you were married because then you'd stay together." It was gradually wearing us down. So we started to plan a wedding.'

Back in Brazil working on her documentary, Trudie was so excited when Sting told her that he wanted to get married that she immediately told all her close friends in Rio.

'It's going to be the wedding of the century,' she exclaimed. 'We're going to have the best of everything and I'm going to get a dress fit for a queen.'

Trudie's friends had no doubt she meant every word.

TWENTY SIX

THE WEDDING

'I'd rather be Frank Sinatra than Ozzy Osbourne.'

– STING

ON 21 AUGUST 1992, STING FINALLY MARRIED Trudie in a brief ceremony at Camden Register Office near their north London home. The ceremony couldn't have been further removed from a royal wedding. The casually dressed couple were accompanied by just two friends acting as witnesses in the fifteen-minute ceremony at Camden Town Hall.

Marriage superintendent Sue Bloom described it as 'a lovely ceremony and very low key which was just what they wanted'. After a small champagne celebration at their Highgate home, they headed for the new country mansion in Wiltshire, where a big blast was scheduled for the following Saturday. It was to be a vast wedding party attended by some of the most famous figures in the entertainment industry. That was going to be Trudie's big day.

That Saturday the union was blessed at the nearby nine-hundred-year-old St Andrew's church in Great Dunford. Both bride and groom were dressed head-to-toe in Versace. All five of Sting's children acted as attendants.

Trudie wore an extravagant hand-beaded creation in ivory satin with a crinoline-skirted ballgown and matching bolero bodice which had taken Versace five months to make, indicating just how long the marriage plans had been in the pipeline. The dress was said to have cost a hundred thousand dollars and also consisted of six underskirts and two silk overskirts.

Sting wore a Beau Brummel-style ensemble that had been specifically designed in order to emphasise his athletic torso, with its classic tailcoat nipped in at the waist and cut away to reveal matching skintight trousers, striped waistcoat and stock tied high at the neck. Both outfits were later auctioned for charity and proceeds from the sale went towards saving the world's endangered rainforests.

More than two hundred and fifty guests crowded into the picturesque St Andrew's Church, including Bob Geldof, Paula Yates, Peter Gabriel, Charlotte Rampling, Meg Ryan, Pamela Stephenson, Billy Connolly and a host of other celebrities.

Guest Deborah Cohen sums it up, 'It was wonderful. It was so over the top.'

When Trudie mounted a horse to ride back to the house from the church, the horse nearly buckled because of the enormous weight of the dress.

As the guests returned to the mansion via a fleet of rented limousines, they were ushered to an enormous tent. Music was provided by The Troggs on a specially built stage. As the hundreds of guests lined up to meet the bride and groom, the MC announced, 'Ladies and gentlemen, Mr and Mrs Gordon Sumner will now receive your congratulations if you would be so kind as to line up and present yourselves.'

Another guest recalls, 'We were all sniggering about that. It all seemed so formal but that also made it kinda sweet.'

The most significant wedding present given to the couple was a fifty thousand pound Jaguar XJS, paid for by accountant Keith Moore and co-manager Kim Turner. It sat in the driveway with a huge red bow tied around it. Miles gave the couple a more modest four-poster bed.

However, it wasn't until about ten o'clock that night when the fun at the wedding really started.

The stuffier showbiz VIPs had gone and there were just close family and friends left. 'We all got good and sloshed and people got thrown in the swimming pool and lots of naughty things happened.'

Those 'naughty things' included a lot of guests swimming naked in the pool and two couples being found making love in a secluded area of the garden, much to the amusement of many of those present. 'Anything seemed to go that night,' explains one guest. 'It was like a throw back to the good old days of rock'n'roll.'

Among those who stayed late were Stewart Copeland, Andy Summers and Peter Gabriel. At about 11 p.m. Deborah Cohen noticed Sting in a huddle with the other three near the stage. Minutes later, The Police were reunited with a little help from Peter Gabriel and Sting's six-year-old son Jake, whose favourite song happened to be 'Rock Around The Clock'. Charlotte Rampling's teenage son Barnaby also joined in.

A guest recalls, 'It was everyone's deepest desire that The Police should reunite for the night but they were so sloshed that they didn't exactly put on their best performance.'

Many of the guests were particularly taken aback by the appearance of Andy Summers who was well into his fifties yet looked about thirty-five. One guest explains, 'He looked as if he'd had a facelift. In fact he looked younger than he was when he played with The Police. It was weird.'

Sting rather put the dampers on the event by later insisting he did not enjoy it. 'But we had to do it. We got up and we hadn't rehearsed or planned anything and we started with 'Message In A Bottle' and Andy starts the riff, he can just about remember it, and Stewart immediately starts fucking speeding up, as usual, as fucking usual, so I turn around and ten years just suddenly evaporate and there I am glowering at Stewart and he's glowering at me and Andy's fumbling with the chords and suddenly it had all come back and Stewart and I immediately caught each other doing it and started to laugh. It was 'very funny. It was actually a very warm moment. That tension was back immediately. People said that the atmosphere was electric watching it.'

Many of Sting's old mates from the North East attended the wedding, even though his one-time writing partner Gerry Richardson did not show up and has never explained why he snubbed the ceremony. 'I don't want to talk about Sting in any way, shape or form,' is all he will say today.

However, Last Exit drummer Ronnie Pearson made it and found himself on one of the guest of honour tables sitting alongside some of Sting's family members and three of the singer's old school pals. 'Nobody knew who the hell we were but they all wondered when Sting spent more time talking with us than anyone else at the wedding,' recalls a proud Ronnie, who was one of the few guests present who had also attended Sting's first wedding, to Frances, sixteen years earlier.

Ronnie was recently very touched when Sting sent him some signed CDs of his latest album after hearing that Ronnie's collection of records had been lost in a fire at his home in Newcastle. 'That's typical of the man. He always remembers his friends.'

The hard core of guests at the wedding stayed until five or six the next morning. And one explains, 'There was a lot of smooching on the dance floor besides excessive consumption of alcohol.'

Next day, all those guests who were staying in nearby hotels and inns were ferried back to Lake House by limousine for a barbecue. Deborah Cohen explains, 'It was freezing cold and raining. People had umbrellas around the pool and everyone was very, very hung over but it was a great ending to the weekend.'

Sting even decided against selling the snaps of the wedding to *Hello!* magazine for fear that it might spell the end of his marriage to Trudie. In recent years the magazine had published slushy pictures of supposedly happy couples who then split up!

*   *   *

With his new four-piece band in place — drummer Vinny Colaitua, keyboardist David Sancious and guitarist Dominic Millar — Sting recorded his new album *Ten Summoner's Tales* on his Wiltshire farm in late 1992.

The crossbred album spanned melodic rock, ambient jazz, folk, reggae and country twang, while also evoking Sting's Police era more than any other solo album he had made.

The title of the album was loosely inspired by Chaucer's medieval masterpiece *The Canterbury Tales*. As Sting explained, however, it was 'a real ragbag of styles and influences; and my name Sumner comes from the medieval Summoner (an enforcer of church law) who was one of the characters in the *Tales*. I thought, "Well, it's a mild joke. They'll call me pretentious but I think it's funny."'

Sting even turned up on the unlikeliest of TV shows when he was persuaded by his children to go on the BBC Saturday morning children's programme *Going Live*. His appearance was completely overshadowed by the scrum for autographs of Take That whose lead singer happened to be a guest presenter on the show.

None the less, Sting enjoyed himself on the programme. He chatted about the new album and took part in a suitably silly sketch during which he was required to pin the 'sting' on an airborne fluffy toy bee. He also got a free plug for the rainforest before he set off for lunch in the BBC canteen with four of his five children, who had come along to the studio with him.

The show enabled Sting to prove to the world what a relaxed father he could be, with Joe, sixteen, Kate, twelve, Mickey, nine, and Jake, seven.

In the spring of 1993 Sting and his band set off on a world tour to promote the album, surrounded by many familiar faces from as far back as the good old bad days of The Police. Co-manager Kim Turner, road manager Billy Francis and the rest of the entourage had practically grown up together.

Sting liked being surrounded by familiar faces and interpreted the situation as such. 'If I'm being an idiot and everyone thinks I'm an idiot, I know it. I know the people around me well enough to know when I'm being an idiot, and they're able to verbalise it without fear that their jobs are on the line. I can be unreasonable sometimes, but someone will stand up and say, "Stop it." I've collected these people over fourteen years, and we're a really close-knit group.'

On stage during that tour, Sting managed to run through virtually all the songs from the new album plus a few solo nuggets and a flurry of Police tunes which always garnered the most furious response.

Sting's album *Ten Summoner's Tales* surprised the cynics by rocketing straight to number two on its release in Britain. Sting was also celebrating the success of the first single from the album 'If I Ever Lose My Faith In You' which became a top ten hit.

Around the same time, Sting started sounding off about being firmly anti-royal and heavily in favour of a republic in Britain. 'I don't see the necessity of the royal family, apart from maybe pulling in the tourist bucks.'

Despite his immense wealth, Sting genuinely believed that Britain would be a better place under a Labour Government. His Marxist/socialist background would never be completely ousted. He actually hopes that the Royal Family would be phased out under such a government.

Sting confirmed his left-wing tendencies by making a point of seeking out Britain's Labour Party leader Tony Blair within months of Blair's election as leader of the Labour Party and a photo of the two men together now takes pride of place on the mantelpiece of Sting's Wiltshire home.

On 18 January 1993, Sting found himself singing on the westbound platform of the Metropolitan line at Ladbroke Grove underground station in West London. Slumped against an underground sign wearing a dufflecoat three sizes too small, he strummed a few Police hits.

At first, most people did not even give the singer a second glance — except for one young girl who fainted. As word got around, travellers gathered around Sting and listened intently to his free concert.

Sting picked nimbly at his acoustic guitar and played a whole selection of Police hits and other songs and augmented his personal fortune by the grand total of seventy-five pence.

The busking performance was all in aid of an article for *Q* magazine but it proved that Sting had lost none of the ability to do anything 'for a photo opportunity' which had been drilled into him by Miles Copeland back when The Police kicked off, fifteen years earlier.

In April 1993, Sting and Chief Raoni's relationship appeared to take a tumble when London's *Daily Mail* published a story claiming that both men had started accusing the other of betrayal over the future of the rainforests. Sting was quoted as having commented dryly, 'They're always trying to deceive you. They see the white man only as a good source of earning money, and then as a friend. I was very naïve and thought I could save the world selling T-shirts for the Indian cause. In reality, I did little. I'm leaving behind my days in the jungle,' although he insisted he would continue to raise funds to save the rainforest.

Apparently, Chief Raoni was just as disillusioned. He hit back at Sting by saying, 'The Brazilian Indians do not need Sting. It would be better if we forgot him.'

The source of the information about this alleged deep rift between the two men was the Brazilian magazine *Vega* which had uncovered details of how the Indians had been earning about six million dollars a year from the sale of mahogany to Europe during the previous ten years. Basically, it was suggested that there had been a complete turn around in the role of the Indians. No longer were they seen as the victims but as the perpetrators of much of the destruction. The *Daily Mail* picked up on the story. It transpired that Raoni had been fed misleading information and once he heard of Sting's continuing love, Raoni re-pledged his support for his 'close friend Sting'.

Sting was fully aware that much of the criticism that had been hurled in his direction throughout the campaign had come from people who were trying to imply that he was attaching himself to such issues as a means of self-publicity, and by people who seemed to want Sting's rainforest efforts to fail.

'People think I did this to be more famous or because I felt guilty for being rich and famous: I don't feel guilty about being rich. I don't really feel that guilty about what's wrong with the world. I didn't create the world. But understanding all those negative perceptions, I still do it. And I still will. Fuck what they say. If, on the first day of criticism about this rainforest thing, I just threw my hands up, I would have gotten a lot less of that. And I'm not looking for praise. I'm doing it because I think it's the right thing.'

That same month, Sting turned his attention to an issue somewhat closer to home. He joined a group protesting over planned improvements at the ancient site of Stonehenge near his Wiltshire home.

Sting spent a lot of time at the house. He adored riding around on horseback and had met neighbours such as the Prince of Wales's close friend Lady Tryon and the Earl of Chichester as well as the novelist Sir V S Naipaul.

In May 1993, Sting recorded a duet with Luciano Pavarotti. Accompanied only by an acoustic guitar playing Franck's century-old melody, the duet opened a new album called *Pavarotti and Friends*.

Around the same time, a rumour swept the music industry that Sting had died of a drugs overdose after a radio station reported that his body had been found at his home. Fun Radio, which broadcasts in the south of France, insisted the report was true. However, the announcement was a sick joke which backfired spectacularly when the station's switchboard became jammed and Fun Radio's bosses had to make a humble apology.

A spokesperson for Sting said at the time, 'He's got a great sense of humour but he is struggling to see the funny side of this.'

In Italy, Sting was banned by local police from giving a concert in the town of Catanzora in Calabria because they feared that his music might incite violence. Sting was bemused by the decision, especially when he heard the local police chief say, 'The young public, in group mania, are willing to exalt themselves, bringing them up to the point of cancelling their inhibitions.'

A spokesperson for Sting said, 'Obviously the police in Catanzora have never heard the music of Sting.'

In June 1993, Sting turned up at another topless bar, this time in New York, with some friends. The singer whooped with joy as he stuffed hundreds of dollars into the girls' garters at Peter

Stringfellow's Pure Platinum nightspot. Sting looked delighted as stiletto-wearing girls stripped down to G-strings and gyrated inches from his face.

Sting had beckoned them over within minutes of arriving at midnight at the club with two friends. For two hours he cheered on the girls before signing a few autographs and leaving the premises.

Owner Peter Stringfellow said, 'Sting had a great time — and the girls said he was one of the best tippers they've ever had.' He added with smile, 'I am sure Trudie wouldn't mind. They have a very good relationship.'

Sting's fascination with such nightspots was growing. He adored exotic dancers. 'They always seem to be giving a lot.' He even sometimes compared himself to a prostitute by saying, 'I don't mind whoring to make a buck now and then. But then I never met a whore I didn't like. I've always found them very warm people. I mean genuinely. The old cliché of the tart with a heart actually is true. They're very giving girls.'

Sting is proud that he has known prostitutes. 'I know a few whores. But you know, I've travelled the world and I've been around for a long time. I think it's an interesting part of our culture. Prostitution will always be in our society because there's a need for it. It's a safety valve, and again it should be legalised and made safer than it is.'

Sting insisted he had never paid for sex himself but his quest for sexual enlightenment has included visiting one of New York's most notorious underground S&M clubs. Sting later insisted to friends that he was 'curious' about the place. The club was filled with people being chained to the walls and whipped. Sting's guide during one visit — a stunning girl in a leather skirt and black polo-neck sweater — told him the place was full of people 'trying to sort themselves out' rather than indulging in thrusting sexual passion. Sting looked on curiously at the dozens of couples indulging in painful practices and did not feel in the slightest bit threatened.

At the Stonewall music gig in 1994, Sting proved himself very adept at striptease by taking off virtually all his clothes in front of a delighted gay audience and co-performer Elton John. 'He seemed to get quite a kick out of it,' explained one member of the audience.

On Sting's forty-second birthday in October 1993, Trudie played up to Sting's open fondness for erotic sex by making and starring in an X-rated video as a 'special present'. In the video, which was shown to friends at Sting's birthday party in Los Angeles, Trudie reclined on a bed, wearing pearls and a black gown. As she whispers sweet nothings to the camera, three toy boys are seen hastily pulling on their clothes in the background and shadowy figures walk about in their boxer shorts.

Sting was delighted by the film. Explains one friend, 'Trudie's attitude was if you can't beat 'em, join 'em, so she decided to give Sting the ultimate piece of porn. It's not really disgusting but it's certainly pretty suggestive and Sting adores it.'

The other side of Sting knew no boundaries.

TWENTY SEVEN

It's Only Money

'Even the term "rock star" is pejorative.
It means maniac, drug addict, egocentric brat.
That may be true, but you try your best to disguise it.'

— STING

IN NOVEMBER 1992, STING CALLED IN THE POLICE after discovering that more than seven million pounds of his vast fortune was 'missing'. Fraud squad detectives were alerted to the situation when Sting and Miles Copeland were told that the money — which represented one-third of Sting's personal assets — had disappeared during a complex series of transactions.

Accountant Keith Moore — who had been loyally retained by Sting despite accusations made against him by other rock-star clients — voluntarily went to Holborn Police Station where he was interviewed by detectives for five hours.

It then emerged that the fraud accusations had first been made in an anonymous letter sent to Sting in September 1992 by persons who had worked with Keith Moore and who had been busy doing their own detective work. Sting read this letter over breakfast at Lake House.

He was shocked by what had happened. 'It made me look very seriously at the idea of wealth, and I came to the conclusion that wealth isn't about what you have in the bank. Your wealth is your friendships, family, health and happiness.'

Moore was charged by the police with theft but it would take another two years before the case came to trial amid a flurry of publicity.

*   *   *

Sting agreed to play a handful of dates as opening act for the legendary Grateful Dead during his US tour in 1993. The two camps never met before the tour but the Grateful Dead member Jerry Garcia (who died in August 1995) reckoned that, 'He's at the stage in his career that he could use a model which is not a conventional show-business model. He's used up what a conventional model can get him. In order to make it to another level, he has to define himself in some other way and use some terms other than "showbiz". I mean, Sting is an intelligent guy. He's no Axl Rose, ya know what I mean? He's a bright guy.'

Garcia was convinced his audiences would love Sting. 'So far our audience has loved everybody we've ever put in front of them.'

The equally legendary Grateful Dead fans — the 'Deadheads' — were still munching on LSD and other hallucinogenic concoctions even in the no-nonsense nineties.

Sting was fascinated by the whole phenomenon but resisted the temptation to reignite his experimentation with serious narcotics. At this time he was still drinking alcohol when the fancy took him and also occasionally enjoying a puff of cannabis.

Sting's attitude towards drugs has changed enormously over the years. By 1993, his about-turn on the subject seemed complete. He told one associate, 'I don't think anyone should take drugs before they're forty years old. I'm talking strictly about casual use. If you're not addicted to drugs by the time you're forty, you're not going to become addicted'.

In a light-hearted aside that summed up his feelings about alcohol, Sting said that when he drank — which was only occasionally — he gets 'happy, then I fall over. I'm no trouble really. And it doesn't take much. So I'm a cheap drunk. I don't cost much. Take me out. Get me drunk. Lay me. Rob me.'

In December 1993, Sting's seventeen-year-old son Joe made his first public appearance with his band, The Australian Nightmare, at a small venue in London's Covent Garden.

The group had been formed earlier that year by Joe and some friends from University College School, Hampstead, where he was studying for his A-levels. Joe had already picked up some useful tips when travelling round Europe as a roadie on his father's tour earlier that year. One member of the group said rather predictably, 'Joe is very strong-willed and determined to make it without his father.'

Shortly after this, as if to confirm Sting's continued obsession with musical experimentation, he agreed to work on an homage album to composer George Gershwin. Sting got together with eighty-year-old harmonica virtuoso Larry Adler to attract such talent as Elton John and legendary Beatles producer George Martin. The result, *The Glory of Gershwin*, was quietly recorded in Britain over a two-month period at the start of 1994. Sting performed 'Nice Work If You Can Get It' and the album also featured Cher, Elvis Costello, Sinéad O'Connor and Meat Loaf, with Adler playing harmonica on every track.

On the domestic front, Sting and Trudie continued to seem determined to prove to the world that they were the most strongly attached couple in showbusiness. They still cuddled on buses and benches like schoolkids and seemed to walk everywhere attached at the hip like Siamese twins. They rarely fought, but when they did, it was generally about subjects far less mundane than the sort of things that cause stress and suffering among the less famous.

The biggest problem between Sting and Trudie seemed to revolve around their respective views of celebrity and stardom. Sting explains, 'She doesn't necessarily see it the way I do. Occasionally, being a celebrity will get in the way of being a human being, and sometimes, for my own survival, I have to be a celebrity, put up a front. And she doesn't like that.'

By 1994, however, Sting was seriously starting to rethink his image and even admitted to one associate that the days when he would happily strip off his shirt to pose for photographers were about to disappear for ever.

Meanwhile, Sting's interest in natural hallucinogenics continues unabated. He takes country walks, looking for and then eating psilocybin fungi, even joking to one friend, 'They're wonderful. The basis of pagan religion was mushroom worship. Stonehenge looks like a mushroom to me. It does when you take 'em!'

Sting never forgot the sensations he felt when taking cocaine years earlier. He never considered himself an addict but he had tried it enough to know that it made him feel paranoid. He preferred the idea of taking the natural ingredients contained in plants. They had a more gentle, reasonable effect.

Also, the criminality of illicit drug-taking really concerned him. He felt strongly (and still does) that all narcotics should be legalised and regulated so that badly cut street drugs could be removed from society.

* * *

In March 1994, Sting proved he was still a mainstream rock star by scooping the Best Male Pop Singer award at the Grammy Awards in the US for his salute to the power of love, entitled 'If I Ever Lose My Faith In You'. Sting's work also inspired a win for Best Engineered Album and Best Long Form Video.

The following month, Sting's Rainforest Foundation returned to Carnegie Hall, New York for its fifth annual reminder to the public that they should help to preserve not only the area that had become so close to the singer's heart, but also rainforests outside Brazil.

Sting and Trudie jointly organised the show which featured Luciano Pavarotti, Tammy Wynette, Elton John and James Taylor. The atmosphere was relaxed and the sell-out crowd enjoyed duets between the various stars.

At home, Sting was definitely slowing down. The old egomaniac edge seemed to have all but disappeared, although ever-truthful Trudie reckoned that certain habits hadn't died yet. She explains, 'He still tries the old star on. In fact, he lives in the mirror. Sucking in his cheeks. I have this quite large mouth, and he curls his lips back and makes himself look like a grotesque fashion of me, which I find very funny. If I am pissed at him, I will whack him across the head properly.'

Trudie was definitely not awestruck in any way by her husband. Sting — who has never raised a finger to her — even told one friend that he sometimes knew what it was like to be a battered husband — and he was only just joking.

'Trudie can get into a dreadful rage sometimes and it's better just to leave her alone on such occasions,' explains one friend. 'But it's usually Sting who bears the full brunt of it and they usually end up kissing and making up real quick.'

*　　　　　*　　　　　*

Sting is not sure exactly when it happened but he became aware that something was wrong with his hearing during the recording of his album, *Ten Summoner's Tales*. Doctors proclaimed the condition was verging on tinnitus. Wherever he went, he started to hear birds singing in his head, like a hedge of twittering sparrows, and he had a hard time telling one mix from another. Sting even hired a man named Bob Ludwig to supervise all the mixing of the tracks for the album because he feared that he might not be able to make those decisions any more.

Sting explains, 'I've lost a lot of mid-range in this ear. And the mid is where the spoken word is so I have to listen very carefully or pretend to hear people.'

Initially, Sting went off to a specialist in Paris for a three-week course which included listening to Mozart through specially adapted headphones with certain frequencies filtered out so that his brain could be retrained to hear them more clearly. However, the diagnosis was grim. He may eventually go deaf — although probably not for a considerable time.

To make matters worse, Sting wanted to ease off on touring but Miles Copeland — ever aware of any golden opportunity — warned the star that his record sales would slide if he did not help to promote them. Miles had become concerned about Sting's heavily introspective interviews to promote his recent albums because he believed that Sting's words to the press made some of his records seem a bit downbeat and that may have considerably hurt sales.

Throughout this period Sting was continuing to fight many other battles — within himself. Having both his parents die from cancer, he was (and still is) concerned that he'll get cancer as well and has his blood tested for every possible ailment at least once every six months. 'This is a guy who needs things to worry about. He's obsessed by keeping in good health. He rarely eats meat and is convinced that he'll die young like his parents if he is not too careful,' explains a friend.

Meanwhile, the practice of yoga was rapidly taking over as Sting's main preoccupation. He spent at least three hours a day 'chilling out' with a variety of body-bending exercises.

Only a few years earlier his attitude towards yoga had been completely different. 'I used to think yoga was a bit wishy washy — a lot of old ladies in leotards sitting around meditating — but it's not like that at all. It's actually a very hard physical work-out, like super-aerobics. When I first started I was exhausted after fifteen minutes.'

Sting's conversion to yoga also brought about an extraordinary interest in Tantric sex because Sting and Trudie enjoyed erotic experimentation. In the early nineties they had discovered Tantric sex through yoga and, as a result, would have intercourse for up to *ten hours* at a time.

Sting explained it to one friend, 'You don't spill your seed; you don't come. You retain it all and go on much longer. You stay erect and your stomach goes as near to the spine as you can make it while still allowing you to breathe and you never lose control, you just keep going.'

Behind these marathon sex sessions lay a theory that was bound not to sit well with the male population. Sting actually believes that, 'The purpose of sex, ideally, is for the woman to attain orgasm and for the man not to. I'm actually serious about this. I think it's about control. For example, we don't use contraceptives. We use the rhythm method, which works, but it demands control.'

When it came to the subject of monogamy, Sting confessed to his friends that it was not easy but he had been working at it for years. 'Monogamy's becoming easier for me as it becomes more logical, so as I get older, it's making more sense to me.'

As a younger man, Sting couldn't understand the logic in sticking to one sexual partner. 'There's all these women that you want to fuck! And they're beautiful.'

Ultimately, that was what had attracted him to Tantric sex. He explains, 'Now I'm much calmer. It makes sense now. Also, sex is better when you can control your, er, behaviour. There's nothing worse than a five-minute wonder.'

To this day Sting has remained fiercely proud of his sexual capabilities. He insists he has never had a problem satisfying a woman. He was so proud of his marathon sex sessions with Trudie that he boasted to friends that he kept going 'for as long as possible'. He even added, 'You've heard five hours? Well, I'm just being modest.'

Tantric sex expert Dominic Collier insisted that Sting should be able to go on for up to ten hours with his partner. 'The key to Tantric sex is self-discipline. It's a form of Buddhism where worship is expressed through the body. Self-discipline is the key and Sting takes it very seriously. The idea is to get in touch with the energy points in your body, and the most important of these are the genitals. Tantric sex can be mind-blowing.'

When Sting and Trudie went on a short holiday to the luxurious eighteen hundred dollars a night Eden Rock Hotel in the French Riviera resort of Cap d'Antibes, they amused other guests by performing a series of complex yoga movements every morning by the side of the hotel pool.

Sting's old buddy Bob Geldof had an interesting view on Sting's appetite for yoga and the change in his character over the years. 'We were both doing a concert in Italy when he started all this yoga bollocks.

I am not into fitness and I said to him, "How can you do that?" He just laughed at himself. He could not have done that five years earlier. I like that about him.'

In early 1993 Sting performed for the first time in South Africa after years of turning down annual invitations on the basis of his opposition to apartheid. Sun City — infamous 'Las Vegas' of the southern hemisphere — was the venue and Sting came away bewildered but intrigued by the country that had finally found freedom under Nelson Mandela.

That same year Sting met up with old pal Bob Geldof and posed for one of the funniest photographs of his career following a marathon six-hour boozing session in a West London pub discussing 'shagging, politics, fame and everything under the sun' for an article in *Q* magazine.

'By the time we got to the photo session, Bob and I were somewhat the worse for wear,' explained a rather proud Sting. 'And when I asked him to lick my boots, he was down there like a shot,' he recalled some months later in reference to the photograph which shows Geldof doing precisely that.

However, Sting's friendship with Geldof was something fairly unique in the fickle world of rock superstardom. Sting admired Geldof's 'no bullshit approach to life' and envied his ability to speak without inhibition about any subject.

Geldof's career had never really hit the heights enjoyed by Sting and he knew it. In many ways his admirable efforts on behalf of Live Aid and the starving masses in Africa probably damaged his musical career more than anything else.

Throughout the late seventies punk era, both Sting and Geldof were seen as little more than bandwagon-jumping lepers. Sting, after all, came from a jazz background and Geldof's band The Boomtown Rats existed on the sweatily unfashionable edge between R & B and pub rock.

Geldof never saw himself as having been a truly famous rock star. He confessed, 'I'm a bit of a prat, actually.' Then he turned on Sting in a good-natured outburst that only Geldof could get away with when Sting asked him if he (Sting) was sexy. 'No, you look like a cunt but you work at your body out of a certain narcissism or vanity. I wish I could be bothered to do exercise because I need to.'

Sting then revealed the gritty details about his newly found love for Tantric sex. Geldof was appalled, 'Where's the fucking fun in that? Why don't you just come? I like to come as quickly as possible. Ten seconds is about my max.'

The conversation between the two then became even more basic.

Sting: 'But that's just a leg over.'

Geldof: 'What's wrong with a leg over?'

Sting: 'Why not have a wank? In yoga, sex is a spiritual focus of energy.'

Geldof was very amused and went on to ask Sting when he actually decided to stop making love: 'So you just fuck for hours? It's a bit boring for the boiler, isn't it? Does she not come either?'

Sting hit back, 'That's not the point. We tend to think that the whole point of sex is about coming and ejaculating. I'm not sure that's a good attitude.' He insisted that he now enjoyed sex much more than before he took up Tantric sex.

Then somehow Geldof got the conversation around to whether Sting would ever consider having sex with his wife, Trudie, and another woman. It was difficult to tell whether the two singers were joking or not. But Sting insisted, 'Yeah. If she was serious. Wouldn't Paula? With you and me.'

Even Geldof was lost for words for a moment. 'What? A fours-up with me and Paula. She wouldn't want to shag you.' It was an ironic comment considering Paula's previous interest in Sting and her later decision to leave Geldof.

Sting continued, 'But would you fancy it? I think Bob Geldof secretly wants to shag me.'

Geldof: 'Fuck off!'

The magazine journalist then asked Sting and Geldof if they would be prepared to watch their wives being shagged by him (the journalist) or would agree to gay sex with Iron Mike Tyson.

Sting was adamant, 'I'd prefer to watch him screw the missus. I could give him a few pointers. You don't want to do it like that!'

Geldof: 'I wouldn't like to see him shag the missus because he's such an ugly fucker. If my alternative is getting one up the arse from Iron Mike Tyson I'd take that as the option, because I don't think he'd be interested. Much as I tried to turn him on, I don't think I could get him going.'

As may be detected, Sting and Geldof appear to have a particularly earthy relationship.

*　　　　　*　　　　　*

By the summer of 1993, Trudie made it clear to her friends that marriage to Sting had made her feel completely secure for the first time in their long relationship.

The couple had even got into the habit of regularly sitting on the front doorstep of their vast Wiltshire home, just like they both did when growing up in the tiny terraced homes of their parents.

To this day Sting never talks at mealtimes. 'Like all northern lads', explains Trudie, 'he was taught to shut up and eat his dinner.'

Trudie worries about the effect that all that immense wealth has on their children who have known no other life. 'When my daughter was five she stayed with my father in the house where I grew up. She came back and said: "Isn't Grandad's house small — it's like a doll's house." I was quite shocked. I don't want her talking like that. I want to show my children that there is a world beyond their back garden.'

The following summer, Sting hosted the wedding of his sister Anita at Lake House. It was obviously a much quieter affair than his own ceremony, but it was a nice gesture, especially as he even insisted on giving the bride away because their father was no longer alive.

Back in Brazil, criticism of Sting and his rainforest campaign was continuing. Explains Gilda Matoso, 'Sting's standing here has been very badly affected. There is no way we could fill a stadium like we did the Macao stadium with a hundred thousand in 1987.'

Gilda admits that the whole rainforest episode has backfired on Sting to a certain extent. But she says, 'Nothing will stop Sting adoring Brazil. Sting likes nothing more than to run on Copocabana Beach, eat seafood and pasta at Satyrico (his favourite restaurant in Ipanema) and workout at the Copocabana Palace Hotel. He says he'll keep coming back here until the day he dies.'

Around this time, Sting's elder son Joe accompanied him to Brazil just before the teenager went off to college in Boston. Getting an insight into Joe proved even more difficult than trying to get a handle on his father.

Gilda Matoso describes the teenager as 'very weird'. She says, 'His hair was half-blond, half-black and he had one nail painted black. He was very quiet but obviously felt under enormous pressure because he was the son of Sting.'

Another friend said that Joe 'found it difficult to come to terms with his father's fame once he reached his teens, but, through thick and thin, Sting has remained incredibly loyal and loving towards Joe'. Joe has since matured into a kind and interesting person, who works hard at his graphic design job and with his band.

In June 1994 Sting was asked to bare all for a photo spread in the American magazine, *Playgirl*. By all accounts, the offer was considered very carefully before being rejected after some heated advice to the singer from his ever-careful manager Miles Copeland. Sting himself still believed he had a good enough body to do it but he realised that, at almost forty-three, he was perhaps a little too old to get away with such a spread of photos.

By September 1994 Sting had ended his own self-imposed ban on playing concert tours of Israel, thanks to the progress towards peace with the Palestinians. 'I think it is important to be sensitive to the complexities of political situations. I am glad things are happening in the way they are happening, so I'm here,' Sting said. His tour included three concerts in Israel.

Times were changing and so was Sting.

TWENTY EIGHT

Tᴇᴀ Tɪᴍᴇ

*'I don't believe you can get into the
spiritual state without drugs.'*
- Sᴛɪɴɢ

Bʏ 1994 Sᴛɪɴɢ ᴀᴛ ʟᴀѕᴛ ғᴏᴜɴᴅ himself with enough free time to reflect more on his life and his abilities as a parent to five children. He was deeply worried that the two oldest might feel less close to him because they had always lived with their mother, Frances Tomelty.

'I tried to balance that out in my life in certain ways,' he says, 'like making specific times for my older children.' However, with eldest Joe away at college in Boston, it was proving increasingly difficult.

'As far as love goes, it's totally expandable and limitless,' explains Sting. 'Whether you're with them or not, you can't help but love them; you love each one differently — not better or worse, but just differently. They're entirely different people and you can't do without any of them. I couldn't see my life without one of them, not without it being irreparably damaged.

'I often wonder what's going through the minds of my children. My kids are blessed, but at the same time the world has encroached upon their childhood too much. Modern children are much more anxious than we were. I've stopped watching the television news because it's usually shown at a time when everyone's there. I don't want to see a massacre in Rwanda with my children. But they know what's going on. The kids are worried about pollution. It's not because I'm drilling them with any dogma, they're just aware and fairly militant in their views.'

Sting's children — Joe, seventeen, Katie, twelve, Mickey, ten, Jake, eight, and Coco, three — had become the epicentre of his life. Sting was incredibly worried that the two eldest felt they had missed out on a lot of the luxuries enjoyed by the younger ones and he tried to more than compensate.

Explains one of his closest friends, 'Sting is incredibly generous with his kids but in a realistic way. He doesn't throw money at them but he tries to give each of them an equal amount of time so that none of them feel left out. I think he is one of the best fathers I have ever met.' However, Sting has warned his children that they will not necessarily inherit a fortune and that they will have to develop their own lives.

Sting tries desperately not to be like his own father but he still retains some of the old-fashioned habits of a parent from the North East. 'He is very strict about their table manners but finds it bemusing the way his children have these posh little accents from their schools while he still considers himself a bit of a rough-neck Geordie at heart.'

Schooling is a very important topic for former teacher Sting. His three kids by Trudie attend a Church of England school in Salisbury near his Wiltshire mansion. Jake even spent some time in a Jewish school in New York where they were trying to help to treat his dyslexia. Sting and Trudie have tried to tackle the problem patiently and with loving care and attention.

In May 1994 Sting made yet another visit to Brazil but this time he embarked on something that greatly concerned some of his closest friends. Ever since experiencing some of that hallucinogenic 'tea' in the jungle with Chief Raoni, Sting had wanted to take the 'tea' on a more regular basis.

TEA TIME

Apparently the tea, long used by the Brazilian Indians as part of their religion, first became known outside the Amazon rainforests in the 1930s, when the rubber-tappers heard about it. The rubber-tappers practised the Christian religion and found the tea put them into a meditative state, highlighting religious awareness and particularly the line between life, death and the possible afterlife. They used the tea as part of their sacrament. A few years ago, the Brazilian Government investigated the tea and legalised it. Apparently, the son of one of the Brazilian army generals was a heroin addict. After taking the tea, the son was cured of his heroin addiction. It is said the tea contains serotonin, an important natural substance which controls the activity of the brain's neurotransmitters. Indeed, once the tea becomes better known in the West, it is likely to cause far more than a storm in a teacup. Will the Government or the Church seek to ban it? Will it give the same self-awareness, spiritual contentment and creativity as it appears to have given Sting? We shall see.

One day Sting and his entourage, including Deborah Cohen, were sitting around the Copocabana Palace Hotel when Sting persuaded them all to try the controversial 'tea' at a place called Jacare Da Dua just outside Rio, run by a religious sect called the Union de Vegetal, which translated means 'the herbal society'.

Deborah Cohen had strong misgivings as did many of the party which included drummer Vinny Colaitua, Ian Copeland and Kim Turner.

The 'tea' is made from ayahuasca, a rare herb found only deep in the Amazon jungle. Sting had first experimented with it during his trips into the rainforest to meet Chief Raoni.

Within minutes of arriving at the Union de Vegetal retreat, each of the party drank a cupful of the 'tea' in a carefully orchestrated ceremony at an old church site. Moments later, virtually all of them vomited, including Sting. It was not a pleasant way to start 'the experience'. Deborah Cohen even recalls that there was a lot of sawdust on the floor specifically designed to soak up the vomit.

According to witnesses at the ceremony, shortly after being violently sick, Sting started laughing uncontrollably.

'Then Ian Copeland started giggling and doing impersonations of his brother Miles. It was completely infectious. Sting was busting himself with laughter as well and we were all getting completely out of control,' reports one witness. 'Then everyone went into this eerie, detached state I can only call "non-being". Afterwards, life felt even more precious to me than before!'

Following an initial thirty minutes of 'feeling like shit', the entire 'trip' took over an hour and a half.

Says one concerned friend, 'We all think that Sting is getting a little too heavily involved in all this. But it's up to him, I guess.'

Deborah Cohen found the whole experience 'rather unpleasant'. She explains, 'I had never taken any drugs before in my life and I certainly don't plan to ever again. It was horrible but each to his own, I guess.'

Also among Sting's friends trying out the 'tea' was Carlos Paiva. He explains, 'Sting told me how great the tea was. I was a bit curious. I believe in fate and destiny and so does Sting.'

Paiva had been shaken by something Sting told him before they set off to try out the trance-inducing 'tea'. He explains, 'Sting was the first person to mention to me that I was obviously having problems with my wife. He had sensed those problems. That made me realise that Lucia and I had lost each other. We split up shortly after that.'

During the 'tea' session itself, Sting became like an unofficial godfather to all the others who were taking it for the first time. 'Sting is deadly serious about the "tea",' says Carlos Paiva. 'He says he had a deep feeling of peace and tranquillity while taking the "tea".'

On 17 December 1994, Sting made a secret trip to the city of Brasilia to take part in a controversial experiment with more of the same 'tea' that had taken his fancy earlier that year. As one friend explains, 'Sting went alone on that trip because he did not want people to know he was in Brazil for that reason. It has become a vital part of his life. Sting sees the 'tea' as part of his quest to experience the very edges of human existence, to understand himself and, through that, life itself. He is, after all, a talented songwriter and musician — all true artists live on the cutting edge of life.'

Sting's trip — which included a visit to one of the Union de Vegetal's leaders — would have gone unnoticed if it hadn't been for a beady-eyed British Airways staff member who told one of Sting's associates in Rio about the singer's hush-hush trip.

Sting's friend couldn't understand why he had not contacted anyone while he was in Brazil. Sting insisted it was such a quick 'in and out' stay that he did not see the point in calling up any of his many friends in the country.

Sting was particularly intrigued by the 'tea' because he felt that, in some way, it helped to awaken his spirits and awareness of things. Some friends say he is 'very impressed' by the 'tea', while others claim he is virtually hooked on it.

The 'tea' itself has been at the centre of much controversy inside Brazil because more and more middle-class professional people are becoming regular users of it. Some politicians in Brazil have tried to ban it. But to date, it is entirely legal.

Psychiatrist Jose Costa Sobrinho has been commissioned by the Brazilian Government to produce a report on the 'tea' and whether it is being exploited.

Members of the Union de Vegetal broke away from the larger Santo Daime group many years ago. The Santo Daime group have been embroiled in controversy similar to that affecting the classic cults in the United States. There have been numerous accusations of kidnap and murder laid against the group in recent years. One teenager abandoned her entire family after taking the 'tea' and her mother had to resort to the courts to try to get her daughter back home. Some years ago, a judge named Carlos Felipe Bruno actually hired armed men to snatch his child after she fell into the clutches of the Santo Daime group.

Some versions of the 'tea' contain not only ayahuasca but also two other hallucinogenic plants grown in the jungle, called *Banisteriopsis kaapis* and *Psychotria viridis*. A Brazilian congressman, Fernando Gabeira, infiltrated the cult and reported that a lot of people were forced to take the 'tea' against their will during vast drinking ceremonies.

One person who drank the 'tea' said, 'I lost track of time. I started to imagine myself after death.' However, others insist that the 'tea' has healing powers. It has even been claimed that, if taken in large doses, it can help to cure people of AIDS.

Everyone who has ever drunk the 'tea' agrees on one thing; the first reaction is to vomit and tremble uncontrollably. People who have come through this stage frequently claim that, afterwards, they have rediscovered things about themselves. It is clear that Sting has done likewise.

*   *   *

On a less spiritual level is Sting's taste in clothes. His preference for the scruffy look is something that has been carefully nurtured for many years. Sting will often keep the same clothes for years on end and he is certainly particularly fond of one tatty denim jacket that travels with him between his homes in London and New York and to his 'wooden shack' in Malibu, California.

However, despite that carefully nurtured, crumpled image, throughout the eighties, Sting developed a virtual obsession with designer clothes. A little Armani here, a lot of Versace there — he seemed to be completely bitten by the designer bug of that era. His favourite shop was (and still is) Browns in South Molton Street. Sting adores their wide choice of clothes and tends to pick things that look old but most definitely aren't.

By the time the mid-nineties came along he was concentrating on purchasing two- and three-hundred pound shirts and two-thousand pound suits that looked cheap — really well-made clothes that tended to make him look like a tramp!

Sting admitted to friends that he bought excessive amounts of clothes when he felt depressed 'because they really cheer me up'. Secretly, Sting had become the most unlikely of shopaholics and, although he was not quite in the Imelda Marcos league, he certainly had a dandyish appetite.

Meanwhile, public criticism of Sting continued to hurt, even though he had become more hardened to the familiar flak. It seemed as if he simply could not win.

To some he was highminded and conceited while to others he was weak, wishy-washy and incredibly safe and boring. 'I've been called everything under the sun — God, they called me pretentious just because I've read Proust,' he says. 'I don't think I'm a genius, but I also don't think I'm a shit. I'm somewhere in the middle. I feel pretty comfortable in that position, and I'm not looking for praise or blame.'

However, one piece of criticism that really stung was when the *Village Voice* newspaper in New York printed a caricature of Sting's face which had been hacked with a knife and headlined 'BRING ME THE HEAD OF GORDON SUMNER'. Sting was furious because he believed that someone reading the piece in New York might take it literally and hunt him down and kill him.

A few weeks later, the kitchen in his Wiltshire mansion was wrecked by fire just a few days after he and his family posed for a photo spread.

TWENTY NINE

ALL IN A DAY'S WORK

*'As far as the money is concerned, I
just don't have time to spend it.'*
- STING

IN MAY 1995 STING PICKED UP a cool two million dollars when he
played at a birthday party for the son of the world's richest man. As
part of the deal, the superstar had to sing 'Happy Birthday' to twenty-
two-year-old Prince Hakim, son of the megarich Sultan of Brunei who
also splashed out a further million dollars for singer Bryan Adams to
sing at the same event. The two stars even managed a duet, much to
the delight of the audience of just two hundred handpicked guests.

A special video was produced of the performance, which was then
distributed among the guests. It was produced by Sting's old
Newcastle-based TV producer friend Gavin Taylor who had first
encountered the singer almost twenty years earlier when The Police
were just starting out.

He says, 'Sting has changed a lot since those days. He takes the
mickey out of himself now in a way he would never have done back
then. He was more standoffish, and Stewart and Andy were not

particularly nice either in those days. But he was a different guy in Brunei. His interplay with Bryan Adams in Brunei was brilliant and he seemed relaxed and happy.'

Sting and Adams even performed a joke version of 'Every Breath You Take' during which Sting changed the words to 'Every Leg You Break' and Bryan replied by singing 'Every Accountant's Mistake'. It was priceless. 'They were fantastic,' says Gavin Taylor, who hopes to persuade the two stars to perform together at a proper concert in the near future.

The day after his performance, Sting went out on ski-boats with Adams and Prince Hakim around the dozens of islands dotted off the coast of Brunei. At one stage, Sting's vehicle flipped over in choppy seas after almost crashing into a rock, but, fortunately, no one was injured.

The same month, Sting's eco-warrior reputation took a knocking when he accepted an estimated five hundred thousand pounds to promote a holiday complex which entailed the destruction of more than a hundred thousand trees.

The singer's endorsement of the hundred and fifty acre Saegaia resort, built in a pine forest on the south-east coast of Japan, surprised British environmentalists. In an advertisement on Japanese television, Sting was seen gazing approvingly from a golf course at the one and half billion pound complex near the city of Miyazaki.

Francis Sullivan, forest conservation officer at the World Wide Fund for Nature, said, 'A two-hundred-year-old forest is likely to support a rich environment and wildlife. This is the opposite of the great work Sting has been doing for the forests.' When Sting was confronted about his involvement, manager Miles Copeland stepped in and insisted that he took full responsibility for the deal and that neither he nor Sting knew about the controversy over the forest until after Sting's work on behalf of the resort had been completed. Ironically, the resort developer had to pay a substantial sum towards the protection of the rest of the massive forest as part of the development deal.

Also in May 1995, Sting and Trudie visited the Cannes Film

Festival where they were showing off their recently completed movie entitled *The Grotesque,* starring Sting, Alan Bates and Trudie. In the picture, Sting portrayed a butler, with Trudie as his onscreen wife Doris the cook and Bates as the eccentric Sir Hugo Coal. Critics hailed it as a tongue-in-cheek, black comedy romp. It was set in a country house in post-war Norfolk.

The film's most controversial scene featured Sting having sex with Alan Bates. There was also another sequence in which he seduced another male character. Sting joked at Cannes, 'I've come out ...'

The couple did admit to the press that they would not want their children to see the movie. Sting disclosed that he had tested his butler technique at dinner parties held at their Wiltshire mansion. 'It's a strange movie so that's why we made it,' he said. 'We don't want to make ordinary run-of-the-mill films.' The rest of the cast included Sir John Mills, Maria Aitken and Anna Massey.

In the summer of 1995, a number of publications had quite a laugh at Sting's expense when it was revealed that he had splashed out thousands of pounds to have a series of new bee hives erected in the grounds of his Wiltshire home.

And Trudie proved she would always be more than just Sting's wife by completing a documentary entitled *Moving the Mountain* which documented the political climate that led to the tragic events in China's Tiananmen Square in 1989.

In August 1995 no one was particularly surprised when news that Trudie was pregnant once again slipped out on the showbusiness grapevine. The child — Sting's sixth offspring — was expected in December. As one friend observed, 'That's what happens when you stick to the rhythm method.' On 17 December 1995, Trudie gave birth to Sting's third son, Giacomo.

However, 1995 was not exactly Sting's crowning year. When *The Times* published its annual list of the highest paid that year, it disclosed that Sting had suffered a 51.8 per cent drop in salary from the previous year, highlighting the knock-on effect of some of the activities of Keith Moore which had allegedly swallowed up many millions of pounds of his money. Sting's actual earnings were in the region of 5.68 million pounds, a drastic drop from the previous year's high of more than eleven million. However, Sting's management contests the accuracy of these figures, pointing out that they do not include Sting's touring income from the USA and other major overseas territories, or his ex-UK songwriting income or the fact that nearly all the monies stolen by Keith Moore have been recovered.

Sting's relationship with his oldest child, Joe, by now eighteen, was becoming more and more intriguing. Sting found that, musically, Joe could barely tolerate his old man. He was keen on young bands like Sonic Youth and Pavement. Just about the only thing they had in common was Nirvana — until Kurt Cobain shot himself.

The rest of Sting's musical taste in the mid-nineties makes fascinating reading. He plays 'So What' by Miles Davis virtually once a week wherever he happens to be in the world. He adores John Coltrane and Wynton Kelly. He also enjoys French orchestral music by such diverse talents as Ravel, Debussy, Fauré and Erik Satie. He even regularly started to listen to Dominican monks singing Gregorian chants, although he admitted to one friend that perhaps that was influenced by his Catholic upbringing.

Back at home in Wiltshire, Sting seemed more capable of handling the fame and fortune that had come his way. His humour about press coverage is summed up by two highly satirical articles in *Viz* magazine, which he had framed and keeps in the study at the house.

In one of them, Sting (real name: Gordon Sting) admits to making such energetic love to Trudie that her head came off. The other cutting recounts his stay at a hotel, when 'four-inch sex monkeys' masturbated into his tea, and fellow guests were not best pleased.

The one thing that all family, friends and associates of Sting continue to admire is the closeness of his relationship with Trudie. Even when they exchange the occasional cross word they are back to stroking, pecking, billing and, indeed, cooing in the rather sickening fashion in which only the seven-pints-drunk or the very-in-love conduct themselves. Sting insists, 'We're very similar in many ways. Both born in the early fifties, both went to grammar school, both from families with a relatively low income. We have the same nostalgias, we remember the same commercials. And she makes me laugh and takes the piss out of me. She's my best friend, my lover, my companion and I really don't want to contemplate life without her.'

Sting had even mellowed to such a degree that, when asked by one journalist if The Police could ever be professionally reunited, he replied, 'I don't have any plans to be in The Police again. But you never know. Who knows?'

It was an extraordinary response considering the acrimony that existed during the lifetime of The Police. However, this was the new, laid-back Sting and anything was possible.

As usual, it is Bob Geldof who perfectly sums up Sting's state of mind in the mid-nineties.

He explains, 'Sting once said to me, "No good conduct goes unpunished". And they have really whipped his back. All the Amnesty gigs long before the rainforests. It's not as if he did anything posy. He said "OK, this is Sting, if I start going on about rainforests then my celebrity will get in the way of what I am actually saying, but I can use that celebrity to get someone who knows something about it to talk about it." He took Raoni on a world tour. He did not get in the way. He was concerned enough about it, but he did it with great dignity. I think he did quite well. Whether it was a success or not is academic. He did it with ability and he still makes great music.'

Geldof's loyalty did not go unnoticed. When the former Boomtown Rats singer's marriage to Paula Yates collapsed in a media frenzy in the spring of 1995, Sting was one of the first friends on the phone offering Geldof a shoulder to cry on.

Yates's very public affair with INXS rock star Michael Hutchence left Geldof completely out in the cold. Sting took him out for a few beers and tried to console him.

In September 1995, Sting's accountant Keith Moore was finally brought to trial over the missing £7.5 million which had been siphoned from Sting's accounts without his permission. Sting himself appeared in court, awkwardly dressed in a suit and tie for one of only a few times in twenty years and sporting a closely cropped haircut.

Southwark Crown Court heard that Sting had received detailed statements from Coutts Bank showing transfers from his account to another created at the Bank of Scotland by accountant and trusted confidante Moore, and that Moore had woven a complex web of deceit to confuse Sting.

Sting insisted that his money was not a 'treasure chest' for others to dip into and that he had always assumed it was protected by bank mandate.

Moore denied the theft charges. Sting was cross-examined, under his real name, by defence counsel Nicholas Purnell who suggested that he had authorised the creation of that account and that it had contained capital saved after Moore had negotiated a deal with the Inland Revenue to protect Sting's overseas earnings. It was then disclosed that £11.6 million of his earnings between 1986 and 1991 had not been taxed (saving him £4.8 million) on condition he spent some time abroad. It was also revealed that Sting had paid nearly £20 million in tax over the years.

Sting replied, 'Are you saying that I agreed that all the money saved from the Inland Revenue should go to an account controlled by Mr Moore? My assumption is that once the Revenue had agreed to a deal, that money would go into my personal accounts to do with as I choose — not that it's some treasure chest that someone can dip into and invest for me. It's my money.'

The jury erupted in laughter when it was disclosed that Sting had obtained an A-Level in economics before working for the Inland Revenue. 'I'm not saying that opens the gates to the financial world but you're not an innocent abroad,' insisted defence counsel Mr Purcell. He went on, 'For an unhappy period you worked for the Inland Revenue. You can't have someone working for the Inland Revenue who is horrified by financial documents.'

To more laughter, Sting replied, 'I'm afraid that's why I was forced to leave.'

A few days after the trial began, it was revealed that Sting had sanctioned the hiring of a private investigator who secretly recorded a conversation to try to extract a confession from Moore. Sting admitted in court that he knew a meeting had been arranged between Moore and the private eye but he denied being a party to any subterfuge.

The court was also told that Moore had broken down and confessed to stealing six million pounds from Sting after being confronted about the missing money. 'If he confessed, why was it necessary for you to employ a private detective to try and get a taped confession?' asked Mr Purnell.

Sting replied that the detective was employed prior to Moore's alleged confession. He then went on to reveal that he had discovered that two hundred and thirty thousand pounds of his money had been used to buy property for one of Moore's girlfriends in West London.

During the hearing it was disclosed that much of Sting's money had been blown by Moore on a number of disastrous investments, such as an aviation scheme to convert Russian military aircraft into huge jumbo jets for civil use and a scheme to launch a chain of Indian restaurants in Australia.

In addition, Moore had diverted cheques payable to Sting totalling £1.2 million to pay Moore's own tax liabilities and a further one million pounds to pay Moore's fees. The trial also revealed that Sting's long-standing trusted adviser and lawyer, Christopher Burley, had masterminded the recovery of nearly all the stolen monies. The recovered monies did not come from the now bankrupted Moore or from the persons who had benefited from the fraud, but from people who were also taken in by the fraud, such as various bankers, the Inland Revenue and a major publishing company.

On 17 October 1995 Moore was jailed for six years after being found guilty of stealing money from Sting between August 1988 and July 1992.

Media coverage of Moore's trial had another, unfortunate, side effect — it publicised Sting's rapidly receding hairline. Since the age of twenty-five, Sting had been particularly concerned about baldness. After his fortieth birthday, however, it really started to bother him because he was becoming noticeably thin on top. Says one friend, 'Sting was and still is an incredibly vain guy. In his thirties he somehow held on to his hair even though it started receding earlier than that. But now it is a real problem.'

Sting visited a hair loss expert in London's West End in 1994 and has spent a small fortune on substances that are supposed to slow down baldness. 'Sting is proud of the fact he has the physique of a thirty-year-old but he cannot come to terms with his loss of hair.'

As the great man recently said, 'Ten years from now I don't want to be the chap in Las Vegas with the balding head and the tuxedo singing 'Roxanne'.

Only time will tell.

THIRTY

FAME AND DEATH

'The nightmare that sometimes hits me is that even if I stopped now and had no further success I'm probably always going to be reconised in the pub as the bloke who used to be Sting.'

IN EARLY JUNE 1997, Sting left his guitar behind at Frankfurt Airport and sparked a bizarre 100-mile chase that ended when a kindly security guard handed over the instrument which had been left on a baggage cart at the airport. Sting rewarded the guard with a sincere thank-you and a backstage pass for his concert in the German town of Korbach.

That same month Sting bought another house in Malibu for $6 million. The 8,000-square-foot, six-bedroom home, which faced the Pacific, and had separate guest quarters and a pool, was previously owned by *Dallas* TV star Larry Hagman. But, perhaps surprisingly, Sting decided not to sell his other Malibu house which he'd bought from Barbra Streisand in 1985.

Also in June, Sting braved appalling weather to perform at

the outdoor Glastonbury Pop Festival in England. Over 100,000 attended the three-day event, which also included performances by Sheryl Crow, the Prodigy, and Radiohead. The weather was so bad that almost 2,000 people had to be treated for exposure and exhaustion, and there were even eight reported cases of the deadly E coli bacteria.

A few weeks later, Sting inked a worldwide publishing deal with EMI that would bring him a lump-sum payment somewhere in the region of $35 million. The deal covered recordings from Sting's days with Police, his solo career, and his future songwriting. Royalties would be split 75–25 in Sting's favor for a minimum of ten years or five albums. The deal was finalized at Sting's Wiltshire home by EMI Music Publishing Chairman and CEO Martin Bandier. 'To be working with an artist of such depth and character as Sting is a once-in-a-lifetime opportunity', said Bandier. 'Particularly as this deal spans such a wide and fruitful collection.'

Sliding across the rainbow from erotic pink to lizard green, the Art Deco structures on Ocean Drive, Miami Beach, were built to uplift the spirits of Americans and to offer a distraction from the Great Depression. Over 60 years later, they helped turn the beach area into a gaudy, head-turning district filled with eye-candy buildings — tacky, faddish and full of showgirl simplicity. They also helped Ocean earn the local nickname of "Deco Drive."

Only 15 years earlier, this area was better known for its derelict buildings, prostitutes and cocaine dealers. Today, it's South Beach, the deco darling of the world and a mecca for the area's vast gay population. Throngs of bronzed and beautiful people fill the district. They roller-blade and stroll past the tables of places like the popular News Cafe, on Ocean Drive, along the sidewalks through the early morning traffic, beneath the palm trees, the wedding-cake deco hotels and a sparkling golden Miami sun.

The News Cafe, favorite haunt of the fashionable and beautiful, is on the beachside boulevard which Miami's rich and successful residents helped turn from a rundown, sleazy ocean front into the American riviera. Ten years ago, this was Skid-Row-sur-Mer, and the main businesses were single shots of cocaine and hard liquor. Now it is transformed. Grunge never made it here, nor did the fear of skin cancer; there is little suntan lotion below the factor six on sale.

The arrival of celebrities like Madonna, Sylvester Stallone and a galaxy of others confirmed the revival of Miami Beach to its glory days of the roaring Twenties, when the police department had to put up boards on the sand to remind the bathing belles: 'Warning: Law Requires Full Bathing Suit.'

The manager of the News Cafe, Ron McLean, even notched himself a place in city history. He set up the News Cafe in 1989, a 24-hour restaurant and bar, another symbol of Miami Beach's renaissance. The idea of selling foreign newspapers as well as Eggs Benedict and Margueritas turned out to have been inspired. It became a mecca for many of the area's most beautiful people.

The News Cafe also happened to be a regular start-of-the-day haunt for one of Sting's best friends, Gianni Versace, a gray-haired, balding, middle-aged figure in white T-shirt, black shorts and sandals. But on the morning of Tuesday, July 15, 1997, Versace seemed more agitated than usual.

Cafe hostess Stephanie Vanover, 30, even noticed that on that day he approached the restaurant from the opposite, beach side, of the street, which was unusual. She had actually seen Versace walk right past the premises before crossing the street and returning 'in a sort of loop.'

When Versace greeted Stephanie he was definitely less relaxed than usual. At the counter of the restaurant's newstand, the man spent $15.01 on five magazines: *Business Week, Vogue, Entertainment Weekly, People* and *The New Yorker*. He asked for *Time* as well, but the store did not have it in stock. Then Versace departed, strolled past a group of tourists staking out places on the beach and walked the four blocks to his home at 1116 Ocean Drive.

Shortly before 9 a.m., as Versace pulled out his keys to unlock the black wrought-iron gates to his palatial, multi-million-dollar home, a younger man in his mid-twenties suddenly approached. He was dressed in a gray muscle T-shirt, black shorts, black baseball cap and tennis shoes. There was an exchange of words. Witnesses later claimed that both men were cursing each other in Italian.

The younger man then took a heavy .40 pistol out from his backpack and shot Versace in the head. The man fell as the first bullet hit him. Then the gunman coolly and calmly bent down to put a second bullet into his skull. The magazines spilled from Versace's arms onto the steps. They were soon stained in his blood. Meanwhile, the gunman pocketed his gun and walked into a crowd of nearby shoppers, leaving his victim dying on the coral pink steps to the mansion.

Eddie Bianchi was at a nearby roller blades store when he heard the two shots. Bianchi rushed out of the store and saw Versace lying on the steps. He was face up and shaking. There was a man walking in and out of the house in a daze, and a woman screaming, 'I saw him! I saw him!'

'We were right there watching and there's nothing you can do', Bianchi recalled shortly afterwards. 'His blood was coming out like crazy. He shook a little bit and stopped moving.'

Police and paramedics arrived at the scene within minutes, but it was already too late. Detectives quickly recovered two cartridge cases from the steps. Then one of the officers spotted a dead pigeon lying at the bottom of the steps, just a few feet from the body. Was it a symbol left by the killer or just a coincidence?

Finally, amongst those magazines scattered on the steps to the mansion was People. *It had just carried a profile of a serial killer who had recently been added to the FBI's 10 most wanted list: his name was Andrew Phillip Cunanan, and that morning he had just claimed his fifth victim, Gianni Versace.*

Sting and Trudi were devastated by Versace's death, as was the entire world. Less than 48 hours after his murder, FBI and police investigators issued a chilling warning to Sting and dozens of other celebrities to be on their guard for Andrew Cunanan, the man suspected of gunning down Versace. Sting and his family were urged to take special care as long as Cunanan remained on the run. Others whom police warned included John Travolta, British actor Rupert Everett, artist David Hockney and designers Giorgio Armani, Calvin Klein and Jean-Paul Gaultier.

The FBI refused to publicly say what had prompted the new warning but they had been talking to some of Cunanan's friends in San Diego. Investigators also believed that Cunanan was carrying with him a photograph taken at a party with *Friends* star Lisa Kudrow, who had irritated him by showing no interest in his acting ambitions when they met at a party almost a year earlier. She was also warned to take extra security precautions.

As more reported sightings of Cunanan flooded the FBI and Miami police, Sting, Trudie and their children stayed put in Wiltshire. Then reports began claiming that Cunanan was believed to be on route to Britain. Several callers to Miami police claimed Cunanan had turned up in London two days after Versace's murder. FBI spokeswoman Anne Figueiras said: 'We've had a voluminous number of calls that have been very fruitful. Our main mission is to locate Cunanan and that's our only focus at this time.'

It also emerged that Versace was Cunanan's sixth victim. And the hunt for Andrew Cunanan reached cyberspace as warnings were issued over the internet worldwide.

Back in Britain, Sting and Trudie remained in a state of complete shock; not only had one of their best friends been murdered but his killer was still on the loose — and the singer and his family were suspected of being on his death list.

Five days later — outside the Versace headquarters on Via Gesu, in Milan, Italy — a simple wreath of yellow flowers hung on the vast wooden door with a small white card beside it. It read 'Mourning for the death of Gianni Versace, Tuesday, July 22, 1997, 1800 local time, a remembrance mass will be held in the cathedral of Milan.'

Just a mile away, inside the magnificent Duomo, Milan's 14th century cathedral, the tiny casket containing the ashes of Gianni Versace sat on the middle of a lace-covered table. To the right was a gold-framed photo of a bare-chested Versace. To the left lay his book, a eulogy of prose and photos entitled *Do Not Disturb*.

Further to the left and the right of the table were ornate gold and malachite candelabra supported by gold cherubs holding aloft seven candles. Towards the front were silver vases holding white, sweet-smelling freesias and roses, Versace's favorite flowers. Yellow drapes darkened the room.

There seems little doubt that wherever Andrew Cunanan was on that Tuesday, July 22, he must have seen TV footage of the extraordinary turnout at the memorial mass for his most famous victim. It was, by all accounts, a remarkable public showing of grief by Sting, Trudie and some of the most famous people in the world. Tragically, Princess Diana — just one month away from her own untimely death — comforted a weeping Elton John for 45 minutes as the heartbroken singer sobbed quietly beside her at the mass in Milan's picturesque Roman Catholic Cathedral. On her other side, Sting and Trudie looked stunned.

At one stage during the church service, Elton John took off his diamond-shaped glasses and wiped his eyes with a white handkerchief. Then he held his head in his hands. He finally composed himself sufficiently to perform, with Sting, the 23rd Psalm, 'The Lord Is My Shepherd.'

Dotted around the church were books of dedication for people to sign. Many did with tears streaming down their cheeks.

Other guests at the memorial service included Naomi Campbell, who had to be supported as she emerged from a Mercedes limousine outside the cathedral. There were other VIPs, including Carolyn Bessette, wife of John Kennedy, Jr., designers Giorgio Armani, Gianfranco Ferre, Valentino and Karl Lagerfeld.

Male mourners virtually all wore dark suits, dark ties and white shirts, while women came in black jackets and trousers or simple black dresses.

More than 20 police guarded the entrance and steel rails were put up on the pavements outside to keep bystanders at a distance as friends and family came and went in the summer sunshine. Inside the cathedral, a Versace aide said proudly: 'Gianni liked things kept simple. He loved beautiful people and beautiful flowers, particularly white roses.'

After the service, the family held a small reception for close friends such as Sting at the Versace headquarters in Via Gesu. The street was closed, with the carabinieri on patrol, but hundreds of onlookers crowded the sidewalk, many carrying bunches of flowers.

Later, Versace's ashes were taken back to that same villa on Lake Como where Sting and his family had stayed, where they were to be scattered in a private ceremony attended by Sting, Trudie and family and other close friends.

Just over a month later Sting found himself attending the funeral of Princess Diana. The similarities between the two occasions were noted by everyone who went to both funerals.

The day after the funeral service Versace's killer Andrew Cunanan was found dead on a Miami houseboat, and the threats to Sting and other celebrities faded. But Sting was shattered both emotionally and physically by his close friend Versace's death, and it actually helped nudge him closer to a much-awaited reunion with his fellow Police Stewart Copeland and Andy Summers.

In late July 1997, Copeland revealed: 'When the band broke up thirteen years ago I wanted it to be a temporary hiatus. I thought it would be temporary and then we all got busy and never got things going again. But I wouldn't rule out a reunion.' And at the same time as Copeland was making encouraging noises about a reunion, Miles Copeland's ARK 21 label was issuing a reggae tribute album featuring both Sting and a never-before-released song by Strontium 90, the pre-Police band that featured all three members. The tribute was to be called *Reggatta Mondatta* and featured cover versions of twelve Police songs.

In December 1997 Sting turned out at the Metropolitan Museum of Art's annual Costume Institute benefit, which was to pay tribute to Gianni Versace. The event showcased a clothing exhibit from the slain fashion designer and featured 90 mannequins wearing Versace's most unique designs.

A couple of days before the benefit, a number of British

tabloids tried to claim that Sting and Elton John had been fighting over who should perform at the tribute. In the end it was Sting who supposedly won the day by performing four songs. Madonna angrily hit back at the rumours, describing them as 'rubbish.'

Elton John, dressed all in black, served as honorary co-chair of the $2,000-a-plate benefit, along with Versace's sister Donatella. 'The final chapter, isn't it really? It's bittersweet tonight', said Elton John.

In April 1998 Sting faced yet another death — this time he was mourning his 92-year-old grandmother Agnes Sumner. The star helped carry her coffin at a moving ceremony in Newcastle, after arriving at the tiny St. Andrew's Catholic Church in a fleet of Mercedes with his brother Philip.

In June 1998, Sting reassembled for yet another tragic event — an emotional memorial service honoring the late Linda McCartney. Once again he and Elton John found themselves in the limelight at the service at the historic St. Martin-in-the-Fields church in Trafalgar Square, Central London. The entire congregation raised their voices to sing 'Let It Be', the moving song Paul McCartney originally penned in honor of his mother, Mary, who died of breast cancer when he was 14.

Throngs of onlookers greeted McCartney, Sting and all the other guests as they entered the church. But the fact that it was the fourth death he'd had to cope with in under a year did not escape Sting. As one of his closest associates said in the early summer of 1998: 'In less than one year, Sting has had to deal with a seemingly endless row of deaths. It's been a difficult period and he's done a lot of soul searching in that time.' With his new lucrative publishing deal in place, Sting responded by keeping out of the limelight as much as possible.

In August 1998, Sting proved that he was still as capable as ever of some extraordinary excesses when he paid out $5,000 to transport his seven-year-old daughter Coco's pet Pony to Italy because she was missing the animal during their summer vacation. Little Gem, Coco's palomino pony, and another horse belonging to Trudie were transported from their Wiltshire estate to the 200-acre Villa Palaggio estate near Florence.

In September 1998 Sting surprised many of his fans by playing Bach on guitar in a short film called *Prelude*. It was the first time he'd ever played classical music in public.

EPILOGUE

'In the end, of course, all I am is this guy.
Just a guy. I shit, I drink, I fuck, I breathe.'

- STING

SO WHAT'S LEFT FOR STING TO DO?

He insists, rather casually, 'I have to enter a phase now where I sit down and say, "What have I learned? Who am I? What have I got to say that's useful or coherent?" And at the end of that period, if I think I have nothing to say, then I hope I have the courage not to say anything. I'll wait and be patient.'

Patience is something which the Sting of today seems to have in abundance. Take the rainforest campaign. He looks on that as 'a useful experience. I learned a great deal about myself and about the media, and human nature generally. I have no regrets about it'.

Sting's attitude is that if you have access to the media and people ask you to help a worthy cause, then why not do it? 'Celebrity is good for kick-starting ideas, but often celebrity is a lead weight around your neck.'

On the front steps of his mansion Sting regularly fills his nostrils with the sharp Wiltshire air and takes a moment to admire the building's fine architectural details. He is lord of all he surveys. You can say what you like about Sting but if you hate him, the news is bad. The news is: it's your problem, not his.

On the other hand, maybe Sting's life is too good. Contentment is reputed to be the enemy of inspiration. There's a view that says, 'nothing like a bit of anguish to get the creative juices flowing'.

'I want to be happy and sane and still make music. People have made great music in these conditions. It can be done. Maybe I'm in a very small percentage of people who are happy. Maybe it's smugness. I don't know. But I am happy.'

For the moment ...

Selected Disc/Filmography

1977 May: The Police's first single 'Fall Out' is released.
1978 April: The Police single 'Roxanne' is released.
Sept: Sting lands his first movie role in *Quadrophenia*.
Oct: Sting acts in *Radio On*.
Nov: The Police album *Outlandos d'Amour* is released.
1979 Sept: Single 'Message In A Bottle' is released.
Oct: The Police album *Regatta de Blanc* is released.
1980 Oct: The Police album *Zenyatta Mondatta* is released.
1981 Oct: The Police album *Ghost in the Machine* is released.
Nov: Sting stars in *Artemis 81*.
1982 Sept: Sting plays the lead in *Brimstone and Treacle*.
1983 May: Sting stars in *Dune*.
June: The Police album *Synchronicity* is released.
1984 Sept: Sting stars in *The Bride*.
1985 June: Solo album *The Dream of the Blue Turtles* is released.
Dec: Sting acts in *Plenty*.
1987 July: Sting stars in *Stormy Monday*.
Oct: Solo album *Nothing Like The Sun* is released.
1988 April: Sting stars in *Julia And Julia*.
1991 Jan: Solo album *The Soul Cages* is released.
1993 June: Solo album *Ten Summoner's Tales* is released.
1995 May: Sting and Trudie Styler star in *The Grotesque*.
Sept: Contributed to Oscar winning *Leaving Las Vegas* soundtrack.

1996	Feb:	Solo album *Mercury Falling* is scheduled for release.
	June:	Contributed to compilation/soundtrack of *Red Hot and Rio*.
1997	Feb:	Contributed to compilation/soundtrack of *Gentlemen Don't Eat Poets*.
1998	June:	Contributed to compilation record produced by Elecktra.

Index

INDEX